10687262

Markets & Institutions in Real Estate & Construction

Markets & Institutions in Real Estate & Construction

Michael Ball

Professor of Urban and
Property Economics,
The University of Reading

© 2006 Michael Ball

Editorial offices:
Blackwell Publishing Ltd, 9600 Garsington Road, Oxford OX4 2DQ, UK
  Tel: +44 (0)1865 776868
Blackwell Publishing Inc., 350 Main Street, Malden, MA 02148-5020, USA
  Tel: +1 781 388 8250
Blackwell Publishing Asia Pty Ltd, 550 Swanston Street, Carlton, Victoria 3053, Australia
  Tel: +61 (0)3 8359 1011

The right of the Author to be identified as the Author of this Work has been asserted
in accordance with the Copyright, Designs and Patents Act 1988.

All rights reserved. No part of this publication may be reproduced, stored in
a retrieval system, or transmitted, in any form or by any means, electronic,
mechanical, photocopying, recording or otherwise, except as permitted by
the UK Copyright, Designs and Patents Act 1988, without the prior permission
of the publisher.

First published 2006 by Blackwell Publishing Ltd

ISBN-10: 1-4051-1099-6
ISBN-13: 978-1-4051-1099-0

Library of Congress Cataloging-in-Publication Data
Ball, Michael.
    Markets & institutions in real estate & construction / Michael Ball. – 1st ed.
      p.   cm.
    Includes bibliographical references and index.
    ISBN-13: 978-1-4051-1099-0 (pbk. : alk. paper)
    ISBN-10: 1-4051-1099-6 (pbk. : alk. paper)
    1. Real estate business.   2. Real estate business – Europe.   3. Construction
industry.   I. Title: Markets and institutions in real estate and construction.
II. Title.

HD1375.B24 2006
333.33 – dc22

                                                                2006001144

A catalogue record for this title is available from the British Library

Set in 10/13pt Trump Mediaeval
by Graphicraft Limited, Hong Kong
Printed and bound in India
by Replika Press Pvt Ltd

The publisher's policy is to use permanent paper from mills that operate a sustainable
forestry policy, and which has been manufactured from pulp processed using acid-free
and elementary chlorine-free practices. Furthermore, the publisher ensures that the text
paper and cover board used have met acceptable environmental accreditation standards.

For further information on Blackwell Publishing, visit our website:
www.blackwellpublishing.com

The Royal Institution of Chartered Surveyors is the mark of property professionalism worldwide, promoting best practice, regulation and consumer protection for business and the community. It is the home of property-related knowledge and is an impartial advisor to governments and global organisations. It is committed to the promotion of research in support of the efficient and effective operation of land and property markets worldwide.

Real Estate Issues

Series Managing Editors
Stephen Brown RICS
John Henneberry Department of Town & Regional Planning, University of Sheffield
David Ho School of Design & Environment, National University of Singapore
Elaine Worzala Real Estate Institute, School of Business Administration, University of San Diego

Real Estate Issues is an international book series presenting the latest thinking into how real estate markets operate. The books have a strong theoretical basis – providing the underpinning for the development of new ideas.

The books are inclusive in nature, drawing both upon established techniques for real estate market analysis and on those from other academic disciplines as appropriate. The series embraces a comparative approach, allowing theory and practice to be put forward and tested for their applicability and relevance to the understanding of new situations. It does not seek to impose solutions, but rather provides a more effective means by which solutions can be found. It will not make any presumptions as to the importance of real estate markets but will uncover and present, through the clarity of the thinking, the real significance of the operation of real estate markets.

Books in the series
Adams & Watkins *Greenfields, Brownfields & Housing Development*
Adams, Watkins & White *Planning, Public Policy & Property Markets*
Allen, Barlow, Léal, Maloutas & Padovani *Housing & Welfare in Southern Europe*
Ball *Markets and Institutions in Real Estate & Construction*
Barras *Building Cycles & Urban Development*
Beider *Housing, Neighbourhood Renewal & Community Engagement*
Ben-Shahar, Leung & Ong *Mortgage Markets Worldwide*
Buitelaar *The Cost of Land Use Decisions*
Byrne and See Ong *Real Estate Investment*
Couch, Dangschat, Leontidou & Petschel-Held *Urban Sprawl*
Couch, Fraser & Percy *Urban Regeneration in Europe*
Dixon, McAllister, Marston & Snow *Real Estate & the New Economy*
Evans *Economics & Land Use Planning*
Evans *Economics, Real Estate & the Supply of Land*
Guy & Henneberry *Development & Developers*
Jones & Murie *The Right to Buy*
Leece *Economics of the Mortgage Market*
McGough & Tsolacos *Property Market Analysis & Forecasting*
Monk & Whitehead *Affordable Housing & the Property Market*
Newell & Sieracki *Property Investment & Finance*
O'Sullivan & Gibb *Housing Economics & Public Policy*
Seabrooke, Kent & How *International Real Estate*
Wellings *British Housebuilders*

Contents

For Asli and Alec,
The two stars in my life

1

Prologue

Focus

Chaucer's *Canterbury Tales* starts with an obvious but arresting phrase: 'Here Bygynneth The Book'. No bogus claim of outstanding literary merit can equate what follows with the work of that ancient bard. Nor for this text can there be much expectation of it being read for more than a handful of years. Even so, there is one important parallel, because the esteemed aforementioned work provides a metaphor for what follows. Chaucer's pilgrims related events while travelling a route trodden each year by tens of thousands through ancient England. Along the way, the variety of their lives and the uniqueness of their expositions brought meaning out of the commonplace. The humble hope of this text is also to tread along some well-worn paths and, in doing so, to cast a little new light on what seems so often to be commonplace in real estate and construction studies: namely, real estate and construction markets and the firms and organisations that populate those markets and provide the goods and services that we all depend on in our lives.

Case studies are presented here of a series of markets, firms and organisations with the aim of understanding how they function and how they interrelate. Sets of rules and practices – institutions – are embodied in those relationships and, so, the reasons why such things exist and their impacts are considered as part of the analysis.

The firms and organisations examined here are part of the supply and transaction chain delivering built structures as market products to investors, business users and consumers. This is one reason why real estate and construction are considered together, though this is an unusual juxtaposition in the literature. Real estate is produced by the construction industry and buildings represent a high proportion of total construction output. In fact, these two industries cannot live without each other. In 2004, around 55% of new construction work in the USA was private housing and about a further 10% was private offices, commercial and industrial building; during the same year in the UK, around 25% of construction output was new housing and around 40% was offices, commercial and industrial. One country was having a housebuilding boom, the other an office and retail-building boom but, in both, roughly two-thirds of new construction was destined for private real estate markets.

Another reason for considering real estate and construction jointly is that they throw up some similar theoretical issues. The product not the process is capital intensive in each of them. Real estate and construction are people businesses, dealing with much the same set of products at various stages of their existence. In many respects, consequently, they face similar issues in terms of the ways in which their business processes and markets are organised.

The study of markets and organisational interrelationships is at the heart of real estate economics and construction studies and there is a truly enormous literature. The arguments here, however, aim to give a some-what distinctive twist to the subject. Broad principles are set out for the general understanding of markets and organisations, as well as in relation to some specific issues. Much of this element of the book draws on a wide body of pre-existing theory. Nevertheless, in what follows there are pre-dominantly examinations of real world markets and organisations. The intent is not simply to regard them as representative of general processes but, instead, to examine markets and organisations as entities that them-selves need explanation.

Real estate and construction enterprises have little resonance in popular consciousness. Their rare appearances in the news tend to be of the critical kind. Leave the shores of the trade journals and journey into more serious academic waters and disdain rules again, usually of a more polite kind. In the real estate and construction literature, with some exceptions, limited attention is paid to understanding its 'industries', by which I mean actual organisations, particularly firms, and how they operate in a market context. They are a backdrop: fabulous generators of data and huge repositories of potential interviewees for those who like the human touch, but generally only of secondary interest. They seriously lack that elusive 'star' quality.

In real estate, there is an enormous literature on market processes, finance and investment but comparatively little on the organisations that function in those markets, that use the finance and that undertake the investments. In the much smaller field of construction economics, there is less of an emphasis on markets and more of one on process issues within and between organisations but, again with some notable exceptions, still not actually much attention paid to organisations within the industry itself. Those topics tend to be left to the financial pages of newspapers and sometimes to business histories rather than being subject to much in-depth theoretical and empirical scrutiny.

This observation should not be regarded as part of a journey to some mythical 'missing link' that would somehow revolutionise real estate or construction studies. Instead, the purpose is to say that these topics are interesting in their own right and analysis of them may provide some useful additions to the armoury of ideas and empirical evidence about real estate and construction. The viewpoint here consequently does not dwell on so-called theoretical failings. Critics frequently declare they have found issues that prevailing orthodoxies cannot explain. Often with sceptics of economic analysis in real estate and construction, the claimed features that economics ignores seem to be treated like the logs on a campfire. The more there are, the greater the blaze. Rather than representing a tearing down of citadels, however, the arguments here apply theories of competitive markets, industrial economics and debates within strategic management to real estate and construction markets and the organisations existing within them, building on a depth of prior research in the literature.

None the less, the analysis remains somewhat distinctive, especially from the frequent treatment of the supply-side in real estate studies. It would be wrong to say the supply-side is missing or neglected in real estate market models. Far from it: many models have supply-side elements within them and there have been a large number of studies of supply-side responsiveness to price changes, especially in housing (DiPasquale 1999; Pryce 1999; Malpezzi & Wachter 2001; Meen 2005). However, they assume a perfectly competitive market with zero transaction costs, stable technology and fixed firm behaviour. The outcome is that only variations in construction input costs, selling prices and interest rates feature. That sort of approach is helpful because of the aggregate nature of such studies. Yet a more detailed understanding of the supply-side can even be of benefit at that level of aggregation, especially as greater concern has arisen with supply-side rigidities in recent years, with expectations formation in examining price fluctuations and in arguing for the need for institutional reform.

Themes

Variety is the obvious word that comes to mind when looking at the types of enterprise operating in real estate and its cousin industry, construction, and diversity has to be the watchword when trying to understand their existence and operation.

Four questions are at the heart of the studies presented in this book.

1. How do markets work in real estate and construction?
2. What actual roles do firms and organisations play?
3. Why is there such an array of different types of enterprise and market practice in these spheres of economic activity?
4. Why in these areas is there such apparent variation in market practices and firm characteristics between countries?

In some respects the answers are simple and contained in any economics textbook: competitive markets are good ways of organising economic activity; specialisation greatly raises productivity and firms are embodiments of such specialisation, etc. Scratch the surface of these issues, however, and a series of difficult themes immediately arise.

- If markets are so good, why have firms at all? (The 'how are markets superior?' question.)
- What is the appropriate size and range of activities for particular types of firm? (The 'firm boundary' question.)
- How can one judge which constellation of market practices is superior? (The 'are country x's procedures better or worse than country y's?' question.)

There are many distinct viewpoints on such matters and a real world that exhibits a wide array of variations. It is infeasible in one book to cover all the issues, so the particular strategy has been adopted of examining particular themes, the choice of which has been partly determined by the author's own research interests in recent years.

Chapter 2 provides an introduction to the analysis of markets and institutions in real estate and construction by examining features of these markets and surveying a variety of potential theoretical approaches. The remaining chapters examine case study themes, using aspects of the arguments in Chapter 2. Chapter 3 examines recent world housing market dynamics and, in particular, experience in Europe. It cautions against, on the one hand, simple extrapolations of market behaviour from one country to another and attempts to measure common cycles and, on the other hand, crude classifications of countries on the basis of supposed institutional differences.

Chapter 4 then reprises arguments about why competitive processes can provide significant benefits in housing provision – arguments that are then applied in Chapter 5 to the housing institutional transitions currently taking place in Central and Eastern Europe. Chapters 6 to 8 look at developments in the analysis of market agents in commercial and residential real estate and how the two types of market have seen divergent trends in their property services industries in recent years. Chapters 9 and 10 examine housebuilding: first, by highlighting how divergent internationally are the characteristics of this industry and, second, by examining why large firms exist and the influence that land-use regulation may have through a UK–USA comparison. Chapter 11 is an integrated analysis of the role of professions, professional bodies and firms in real estate and construction. It is then followed by consideration of why very large firms exist in the construction industry, despite its typical classification as a highly competitive industry in the traditional sense of a mass of small-scale producers. The final chapter studies the recent but already popular development of community–developer–local-government governance processes in urban regeneration, asking how feasible they are and providing some empirical evidence on their effectiveness.

The topics in this book are varied in theme but have a common underlying approach. The aim is both to provide an analysis of each topic and to present a particular viewpoint about studying the real estate and construction industries. Considerable effort has been put into describing the material in a simple, readable way, though some elementary knowledge of economics would be of benefit when reading the book. The chapters have also been designed to be self-contained, as well as interlinked, so that they can be read individually or in terms of dipped-into subjects of interest.

2

An introduction to the analysis of markets and institutions in real estate and construction

Introduction

The themes of this book look at real world markets and organisations operating within them. The objective of this chapter is to justify the focus on these issues and to examine:

- some special characteristics of markets, firms and other types of organisation in real estate and construction;
- the interrelationships between markets, industries and firms;
- various theories used in the study of markets, firms and institutions; and
- when such an institutional analysis is appropriate and when it is unnecessary.

Some key features of real estate and construction

Varied and competitive markets

In the real estate and construction industries, the transactions of goods and services predominantly take place through market exchange. A myriad of markets exist, distinguished by such features as building type, location and property rights. Unless governments impose restrictions on transactions, they are also highly competitive markets because there are a multitude of buyers and suppliers in virtually all spheres. In order to corner a housing or office market, for example, not only would a would-be monopolist have to control all new production, he or she would also have to buy up all the existing stocks of such buildings in a locality and all the potential land on which other buildings could be built. In a market system, in all but the smallest towns and cities, this would be exceedingly expensive. Similarly, in construction, suppliers are always threatened, because firms and labour are highly mobile, by the fear of someone offering a lower price to undertake the work.

Technology is an important influence on this competitive environment in the broad sense of the physical characteristics of built structures and the ways in which they are made. It is because built structures last a long time that the existing stock of a building type can always compete with new supply. Within new supply, most techniques of production are freely available and widely known. There are few proprietary technologies, unique specialist pieces of equipment that require huge dedicated plants, or essential operating systems under patented ownership. Yet these are common in a whole variety of other industries. Even where technology restrictions do exist, near substitutes abound.

Property rights are another key factor in the maintenance of a competitive environment in real estate. Ownership is widely spread across a broad range of organisations and individuals. Rights are generally clearly understood and enforceable in law. It is also easy in market economies to set up real estate development and construction companies. Failure rates may be high, but so are successes. With a steady flow of new entrants, incumbents are kept on their metal.

This is not to say, of course, that monopolistic practices and restrictions are never imposed. Constraints are rife across the world, many of which are state enacted. The housing and land markets are generally the most vulnerable to such constraints. Restrictions are often introduced with the highest of motives by governments, and with widespread popular support for their actions but little understanding of the consequences. Historically, real estate has probably been the most common area in market-oriented countries where governments have felt emboldened to pass edicts that wipe out, in perpetuity, ownership rights worth billions with little or no compensation. Think of changes in the right to develop land or property altered by the introduction of planning regulations. Think of rent control.

Disparate enterprises

It is possible in many industries to identify immediately some key players in the supply chain, such as a major motor producer, computer firm, film

studio or food processor. Around them hovers a mass of specialist enterprises, either linked into a major's activities or trying to carve out market
niches beyond their reaches. In contrast, in real estate, there are no obvious focal firms. Furthermore, concentration ratios are frequently low in
construction (Chapter 12). Instead, there are a myriad of distinct types of
enterprise. The spheres in which they operate may even be industries
or unique domains in their own right. The list is long. A few of the most
important are: house builders; real estate developers; estate agents/real
estate brokers; construction firms; real estate investors; mortgage lenders;
mortgage brokers; and professional practices, such as for planning, valuation, surveying, architecture, engineering and property law.

Not only is there such a variety of firms and markets but also a considerable lack of correspondence in their characteristics between countries.
For ostensibly the same product, there are diverse types of producer and
varied markets in which they operate. For instance, in countries such as
Germany and France, much new single-family housing is created by people
who buy a serviced plot of land for their residence and get someone else
to organise the design and building of it for them. More comprehensive
market processes exist elsewhere. In Australia, Ireland, the UK and the USA,
for example, most housing is mass-produced by specialist builders and
developers. They build for a general market of potential buyers throughout the quality chain, from the cheapest to the most expensive types of
property. Other countries do not even have a distinctive housebuilding
industry. Instead, in Spain, and in much of the rest of Europe and large parts
of Asia, large general-purpose construction firms are the main developers
and producers of housing.

Inevitably, people understand the broad functioning of markets from
their own experience of them. Normally, that is a perfectly reasonable
procedure because many markets function in similar ways right across
the globe. However, in real estate and construction the assumption is more
circumspect because of the degree of variety that can be observed. This
does not mean that it is impossible to apply common forms of analysis
to them but it does mean that the phrase 'in this context' can be more
important than usual.

Setting the focus

The list of cross-country differences in enterprise types and markets in
real estate and construction could be very long. An obvious question is why
does such cross-country variation exist, especially when it does not occur

to such stark extremes in many other industries? Can it simply be put down to the vicissitudes and impact of distinctive government polices, to something vacuous like the strange ways of foreigners, or are there other more systematic factors at work?

Undoubtedly, such variety and cross-country complexity is interesting in its own right, yet what inferences should be drawn from such diversity? In everyday life, for example, people delight in the minutiae of personal differences. The media draws on this aspect of human nature when it feasts on beauty, idiosyncrasy, celebrity and fashion. To heart surgeons, however, people are far more mundane in nature. Patients come to see them because of defects in a vital organ, one that when healthy beats in almost exactly the same way in all of us and that, when malfunctioning, surgery may be able to fix. Differences obviously matter but, equally clearly, only in specific contexts.

The problem is in identifying the characteristics on which attention should be focused. This is a key issue when looking at markets and the entities that operate within them. Which features are important depends not only on the questions being asked but, in addition, on the theories being applied in the attempt to understand causality and change. Moreover, any theory contains assumptions about what to ignore or to hold constant.

Within theories, assumptions play an often-misunderstood role. They form the building blocks of the analysis. The misunderstanding arises because the use of assumptions is different from the typical everyday meaning of the assumption, as when making descriptions of events or people. When describing something, everyone needs to make implicit assumptions about what features are important to relate. In contrast, theorists when making assumptions do not necessarily believe that these assumptions are realistic or even good shorthand for a specific empirical situation. Instead, assumptions are used because they are relevant in solving the problem at hand, by helping to build up theories and derive useful insights from them.

Product and process specificities

The array of real estate and construction enterprises and markets is obviously influenced by the type of products being produced, sold and owned and the technical nature of the value creation processes being undertaken. In broad form, these features are no different from those associated with any other product or service in a modern economy. Nevertheless, detailed characteristics of real estate and construction do matter. So, at this stage it is useful to delineate and justify the selection of some key features of real estate and construction as they form the building blocks of the analyses of subsequent chapters.

Longevity and expense

Buildings are large, valuable, indivisible and last a long time. These factors are interlinked. Buildings last a long time, partly because of their durable nature, but also because it is costly to build and demolish them. The time and irreversibility dimensions make a building a significant commitment. Most of the benefits from them will arise in the future for both investors and users in a climate of considerable uncertainty, while most costs are front-loaded unless spread out through borrowing. A building's high worth arises because of its highly prized usefulness to firms and consumers and because scarce land is consumed in its creation. In addition, its construction is expensive and transaction costs are significant.

The economic ramifications are substantial. Built structures typically represent a substantial proportion of a country's capital stock. In terms of value-added, around 10–15% or more of a country's annual economic activity is devoted to real estate and construction, if one adds together all the activities associated with production, maintenance, exchange, monitoring, finance, defining and enforcing property rights, regulation, education and training. Employment-wise, thousand of people are engaged in building and maintenance, in buying, selling and financing and in other ancillary services. In terms of finance, large volumes of investment funds are absorbed, short-term loans extended, debt issued, equity purchased and other financial instruments traded. Moreover, considerable volumes of public revenues are absorbed.

Varied end users

End users come in many varieties because built structures are used in so many aspects of life. The obvious divisions are between final consumers, typically in relation to housing, and the business users of commercial property. Construction-related enterprises may similarly have final consumers or other businesses as their clients. The property rights of owner-occupiers, who are both users and investors, are different from those of landlords and tenants.

The expenses associated with built structures and the time horizons involved make it worthwhile for building owners to employ – usually indirectly – people to ensure that the structures are maintained and that future marketability is sustained. Moreover, most investors and users undertake transactions associated with buildings infrequently. So, it rarely pays them to become experts in any aspect of real estate provision but to leave matters, instead, to professionals.

Product and process heterogeneity

For the discussion here, it is useful to highlight three features with regard to heterogeneity: physical characteristics, location and information. They identify particular issues within economic analysis as being of particular relevance.

1. Physical characteristics

Few buildings are identical. Instead, they differ in use, size, height and many other characteristics. Nor is there standardisation in the processes by which they are created. Attempts are made at standardisation in construction but preferences, designs and locations militate against it.

With such prevalent variety, it is unsurprising that a considerable amount of *specialisation* occurs in building production, exchange, finance and ownership. Few people or enterprises can have expertise in more than a limited sphere and the principle of comparative advantage highlights the wisdom of concentrating on what one does best.

The *arbitrage principle* of buyers and sellers searching out the best exchange opportunities in a competitive environment is important in relation to heterogeneity. It explains much about the nature of market exchange and the formation of prices. As long as built structures are relatively close substitutes, trades occur until their prices vary only by the differences in their attributes: size, age, location, etc. In other words, these underlying attributes have a uniform price and built structures vary in price only according to the characteristics bundle they embody. This type of causal mechanism underlies cross-sectional hedonic price indices and time series quality-adjusted price indices in housing (Sirmans *et al.* 2005). Arbitrage, furthermore, provides a useful definition of the extent of any market. As suggested by Cournot in the nineteenth century, it is the sphere within which arbitrage takes place (Gallet 2004). Equally relevant, arbitrage principles explain how competition operates in the midst of variety.

2. Location

Location differentiates and segments real estate markets and requires that construction be a mobile production process. Buildings are useful only when plugged into some network of economic and social life at a specific geographic place. Moreover, within any locality, built structures compete with near substitutes. Distance erodes the area over which such substitutes exist, so that real estate markets are delineated across space. Spatial differentiation determines many characteristics of real estate and related construction industries. Much market information and competitive interaction is inevitably local in nature. Local markets also vary enormously in size and value, affecting the fortunes of the enterprises that operate in them.

Developers and producers have to create new buildings at specific sites and, so, resources have to be assembled and used there. This contrasts with most manufacturing processes, where goods are first produced at one location and then distributed to customers via networks of distribution outlets. When creating new buildings, instead, production and distribution are simultaneous events with significant implications for the commercial development and housebuilding industries.

Location in the context of substantial product differentiation has another important impact in real estate and construction via the consequences for the development of specialisation. Specialisation has long been recognised to lead to significant increases in productive potential. The degree of specialisation, however, is limited by the need for a sufficient volume of demand to employ specialist processes fully. When products are highly spatially differentiated, demand can quickly act as a constraint on specialisation. To extend their markets, specialists have to operate at more distant locations. This is problematic because of the costs of transportation, the feasibility of travel, spatial constraints on available information and the degree of commonality between the distinct markets and the competences of the organisation. Demand for an enterprise's products or services are consequently often highly finite. That demand is also likely to be quite variable and pooling it with activities elsewhere is costly.

Specialist activities in the face of finite and variable demands have two choices. They can spread out spatially (or functionally), becoming large firms. By doing so, they incur the cost penalties just identified, so there have to be good offsetting benefits if that option is to be worthwhile. The other option is to stay within the constraints of a particular market and stay small. There they can come together with other specialists on a project-by-project basis.

This option of functional and localised specialisation in a context of market exchange is observed time and again in real estate and construction in the form of local producers, specialists and subcontracting. Labour-intensive specialisation is at the heart of many activities in real estate and construction, operating through market rather than intra-firm relationships, and networks are key elements in the functioning of those markets. Clients may have to go round independently to each type of specialist, assemble teams themselves, or employ someone like a project manager to do this for them. Alternatively, specialists may offer their services to clients in formal or informal teams or build up long-term relationships of being available when required.

Nevertheless, frequently observed in real estate and construction is the other option of a widening market spread. Any centralising pressures, if they are to occur, have to more than counterbalance the centrifugal forces of localisation. Some exceedingly large enterprises that are on a par with major firms in other industries in terms of their turnover and market capitalisation can be identified empirically. This implies that scale is an important economic factor in certain areas of real estate and construction, though typically large firms co-exist with many smaller brethren in the same specialist area, being differentiated by their degree of market spread rather than by their production technologies.

Unsurprisingly, different enterprises make distinct choices about the degree of market spread of their operations. These depend on their leaders, their assets and other characteristics, their prime activity and the market contexts that they face. Furthermore, these choices are constrained by pressure from competitors, who are out to be able to deliver cheaper or better, or both, and by what customers find acceptable. The general predicament of whether assets and activities should be combined within a firm or separated in ownership and brought together through market exchange is often termed the *boundary of the firm* debate.

3. Information

Within markets characterised by vast arrays of highly differentiated, long-lasting buildings spread across locations, information becomes a key asset. Nonetheless, in real estate and construction, this information is often of relatively poor quality and expensive, if not impossible, to acquire. With most manufactured goods, particular product models are identical no matter where in the world they are purchased, buyers can read countless reviews and, knowing the age of a second-hand model, they can get a good idea of depreciation rates and condition. It is also easy to find out purchase prices from different suppliers and to compare them on a like-for-like basis. With built structures, none of these conditions hold. Knowledge of markets, networks and detailed events, therefore, is at a premium in all aspects of real estate. Much the same is true in construction. The same uncertainty occurs with production costs. The revenue streams to be expected from buildings and their future prices are also highly uncertain.

The ability to assemble, process and analyse information has greatly increased over time. This trend has accelerated in recent decades with the evolution of modern information and communications technologies. These developments have weakened the barrier effects of localised knowledge in real estate and construction, though by no means eradicated them. Such technical changes help to explain the historical development of enterprises that have gradually broken out of the confines of extreme locality to embrace regional, national and even global markets. Yet, no matter what spatial scale is attained by such firms, the products they deal with – buildings – still have local grounding, literally.

Knowledge is fragmented and information in many real estate and construction contexts is asymmetric between parties to negotiations and exchanges, in the sense that one person or agency knows something that another does not and often has no incentive to reveal what it is. It is very hard, for example, to find out the actual construction cost of a building unless an owner or supplier for some reason wants to publicise the fact. Generalising about such *information asymmetry*, it can be said that real estate and construction processes are associated with much private knowledge rather than with a prevalence of public information that is available to all at low cost. Information and its lack consequently are likely to have considerable impacts on the organisation of activities.

The prevalence of private information is not simply about the condition and general quality of a building but, of equal importance, about the effort and honesty of the myriad of enterprises and people in situations where specialisation is substantial and processes are non-standardised. This 'people issue' is a key influence on the industrial structure and organisational forms found in real estate and construction and is a key theme of several later chapters.

Markets, bureaucratic administration and firms

The prime justification for competitive markets is that they are efficient in the two senses of creating 'least cost' outcomes – minimising the resources required for a given array of outputs – and providing an 'optimal allocation' of resources, meeting preferences between competing ends on the basis of consumer sovereignty. The only external information that market participants require to achieve these ends is the price. The price mechanism in Adam Smith's famous phrase acts as an 'invisible hand' co-ordinating self-interested actions into collectively superior outcomes. Their role in facilitating and driving change is perhaps one of the most widely observed benefits of markets. They create enormous incentives to profit from innovation and sweep away outmoded processes and this leads to perpetual increases in wealth and living standards. In contrast, non-market allocation systems based on administrative processes are inefficient for four fundamental reasons.

1. *Information constraints* They require far more information than markets and so suffer problems in data gathering, comprehension and measurement. Data are also poor or non-existent for many key issues on which decisions have to be made.
2. *Complexity* Administrative rules have simultaneously to be comprehensive, fair and flexible, which is hard to achieve.
3. *Conservative outlook* Once set up, administratively-based systems are resistant to change.
4. *Special interest group takeover* Such systems can often be taken over by special interest groups. For instance, producers in organisations may wish for an easy life, be resistant to change, or have their own agenda of interests. Alternatively, particular sets of consumers may know how to work the system in their own interests, or lobbyists with specific agendas may be able to take control.

No society, of course, works purely on a market basis; societies tend to be a mix of market and primarily administratively-based systems, with the latter prevalent in the public sector. Administratively-based systems widely exist in real estate and construction: land-use planning is a case in point; professional bodies are another.

Firms, of course, are administratively based, hierarchical organisational forms as well. However, they differ from other organisations in having direct relationships to markets as suppliers. Moreover, they have to make profits and, so, are constrained in their behaviour by that requirement.

In terms of their internal operation, firms often mimic markets by setting up multi-divisional organisational structures. These often operate as independent profit centres and internal transfer pricing prevails. The administrative characteristics of firms, nevertheless, highlight constraints to their existence – they may be less efficient than market processes.

Approaches to understanding markets and organisations

Several approaches need to be outlined. Many of them are not actually radically distinctive theories but, instead, may be complementary. Differences in terminology and emphasis tend to cloud such complementarities, as do some of the assertions about the dynamic behaviour of systems (Milgrom & Roberts 1992; Holmstrom & Roberts 1998).

Production technology focused

Production technologies and relative input prices are the basis of the constrained optimisation cost functions found in standard micro-economics textbooks. They emphasise that firms' production choices vary with available technologies and prices. Firm size in a competitive market depends on the characteristics of the available technology set and production takes place at the minimum average cost output.

Within the production technology approach, the size of firms depends on whether scale economies exist. Optimal firm size is also important to the understanding of an industry's competitive context. When scale economies are limited, entry and exit from an industry is likely to be easy and competition consequently high. When scale economies are high, only a handful – or even one firm – will exist and competition will be low. (In fact, market equilibrium may be impossible to reach with pervasive scale economies.) That eventuality aside, the production-technology focused approach is useful for examining how industries in the aggregate behave, because many markets are broadly competitive.

Much of the history of industrialised economies over the last two hundred years has been associated with increases in scale of industries and the evolution of giant enterprises (Chandler 1990). Once technology pushes the size of firms beyond the threshold where they begin to produce a significant proportion of an industry's total output, the nature of inter-firm competition becomes important. In such contexts, key conclusions on firm strategies can be derived through extensions of the production-technology focused approach, because they define how firms can interact (Tirole 1993; Martin 2002).

In many parts of real estate and construction, scale economies are not that great and, as noted earlier, market structures are typically competitive. However, there are areas where large firms do exist and this is likely to be because of scale (and scope) economies. Therefore, as a rule-of-thumb, it is useful at an early stage of a study of firms to consider the technological conditions of production and the resultant impact on market structures. Therefore, it is instructive to examine how they might be changing and explore what inferences might arise as a result.

Agency

Focusing on production technologies and market structures assumes away incentive problems. These are encapsulated in the question 'How do you get someone acting as an agent on your behalf to do what you want them to?' 'Principal–agent' problems arise when some crucial agent-related events are unobservable by the client, such as the amount of effort the agent puts into undertaking a task. Organisational forms may evolve to limit the potentially adverse impacts of such information asymmetries (Sappington 1991; Molho 1997; Laffont 1999).

Principal–agent issues arise within firms – for instance, how do shareholders get salaried managers to work in their interests? They also exist in contractual relationships – for instance, how do you incentivise a broker or agent to sell your home for the best price in the shortest time? As a result, principal–agent analyses can provide rich insights into both how firms and markets are structured and function.

Unsurprisingly, as information issues are important in real estate and construction, information asymmetry factors have proven useful avenues of enquiry. For example, they provide good insights into the study of real estate brokerage and in analysing professions (see Chapters 6 and 11 below.) Yet they tend to examine particular business relationships rather than explain what firms do. For one thing, incentive structures are needed for relationships within firms as well as those that take place through market exchange, so when is a within-firm form better than a market one? Why should it be easier to monitor an employee than a contractor? The questions of why firms and other organisations exist and what they do consequently are by no means completely answered by the principal–agent approach (Hart 1995).

Transaction cost economising

Transaction cost economising highlights the fact that exchange is expensive. Costs vary depending on the type of transaction and the way it is organised. This observation is converted into an operational theory by arguing that observed organisational forms, particularly the extent of market exchange and within-firm direction, are the outcomes of evolutionary processes leading to a minimisation of transaction costs (Williamson 1985).

Transaction cost issues can be broken down into two broad types: (1) co-ordination ones – making transactions happen, and (2) motivational factors – ensuring a mutual alignment of interests between the transactors (Milgrom & Roberts 1992). Both raise a whole series of issues, so that the ramifications of this type of analysis are complex and the possible outcomes in terms of organisational framework are varied. However, some broad generalisations about industrial organisation do arise.

Firms and markets, along with other potential organisational forms are classified as potential 'governance systems' (Williamson 1996). Transaction cost economics regards markets generally as superior. In fact, they are treated as the standard against which to compare other sorts of governance systems. Yet there may be situations where alternatives to markets are better at keeping transaction costs down. Highlighting such situations is where the theory's key hypotheses are generated.

Emphasis is placed on three characteristics of exchange. Standard types of market transaction, it is said, become inferior the greater the frequency of transactions, the less certain the outcomes and the more specific the assets used. These features are multiple dimensions of transactions, so that outturn governance systems are products of combinations of them. For ease of exposition, however, it is useful to illustrate their impacts separately.

1. *Frequency* When transactions are infrequent, parties have limited opportunity to learn about each other, market exchange under standard forms of contract tends to prevail, and recourse is made to the courts when things go wrong. For many goods and services, this situation works well. For instance, it is how most people operate in market contexts in their day-to-day lives. Yet, for some transactions, particularly when they feature uncertainty and asset specificity (see below), problems may arise. As a result, in situations with greater transaction frequency, procedural and organisational innovations may emerge that lower costs, are quicker, and resolve problems with limited conflict. Where the outcome is a non-market form of governance, its fixed costs are spread across a large number of events, making it more economical.

2. *Uncertainty* When the outcomes of a transaction are potentially variable, it is more difficult to specify simple contracts to cover all possible eventualities and so many are likely to be 'incomplete'. Such situations are most likely to arise with complex transactions and when performance is hard to measure; both of which are common in real estate and construction. The outcome is either ever more complex contracts, which will almost certainly never manage to cover all eventualities, or behavioural and organisational alternatives to simple market relations.

Uncertainty and complexity are often tied to the observation that individuals are only able to comprehend limited sets of information, often termed 'bounded rationality'. Putting bounds on rationality is not the same as a full-blooded critique of rationality. Instead, the suggestion is that institutions evolve to deal with some of the issues associated with uncertainty and complexity, while agents still focus on the most relevant matters for them. Therefore, the consequences of bounded rationality are similar in dynamic to other elements of the transaction cost economising process in that they generate organisational responses which lead to rational outcomes (i.e. those claimed to be most efficient).

3. *Asset specificity* With most exchanges, suppliers and customers do not have to undertake specific investments to make them but, in some, they do. The classic case is a car body manufacturer supplying formed parts for a particular car model assembled by another firm. Another example is learning a firm-specific skill in order to be able to work. A third is making a commitment from which it is costly to exit, as when signing a contract to build a large structure.

In these types of transaction, parties suffer high costs if relationships break down through unexpected, early termination or other self-interested behaviour by partners to the transaction. This is often called the 'hold-up' problem, as feared future actions by one party can hold up investments by another, leading to market inefficiency. Possible suggested solutions are compensation clauses in contracts or the combination of the activities under the auspices of one enterprise.

Even in this brief summary, it can be seen that transaction cost economics provides some interesting hypotheses about why firms exist. Unsurprisingly, therefore, this perspective has captured the imagination of many industry researchers. In particular, it is the most common approach used in analysing the structure of the construction industry and project management (see Chapter 12). It has been applied to land-use planning systems (Alexander 1992; 2001; Buitelaar 2003; 2004), though less so in other areas of real estate.

Drawbacks of the transaction cost approach

The transaction cost economics, as was noted earlier, not only examines transaction costs, which production-focused theories tend to assume away, but also argues that economic activity and organisations are structured to minimise transaction costs for all parties. Markets are the default option unless other governance modes offer superior benefits by reducing transaction costs.

A specific research agenda for empirical work on market and firm analysis is laid out in this viewpoint: compare transaction characteristics, impute costs to them and then deduce transaction reasons why current organisational forms exist. Much empirical work has been undertaken using transaction cost economics and its proponents argue that this demonstrates the usefulness of its hypotheses, especially those regarding asset specificity and process integration within one firm (Shelanski & Klein 1995; Rindfleisch & Heide 1997). Economic historians have also found the approach beneficial in understanding the rise and fall of economic systems (North 1990; 1991; Alston *et al.* 1996).

However, some have suggested that the correspondence between transaction cost economics hypotheses and empirical situations is simply that, with other options producing similar results, because there is a difficulty in designing sufficiently discriminatory tests (Holmstrom & Roberts 1998). Problems arise in the applicability of transaction costs economising as the core research programme for studying industrial structures for several reasons. Only a brief summary of the issues can be given here.

The first and major difficulty has already been alluded to. The theory is predicated on a comparison of the effects of different governance states but frequently it can only be done by conjecture rather than precise empirical measurement. Though it may be true that market exchanges generate different cost profiles from within-firm ones, quite how is unclear without such measurement. Therefore, the analysis has to assume the superiority of one governance form over another, instead of being able to provide categorical identification. (This comparison problem has more general implications beyond the transaction cost economics approach, because it highlights the empirical difficulties of, say, cross-country analysis in general.)

Measurement problems arise in both the practical and theoretical senses. Practically, there are often many intangible transactions costs, such as time expended. Theoretically, problems arise with apportioning costs when many joint transactions exist as is typical for firms and in projects in which many agents and organisations participate. In such contexts, measurement becomes difficult, if not impossible. So, although transaction cost hypotheses have been subject to empirical testing, the results cannot be definitive.

Another take on this issue relates to the fundamental exercise in transaction cost analysis of governance comparison. It assumes that an observed switching from one governance type to another leads to lower transaction costs, yet that assumption can never be verified. Instead, the analysis tends to adduce superior features of governance systems, such as those in firms. Firms, for instance, are identified as hierarchical governance structures and are assumed to be better able to deal with 'opportunism', that is self-interested behaviour, than market exchange. Yet, the number of decisions made within a large organisation and the vast amounts of information on which they are based inevitably lead to a decentralisation of information, decision making, and control (Sah & Stiglitz 1986; Radner 1992). Therefore, it may be unsatisfactory to assume that informational structures change simply as a result of a different governance structure – the same problem, as noted earlier, that confronts principal–agent analysis.

Second, it is conceptually difficult to separate costs into production and transaction ones, as production costs tend to depend both on technology and organisational form. Therefore, production costs cannot be assumed to be conceptually given prior to the formation of organisations through transaction cost minimisation (Milgrom & Roberts 1992). More generally, production technology may have wider implications for firms than simply constituting the background conditions to transactions, such as by defining the degree of asset specificity.

Third, there are the general issues of motivation and whose costs are being minimised. Specifically, why should any one entity be interested in minimising the transactions costs of others as well as its own? In which case, how can the actions of one party necessarily lead to cost reductions for others?

Fourth, transaction cost economics takes a transaction as the object of enquiry and unit of measurement. Therefore, in its view, firms and markets are aggregates of transactions. This may be a rather limited view of what firms and other organisations do (Bolton & Sharfstein 1998). For instance, it means that little can be said about why firms come in many different forms and sizes within one industry. Firms also are likely to gain little benefit from adopting strategies in many areas because evolutionary transaction cost economics processes ultimately determine their boundaries.

In summary, transaction cost analysis provides many useful broad conjectures. Yet the 'what do firms do' question is likely to be more complex than 'sometimes reduce transaction costs'. Williamson himself, while by no means accepting all criticism, has suggested the need for broader perspectives on the nature of the firm, incorporating more features than solely transaction cost minimisation and has suggested ways in which a variety of theory of the firm approaches are, in fact, interlinked (Williamson 1999; 2000).

Property rights

Economic property rights differ from legal ones, though typically are supported by them. Legal property rights are what the state assigns to a person and are enforced by the courts, whereas economic property rights relate to an individual's ability to consume a good or service, including the services of an asset. Economic property rights are not absolute but depend on the recipient's efforts at protecting them and others' attempts to capture them. In this framework, for example, squatters are less secure in their land rights because they can expect less police protection rather than just through a lack of property deeds.

The notion of economic property rights is linked to transaction costs because there are costs associated with the transfer, capture and protection rights. It is the existence of these costs combined with the benefits of particular outcomes that set up the inter-agent dynamics in this theory. The analysis differs from transaction cost minimisation in that it typically traces out the consequences of bargaining situations. Via bargaining models, an analysis of inter-agent behaviour is developed in which rational individuals aim to maximise the value of their property rights whenever the opportunity arises (Barzel 1989).

In real estate economics, the property rights approach has been used in a number of contexts. They include rent control (Cheung 1975); markets (Jaffe 1996; 1998); international comparisons (Jaffe & Louziotis 1996); and studies of zoning and land-use planning (Fischel 1980; Fischel 1985; Lai Wai Chung 1994; Webster & Lai 2003). It has not been used much within construction studies.

One of the most fruitful outcomes of property rights analysis for understanding the role of firms is the view that the owners of a firm have residual control rights over the use of the firm's assets, so they can use them in whatever way they want, unless prescribed by law or any contracts (Hart 1995; Bolton & Sharfstein 1998). In terms of the hold-up problem, noted earlier, when assets are under a firm's control, this influences incentives and bargaining outcomes. Models can then identify the efficient allocation of ownership between agents/firms depending on which party has the more specific assets tied up, although the results are sensitive to the assumptions used (De Meza & Lockwood 1998).

This approach to the theory of the firm has had little impact on real estate and construction research. In part, this is because the property rights approach to firm boundaries is worked out in mathematical models, which present only partial pictures of the real situations in which firms exist. Generalisations about real world firms are consequently difficult, though some interesting insights have emerged (Hubbard 2004). It has been most successful in the analysis of the choice of capital structure, because this type of problem is amenable to such approaches.

More general property rights approaches face similar problems about the appropriateness of the bargaining solutions proposed, especially when many people are expected to negotiate over a basket of outcomes (Mueller 2003). Imperfect information can also lead to inefficient bargaining outcomes (Farrell 1987).

Institutional theories of markets and firms

Transaction cost economics and property rights analysis are generally treated as two strands in new institutionalist theory. They are intuitionalist because they examine laws, practices and customs. North's definition is: 'Institutions are the humanly devised constraints that structure political, economic and social interaction. They consist of both informal constraints (sanctions, taboos, customs, traditions, and codes of conduct), and formal rules (constitutions, laws, property rights)' (North 1991).

Of course, new institutionalist theories do not examine all such institutional phenomena but, rather, specify procedures for understanding their consequences. Moreover, they highlight the institutional features seen as being of most relevance to the hypotheses being propounded in relationship to particular economic and social problems. Some extensive surveys of institutional research in economics exist (Eggerston 1990). North and other economic historians have also provided accounts of the evolution of economic institutions (North 1990; Alston *et al.* 1996).

Rules and organisations

It is typical, particularly within the transaction costs 'new institutional economics' approach, to suggest that the study of institutions breaks down into two aspects. Terminology varies but, most commonly, there are *rules* by which actions take place, which may be formal or informal and explicit or implicit in nature, and there are *organisations and agencies* that operate under those rules. A common analogy is with a team game.

This separation is not one of equals because the form and content of organisations is essentially determined by the rules. The study of markets and institutions, thus, becomes an unravelling of the riddles of pre-given rules.

The lack of firm-specific 'strategic' behaviour inherent in such rule-driven processes is distinctive from much modern industrial economics when considering firm behaviour in imperfectly competitive markets. In that analysis, for instance, even though it is often highly abstract and mathematical, firms set prices, react to real or potential threats from others, set advertising budgets, product differentiate, merge and undertake research and development with real effects on markets (Martin 2002).

This point about the passive role of firms and organisations in new institutional theory raises broader issues about the complexity of what firms actually do, the myriad of relatively independent decision-making agents within them and how they affect and interrelate with markets. Empirically, it seems unlikely that one strand of institutional analysis will provide all the answers or even that new institutional theory necessarily provides superior analytical devices to apply to real world contexts.

Other institutional theories

There are a large number of institutional approaches in the other social sciences apart from economics. Some relate to the theories discussed above, while others suggest alternatives (Hall & Taylor 1996; Blom-Hansen 1997; Healey 1998). Most are not of particular relevance here, because of the topics they investigate or the theories expounded. A series of alternative institutional viewpoints have been used in studies of real estate. They generally promote radically different theories to the broadly economic approach adopted here (Ball 1998; 2003). Some claim that such viewpoints can provide additional insights to economic analysis despite the inconsistency of the underlying theories. Those claims find little support in the case studies examined in this book.

Other firm theories

Industrial economics apart, there are several approaches within the strategic management tradition examining enterprises from a firm-oriented rather than an institutional perspective. Porter's work is perhaps the most well known and relates to strategies for firms and national economies in terms of the market conditions and industrial technologies facing firms and industries (Porter 1985; 1990). Firms adopt strategic responses to threats that exist in a general state of rivalry. Rivalry in the Porter framework is determined by five forces: two relate to the power of buyers and suppliers, another concerns barriers to entry and the final two are identified as the threat of substitutes and the degree of rivalry between enterprises. A series of factors are then hypothesised to influence each of those five forces.

Much of Porter's analysis is an extension and reinterpretation of traditional industrial economics, which emphasises features like scale economies, market size and entry barriers (Bain 1956; Scherer 1980). This traditional approach is often termed the structure–conduct–performance paradigm, because of the way it sets up the market–firm relationship. Its main hypothesis is that market characteristics determine the behaviour of firms and that firm behaviour then determines market performance (Martin 2002).

The structure–conduct–performance paradigm of traditional industrial economics has been widely criticised on a number of counts with regard to the study of firm dynamics. It is pointed out that the paradigm studies industry structures rather than firm resources: it treats markets statically as being in a particular competitive state, ranging from monopoly to perfect competition, in which firms are identical and, so, can have little strategic input; and that it places considerable emphasis on barriers to firm entry. Contrasted with this approach are theories putting emphasis on within-firm competences (McWilliams & Smart 1993; Teece *et al.* 1997), variously termed the efficiency or resource-based view.

In broad terms, this perspective has a long pedigree. For example, in the 1940s Schumpter was treating competition as a process of strategic rivalry that led to few survivors. Even the survivors' existence was probably temporary, as they might succumb to economic downswings in processes of 'creative destruction' that left less efficient plant and machinery abandoned (Schumpter 1942).

The modern resource-based view is associated with the work of several authors and particular antecedents (see Penrose 1959; Barney 1991; Barney *et al.* 2001). In it, firms have specific tangible and intangible 'resources' or 'assets', which are more or less embodied in, or tied to, the firm in question. From these resources, firms earn economic rents (i.e. the returns from them are greater than their cost), because no other producer can quite match what they do. A firm's bundle of resources depends on its physical assets, knowledge, organisational processes, etc. With firms regarded as unique bundles of resources, they are heterogeneous rather than uniform in nature. Firm resource bundles are unique because they are costly to copy or inelastic in supply (Barney 2002). Firms' resource mixes can be categorised on the basis of whether they strengthen or weaken a firm's competitive position. Identifying the ideal resource mixes and achieving them, consequently, becomes an objective of firm strategies.

The resource-based view is not without its critics. It has been argued, for example, to be too focused on internal competences and to produce tautological or descriptive statements rather than causal, empirically testable hypotheses (Barney 2001; Lockett & Thampson 2001; Priem & Butler 2001a; b).

Synthesis

A growing number of commentators have argued for some sort of merging of the resource-based view and transaction cost economics (Mahoney 2001; Leiblein 2003), reflecting concern at the wide variety of firm–industry theories currently in existence and recognition of the commonalities and the possibility of a cross-fertilisation of ideas. However, conceptual inconsistency may remain a barrier to such efforts.

The 'partial explanation' nature of the insights of the various theories of the firm and industrial structure surveyed in this chapter has influenced the analyses in the case studies of later chapters. Distinct arguments from the theoretical literature, rather than one uniform approach, are applied to the issues under investigation. For example, principal–agent and transaction cost type arguments together prove useful tools in understanding both estate agency/real estate brokerage and the professions; structure–conduct–performance perspectives are fruitful when examining housebuilding; and resource-based view and other firm theories underlie the discussion of large construction firms. No particular hierarchy of these concepts is found in what follows, just what seemed appropriate in the context. However, underlying the analysis, always is the significance of competition in a dynamic context.

One broad area of organisational theory remains to be evaluated. Many of the empirical situations studied in later chapters involve networks of agencies and international comparisons. So, some consideration must now be given to these themes.

Institutional networks and international comparisons

Organisations in real estate and construction markets are often interlinked through networks of markets and other types of formal and informal relationships. These networks can be regarded as taking on institutional forms in terms of their underlying rules and practices. Such institutions have significant implications for organisations, industrial structures and market performance. Three interrelated dimensions of network types of relationship are of particular relevance when examining real estate and construction: the grouping of providers, market-based and country-specific factors.

1. Intermediate or joint providers of services

Suppliers often come in groups, as in the various parties that come together in building projects (Powell 1990). They may either be intermediate suppliers and subcontractors, or one of a series of functionally distinct agencies brought together in project teams. Institutional frameworks evolve within which these groupings take place and typically such networks are repeated many times across discrete projects rather than being one-off events.

2. Market-based networks

The markets for particular types of built structure and ownership forms have their own distinctive array of agencies and modes of operation. This can be seen by thinking of owner-occupied or rental housing and the various types of commercial structure (offices, retailing, etc.). There are distinct types of providers active in them in the transaction, finance and production spheres, and the frameworks with which they operate differ substantially.

3. Country-specific networks

Country-specific characteristics – 'national business systems' – are widely recognised as being important in terms of how firms compete. In this institutional viewpoint, comparative advantages are generated by nationally specific societal environments and the institutions associated with them (Porter 1990; Quack *et al.* 2000).

There is generally a much greater degree of country-specific features in real estate and construction markets than is typical in many other industries. For example, the levels of ownership of real estate assets by their users vary considerably between countries in both the commercial and residential sectors. In terms of providers, the differences relate to a whole range of issues, such as firm structures, legal frameworks, land-use planning regimes, valuation procedures, and educational and professional qualifications, to name but a few.

Part of the reason for such variety is that there is a weaker influence of international trade in real estate and construction than in many other industries. Even when foreign players are active, they generally have to act within the same institutional frameworks as the home teams. The dynamic of competition is thereby 'domesticated'. Therefore, the country-specific perspective in real estate and, to a lesser extent, construction is somewhat different from that envisaged in national business systems. It is not so much what firm endowments are bestowed on the global stage by national characteristics but, rather, what institutional framework does any organisation have to operate within to do business in a particular real estate or other construction market in a specific country.

Not all cross-country differences have specific real estate and construction roots. Other characteristics obviously play significant roles, such as the nature of financial systems. There are widespread differences in countries' mortgage markets, for example, and investment ownership patterns in commercial real estate are similarly variable. Organisational structures amongst real estate and construction providers may also be affected by whether a country's financial system is relationship or market dominated. Relationship-based financial systems are those in which banks and other financial enterprises build up significant long-term lending relationships with firms, such as in Germany, France and many Asian countries. A market-based one is more arm's length and impersonal, where greater use is made by firms of equity and debt issues and less weight put on other borrowings, such as in the UK and USA. There are also further variations within these two subdivisions (Rajan & Zingales 1995; 2001; Degryse & Ongena 2002).

The impact of institutional networks on research approaches

Much of the previous discussion of theoretical approaches centred on a single transaction or business relationship. This reflects the focus in the literature. A broader research strategy, however, is required in real estate and construction because of the wide prevalence of networks and their country-specific characteristics. This does not necessarily mean rejecting particular theoretical approaches, rather it implies a need to circumscribe analysis within an appropriate institutional framework when necessary.

In previous work (Ball 1998; 2002), I have argued that one approach to undertaking this contextualisation is to define specific 'structures of pro-vision' – that is, the networks of organisations (firms, regulatory bodies, etc.) and institutions associated with production and transaction of parti-cular types of built structure. The differentiation of structures of provision in real estate usually depends on four interrelated dimensions:

1. the type of building use: residential, office, etc.;
2. the property rights of investors and users: owner occupiers, renters, land-lords, etc.;
3. combinations of organisations involved in networks of production and exchange;
4. institutions used in the sense of customs, laws and practices, which in many aspects are country-specific or, even, provision structure-specific (e.g. in social housing).

Structures of provision may be an institutional approach in the general sense of the term, but the idea is not put forward in order to develop an alternative to other institutional theories. Instead, the aim is to ground analysis of certain empirical situations by identifying the need to understand networked contexts.

New institutionalist theories have what can be called a 'meta-causal dynamic', a set of features that are argued to drive organisational outcomes, such as transaction costs minimisation or the actions of rational agents in maximising the returns from their economic property rights. (Economics, more generally, adopts the meta approach of constrained optimisation by rational agents in the context of given preferences and technologies.) Structures of provision do not have such a theoretical status, because causal theories are still required to understand real world networks even after the specification of empirical contexts. Those causal theories will, to a great degree, also define the precise network arrangements that need to be defined, because theories focus on particular elements that they hypothesise to be crucial.

The need for some general institutional grounding is particularly important in real estate and construction because of the significance of country- and market-specific organisational interrelationships, as argued above. Furthermore, there is an important element of path dependency in the way in which these networks change, so that widespread differences remain between countries and within countries over time. Why these differences remain is itself an important research question in its own right. At the same time though, there is no obvious reason why convergence in them should take place.

When is an institutional analysis appropriate?

Those who have been diligently reading this chapter have worked through many pages discussing specificity in real estate and construction and a variety of approaches to the understanding of markets and organisations. Does this mean that acres of institutional specificity are required when examining these industries? To answer this question with 'yes, always' is misguided. A better reply would be: 'it all depends on the questions being asked'.

The chapter started off with an analysis of why real estate and construction markets are generally competitive. For many real estate and construction analyses, a competitive approach seems a perfectly reasonable assumption and the abstractions of the competitive model are likely to be good predictors of real market features. This is particularly the case with the aggregate performance of these industries and also with many more micro-analyses, such as the implicit values of housing attributes in hedonic studies, as discussed earlier. It seems utterly wrong, therefore, to dismiss the many important studies of these industries simply on the grounds that they ignore some real world complexities. To take such a position to its logical extreme would be to deny any role for theoretical abstraction. The competitive principle within an abstract optimising analytical framework should surely remain as a central element of most analyses because of the power of its results.

For particular research questions, however, institutions in some form or another may matter far more. For example, explaining what actual real estate and construction firms do and how they are changing is likely to require a firm empirical grounding in institutional factors. Similarly, in studying differences in market performance and behaviour between countries one might well be advised to recognise key country peculiarities. Yet, even in these contexts, the significance of institutions should be treated as a working hypothesis that needs to be subject to scrutiny. In the next chapter, on recent international housing market performance, for example, it is argued that easy answers to country differences cannot actually be found by reference to institutional variations alone.

Furthermore, even when one examines issues that have a key institutional element, it is unnecessary to specify the full range of institutional factors. Instead, only particular ones may be relevant. Many of the following chapters treat institutional frameworks in such partial or implicit ways.

It might be argued that there is a contradiction in a viewpoint that sees institutional analysis in its broadest sense as being empirically, as well as theoretically, contingent. The principles of aggregation would surely suggest that something that holds at one level of detail must equally hold at others. The answer to this conundrum again rests on the meaning of abstraction. The elements of the real world that get classified as 'institutional' in some of the above theories implicitly 'appear' within empirical analyses based on relatively simple competitive market models. This is because they help to determine the parameter values of variables – response coefficients, elasticities and the like. As long as there are no significant changes in institutional frameworks, it is reasonable to assume that those parameter values remain stable. In fact, parameter stability is a fundamental assumption of modelling work and, generally, institutions and the like may reasonably be ignored. However, shift factors may periodically occur in institutional frameworks, in which case they should be empirically investigated.

A common finding in housing market studies, for example, is that house price dynamics react to institutional changes in mortgage markets, such as a sudden relaxation of credit constraints (or 'liberalisation'). Models have to deal with such changes but that does not deny their general usefulness; quite the opposite, as they can help identify the relative importance and consequences of such changes.

Instances of several currently-occurring institutional shift effects can be found in several of the later chapters. One shift, for example, may be currently taking place within commercial markets (Chapter 7), because of the globalisation of real estate service providers. This is likely to be affecting the performance of individual commercial real estate markets by enhancing the international availability of market information and the ease of investment. Another institutional parameter shift argument relates to the increasingly restrictive regulations on housing land supply being brought in in a number of countries in recent years. These may not simply be having a direct impact on housing supply but, also, be inducing further constraints indirectly via house-builder behavioural responses to the new land supply situation.

Institutional approaches can also offer valuable insights into understanding what sorts of market reforms may be needed. This is brought out clearly in debates over the efficacy of markets in relation to other forms of allocation. Real world markets may be uncompetitive, in which case the claimed benefits of markets do not necessarily materialise (Rajan & Zingales 2004). This may be the case in developing countries, where political opposition to market reforms is frequently strong. A poor slum dweller, for instance, when required to buy water may only face one monopoly provider that has little incentive to do anything but command the highest possible economic rent out of the transaction. Reforms, therefore, may only work in specific institutional contexts. Institutional arrangements have to exist that ensure the existence of competition or, where this is impossible, lead to the setting up of regulatory regimes to provide incentives that mimic competitive outcomes.

This conclusion about the proper institutional context extends to networks of relationships, which have been argued above to be so widespread in real estate and construction. Creating competition in one part of a network might easily fail to generate the hoped-for outcomes if competition does not exist elsewhere.

This point about the need for system-wide competition comes out clearly in policy debates over reforms in transitional economies, where extensive state intervention and support for particular enterprises is being replaced by more market-oriented programmes. The analysis of housing market reform in Central and Eastern Europe in Chapter 5, for example, suggests that supply-side competition is often weak. The situation consequently is at variance with the conclusion drawn earlier in this chapter that the supply-side is a prime guarantor of competition in real estate.

Once again, however, these points about institutional networks are contingent on actual empirical situations, the questions being asked and assumptions being made. In many of the following chapters, for example, institutions do not play the key role. Instead, as already noted, a range of theoretical perspectives is adopted, which ones depend on what seems more applicable.

3

House price cycles: evidence from recent European experience

Introduction

An examination of recent house price behaviour in Europe illustrates the problems of housing market generalisations:

1. Several European countries have seen very high real house price rises over the past two decades, notably in order of scale of increase: Spain, Ireland, the Netherlands, the United Kingdom and Belgium. They have all significantly surpassed the leading non-European highest price rise contender: Australia (see Table 3.1).
2. Many other European countries have experienced significant real rises in house prices over the same time period.
3. In contrast to the booming countries, others have had declining or stagnant house prices over the past decade: notably, Austria, Germany and Switzerland.
4. Housing market cycles, their scale and associated volatility vary significantly across Europe. This is true for countries within the Euro-zone as outside of it, so uniform short-term interest rate setting is not leading to uniform housing market behaviour.

European countries contain housing markets with a myriad of relevant policies, institutions, tenure shares and market performances. Trying to capture those differences into a few features is a hard task. Even so, considering what has happened to house prices across Europe in recent decades enables insights into some key housing market differences to be discerned. An advantage of such variation is that it provides some useful empirical evidence on how housing markets work. Unfortunately, the available data are insufficiently good or comprehensive to undertake modelling

Table 3.1   Characteristics of the most recent house price upswings[+] in Europe.

Country	Approx. 2003 real house price (1985 = 100)	Approx. real house price rise in latest upswing (to 2003 %)	Start date of most recent real house price upswing	Current length of upswing (years to end 2004, brackets where period was earlier)
Austria	100	6[*]	1986 (to 1991, then declined, flat post-2000)	0 (5)
Belgium	210	110	1986	18
Denmark	120	65	1993	11
Finland	120	55	2002 (1 yr dip, otherwise 1996)	2 (8)
France	160	45	1996	8
Germany	95	15[*]	1985 (peaked 1995)	0 (10)
Ireland	260	160	1995	9
Italy	150	40	1998	6
Netherlands	255	160	1991 (zero real price change since 2002)	0 (10)
Spain	315	75	1998	6
Sweden	150	50	1997	7
Switzerland	95	4	2000 (1–2% annual price growth only)	4
UK	240	100	1996	8

+ Upswing is defined as a period of continuous positive real price growth.
* Upswings in Austria, 1990–94; Germany, 1988–1996.

Sources: Own calculations based on Ball, 2003, 2005b and BIS data.

work on these issues. All the same, some useful indicators are at hand with which to address these topics.

Three specific questions are addressed here:

1. To what extent do European countries' housing markets exhibit a similar price performance over time in terms of trend growth and fluctuations around those trends?
2. Apart from the scale of price changes, what are the comparative temporal patterns? That is, do European countries' house price cycles approximately follow each other over time?
3. What can explain any discovered differences in European countries' house price behaviour? In particular, to what extent are those differences systematic and caused by stable institutional factors or how much are they a result of unpredictable variations in historical events?

Attention will be paid to the old EU15 countries plus Norway and Switzerland, with comparison made with the housing markets of other

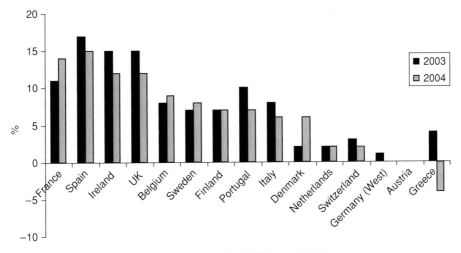

Figure 3.1 House price rises in Europe in 2003 and 2004.

Source: M. Ball, RICS *European Housing Review*, 2005.

advanced economies, because these are the ones with mature housing markets and so they can be examined over a long period of time. In contrast, the new EU accession countries have distinctive and relatively new markets, particularly those in Central and Eastern Europe, and they are considered in Chapter 4.[1]

2003–2004 was the peak period of house price inflation for most EU housing markets, particularly when account is taken of a mixture of indicators – prices, transactions, housebuilding and mortgages. Figure 3.1 shows 2003–4 out-turn rates of house price inflation across Europe.

Of the larger countries, only Germany had a stagnant housing market throughout the period, a market situation that has existed for a decade. Even there, signs of increased mortgage demand by owner occupiers in the second half of the year suggested that the long downswing in its housing market cycle was finally over. Elsewhere, Austria also had a long-term stagnant housing market and Greek house prices fell slightly, though transactions, as indicated by mortgage demand, were high.

With the exception of Austria, Germany and Switzerland, housing markets have been strong in Western Europe for seven years or more. Some countries had already seen the end of major price booms, notably the UK from mid-2004 and the Netherlands, from 2001. However, in neither country did it seem that house prices were about to crash, rather that prices were levelling off in real terms.

The most recent housing price cycle in context

The house price boom has been quite a long one (see Table 3.1). Other advanced economies, such as the USA from 1995 and Australia from 1996, have also had long periods of rising real prices.[2] In contrast, Japan has experienced falling prices since the early 1990s.[3]

Belgium's upswing is the longest. It seems to have been going on for almost two decades. However, other countries have experienced prolonged growth: Denmark for 11 years and others for 6 years or more. Prior to that homeowners in many countries saw house prices fall in real terms for several years in the early 1990s after an earlier 1980s boom. In summary, a common historical experience of fluctuating house prices exists across Europe, though there has not been a particularly close correspondence in the timing of the price cycles of each country, as Table 3.1 shows.

The last two decades for many countries, furthermore, stand in stark contrast to the previous era from the early 1970s to the mid-1980s, when house price growth rates were generally far less. Denmark, Italy and the UK are the only European countries to witness substantial trend price growth in both eras (Table 3.2). In fact, there is a generally negative correlation between the ranks of house price growth in the first period and the second one. This suggests that countries cannot be divided broadly into low and high house price inflation sectors beyond fairly narrow time frames, with the possible exception of the UK.

The temporal changes in Europe, in addition, map those occurring elsewhere in advanced economies. The average rate of real house price inflation grew in Europe from a modest level in the 1970s and first half of the 1980s to far more substantial levels in the second half of the 1980s through to the mid-2000s. The 'English-speaking' world in general, as well as Europe, experienced such an event, while Japan did not.

The length of the most recent house price upswings in European countries is by no means historically unique. House prices in France, for example, rose for two decades in real terms up to the late 1970s, pushing prices up almost threefold. Other countries have had similar long upswings in the past (Ball & Grilli 1997).[4] This suggests that house price fluctuations and relatively long cycles in them are a fact of economic life. Tantalisingly, such price fluctuations do not come in neat regular cycles; instead both the length and amplitudes of upswings and downturns are highly irregular.[5]

Table 3.2 Real house price growth 1970s–80s and 1980s–2000s compared.

Rankings	Growth % pa average	
	1971–1985	1986–2003
Europe		
Spain	−0.2	6.8
Ireland	0.4	5.9
Netherlands	0.0	5.3
United Kingdom	2.3	4.7
Belgium	−0.3	4.1
France	0.7	2.6
Sweden	−1.5	2.6
Italy	1.9	2.6
Norway	0.8	1.9
Finland	0.4	1.6
Denmark	1.9	1.2
Germany	0.2	0.0
Switzerland	1.2	−0.6
Other countries		
Australia	1.6	3.7
Canada	0.8	2.5
United States	0.7	1.7
New Zealand	0.0	0.9
Japan	2.1	−0.6
'Europe' average	0.6	3.0
'World' average	0.7	2.6

Source: Based on IMF data.

These fluctuations, moreover, occur around a varying, but positive trend, with average house prices rising by less than 1% annually in Europe between 1971 and 1985 and 3% between 1986 and 2003. Of course, the trend figure would be different with distinct end points to the periods, yet this simple division does suggest that the trend is not constant. However, it is positive – although noticeably variable between countries.

If housing supply was perfectly elastic over the long run, there should be no trend in house prices. A positive long-run supply schedule may be attributable to three factors:

1. An increasing shortage of land, which may have planning or accessibility (e.g. increasing congestion) causes.
2. Rising costs in housebuilding, due to a mix of either slower relative productivity growth or mounting skill shortages caused by an increasing reluctance of working populations to undertake construction work.

3. An identification problem, whereby house price indices fail to take account of housing quality changes that households are willing to pay more for.

Although there are few studies of these issues, land shortages and productivity factors seem to be the most likely influences on long-run house prices (Ball 1996; Barker 2003).

House price volatility

The irregularity of house price cycles shows through in house price volatility. Table 3.3 shows price volatility for the same sample of countries as listed in Table 3.2. It can be seen that volatility varies considerably over time – both between countries and within each one. This suggests that it is going to be difficult to identify countries with housing market regimes that induce greater price stability over the long term than others.

Table 3.3   Real house price volatility 1970s–1980s & 1980s–2000s compared.

	1971–1985	1986–2003	Difference*	Rank 71–85	Rank 86–03
Europe					
Finland	6.9	11.8	4.9	7	1
Spain	8.6	9.4	0.8	5	2
Norway	4.5	8.5	4.0	11	3
United Kingdom	11.1	8.4	−2.7	3	4
Sweden	5.9	7.6	1.7	10	5
Italy	12.3	7.5	−4.8	1	6
Denmark	10.1	6.4	−3.7	4	7
Ireland	6.6	6	−0.6	8	8
Switzerland	6.5	5.9	−0.6	9	9
France	4.3	4.7	0.4	12	10
Netherlands	11.7	4.1	−7.6	2	11
Germany	3.3	2.6	−0.7	13	12
Belgium	7.9	1.7	−6.2	6	13
Other countries					
Australia	5	6.6	1.6	4	1
Canada	6.8	5.6	−1.2	3	2
Japan	8	4.6	−3.4	1	3
New Zealand	8	4.4	−3.6	1	4
United States	3.4	2.7	−0.7	5	5
'Europe' average	7.7	6.5	−1.2		
'Other' average	7.3	6	−1.3		

* Period 2 minus Period 1.

Source: Own calculations and IMF.

The reduction in volatility overall from the first high inflation period to the second lower inflation one is similar in Europe to elsewhere. However, the reduction is quite small. Furthermore, there are only a limited number of countries that are either high or low volatility countries over both periods. In Europe, Spain and the UK are towards the more volatile end of the spectrum in both rankings; whereas France and Germany are towards the lower ends and Ireland and Switzerland somewhat below average. Elsewhere, the USA consistently ranks as the least volatile country – though it has greater price fluctuations than Belgium and Germany in the second period.

The historical specificity of these volatility data is highlighted by the current behaviour of house prices in France. Although it has traditionally been a low price volatility country, in the 2000s French house prices surged and, so, its erstwhile price stability is rapidly disappearing.

Causes of house price changes

Table 3.4 identifies several factors that are generally regarded as influential on house price change:

- economic growth
- increases in housing supply
- share of owner occupation
- mortgage debt to income ratio
- increase in mortgage indebtedness
- extent of use of fixed and variable rate mortgages
- existence of mortgage interest tax relief.

It can be seen from the table that there is not a simple systematic relationship across countries between house prices and economic growth, housing supply, existing degree of mortgage indebtedness or whether mortgages are fixed or variable interest rate based. Therefore, singular institutional or economic performance factors are unlikely to be straightforward explanations of contrasting housing market performance.

Perhaps the one factor that stands out most strongly in Table 3.4 is the scale of mortgage interest tax relief (MITR). The most generous countries tend to have had the highest recent increases in house prices, namely Ireland, the Netherlands, Belgium and Spain. (Italy has traditionally had poor mortgage availability and so is not directly comparable with the other MITR countries and Switzerland's tax system is tenure neutral with respect to MITR and generally more favourable to renting.) However, the

Table 3.4 Potential causes of house price inflation.

	Approx. real house price rise in latest upswing to 2003 %	Average annual growth 1995–2003 in:		Owner occupation % 2001–3	Mortgage debt to GDP ratio % 2002	% change in M/GDP ratio 1996–2002	% variable rate mortgages 2002	Mortgage interest tax relief
		GDP	Res. invest					
Ireland	160	8.2	11.6	77	37	32	70	Y
Netherlands	160	2.5	1.2	54	88	40	26	Y
Belgium	110	2.0	1.4	68	28	21	25	Y
UK	100	2.7	2.6	69	62	2	72	N
Spain	75	3.2	6.3	81	38	61	75	Y
Denmark	65	2.1	5.0	51	82	22	25	Y+
Finland	55	3.6	4.9	58	32	3	97	Y+
Sweden	50	2.8	0.9	60	48	–17	62	Y+
France	45	2.2	2.2	56	19	5	20	N*
Italy	40	1.7	1.2	80	11	36	56	Y
Austria	0	2.0	–1.3	56	27	22	30	Y+
Germany	0	1.3	–1.6	43	51	4	30	N
Switzerland	4	1.3	–2.1	31	–	–	–	Y

* France has many subsidised mortgage schemes.
+ MITR is limited.

Sources: Based on Ball, 2003b, 2005b, BIS, OECD, *Housing Statistics in the EU*, 2003.

UK provides illustration that abolishing MITR is no guarantee of a slow rise in house prices.

Higher house price inflation countries also tend to have high ratios of owner occupation, with the exception of the Netherlands; whereas lower house price inflation countries tend to have 40% or more renting. This may suggest that higher entry costs to owner occupation discourage tenure transfer to home ownership and the resultant lack of first time buyer demand stops prices from escalating too fast. However, this argument is one-sided as it looks only at the consumption of rental housing. In order to absorb the increases in housing demand that are the potential stimulus to house price rises in the first place, vacancies or additional supply have to exist in rental housing. Where do they come from? Does not that demand raise house prices itself? In other words, investment behaviour by landlords has to be incorporated into the picture. The very price rises that deter first-time buyers from owner occupation may encourage investors into rental housing. Moreover, they might have higher expectations of future house price rises than first-time buyers and are prepared to put up with low yields from rental income on the expectation of future capital gains. Hence, they can have higher housing demand than the potential first-time buyers they displace from purchase and accommodate in their rental homes during price booms. A rush of investors into rental housing has occurred in Australia, Ireland and the UK, for example, over the last decade. It is debatable consequently whether a higher share of rental housing actually stabilises housing demand and house prices.

An alternative interpretation of the impact of higher shares of renting may be that it is acting as a surrogate indicator of somewhat different processes associated with the process of buying and selling dwellings. For example, it may be highlighting a transactions effect in that high homeownership countries have more liquid housing markets where buying and selling is easier and so price changes are more rapidly transmitted through the housing stock as a whole than in higher renter share countries.

Weight is given to the transaction argument when it is recognised that some high renter countries' housing markets are more segmented than others and such segmentation limits price transmission effects and/or influences the rate of change of measured housing prices. In a country like Germany, for example, many new owner-occupier dwellings do not appear in the house purchase statistics because they are individually built on purchased land sites. Increased demand for such properties, therefore, will transmit potential price effects through the land and construction markets not the housing market.[6] The same is true in France, where around

40% of new dwellings are built in such a way, and in Belgium, Greece, Italy and several other countries. Such 'self-organised' building may also be a way of avoiding paying tax and so not be associated with large increases in mortgage finance either.

A reduction in new building or a greater capture of such housebuilding in the statistical net may also explain some house price changes. In Belgium and Italy, for example, land shortages have encouraged a significant switch from new housebuilding to improvement of the existing stock. The price of existing dwellings has consequently risen relative to new ones. As house price indices in those countries are predominantly based on estate agent sales of existing dwellings, they may consequently be exaggerating the true extent of house price inflation. In more integrated house markets, especially those that rely most strongly on second-hand sales, demand transmission is more likely to occur through a succession of well-recorded purchases and sales by different households in transaction chains (and be clearly measured as housing market activity).

One conclusion that comes out strongly from these observations is that the institutional structure of housing markets not only affects their operation but also their measurement. Consequently, care has to be taken when comparing country data to avoid spurious results.

One factor missing from Table 3.4 is information on mortgage credit availability. This is some of the most difficult information to come by systematically but, obviously, most households in situations of rising house prices are going to have to borrow ever-larger sums to fund home purchases. Mortgage availability, therefore, may be a crucial variable in understanding whether a country's financial system is accommodating to significant house price increases or not. A number of countries do seem to have had noticeable increases in mortgage credit availability over the last decade, for one reason or another, including most of the higher house price inflation countries. France and Italy have also seen more recent relaxations in mortgage lending criteria and those two countries have experienced somewhat later house price accelerations in recent years.

According to a recent study by the European Central Bank (ECB 2005), competition in mortgage markets has increased markedly throughout the EU. Nevertheless, much of this competition has been within country with little cross-border lending taking place, and there has not been much cross-border movement of, or consolidation between, financial institutions. Structural differences remain great in the institutional frameworks of mortgage finance: in legal, tax and intermediation structures, mortgage products and lending procedures. Mortgage finance rationing, where it previously existed, is likely to have been eroded – though lending criteria are still highly variable. Even so, a simple correlation between the most relaxed mortgage lenders and the rate of change of house prices is unlikely.

Another absent element is the degree to which rising price expectations have become ingrained in popular perceptions of housing markets. With substantial price increases lasting for 6 to 18 years across many of Europe's housing markets, many consumers have ingrained expectations of future rises, especially when pundits' forecasts of future stagnation or falling house prices fail to materialise. Obviously, prices cannot rise forever, so that each year the major price rises continue the more likely they are to be driven by unrealistic investment expectations and the greater is the probability of a period of falling real prices in the future.

Housing regions?

The ranking in Table 3.4 does suggest that there might be some regional similarities across Europe in house price behaviour, although the correlations may be chance events. Adjacent countries seem to be behaving in broadly similar ways, enabling four house price regions to be loosely identified.

1. *Nordic countries* Denmark, Finland, Norway and Sweden. They have experienced broadly similar 'mid-range' house price inflation for many years. They also all suffered from housing market 'bubble' shocks in the late 1980s/early 1990s, which has left them with relatively high measured price volatility. They have high shares of rental housing, which itself is subject to strict controls, with the partial exception of Finland. They have comparatively high levels of housing output, with the exception of Sweden. Economic growth has been strong and geographically focused in recent years. Mortgage markets are highly concentrated.
2. *Central European countries* Austria, Germany and Switzerland. They have had stagnant housing markets for many years. Economic growth has been poor. Housing supply is relatively elastic by European standards. Rental sectors are large and strongly regulated. Housing markets are weakly integrated. Mortgage finance is strongly regulated as well.
3. *Northern Atlantic countries* Belgium, Ireland, the Netherlands and the UK. They have experienced the greatest recent house price rises.

Economic growth has been strong, particularly in Ireland, and geographically focused. Mortgage markets are moderately concentrated. Housing supply has been poor, with the partial exception of Ireland (though there much new housing is in the wrong places). Two of the countries in this group have recently experienced stagnation in their house prices: the Netherlands and the UK.
4. *Mediterranean countries* France, Italy and Spain. Experience here has been more mixed, but all three have had substantial house price inflation, which has been accelerating in recent years. They share different institutional traditions from countries in the other groupings, though they are generally unique traditions, rather than reflecting the common features of the first two groupings.

The importance of supply

As with all other goods, the long-term price of housing is determined by the costs of its supply. Supply is slow to come on stream in housing markets, so that short-term house prices tend to overshoot longer-term ones. Two supply-side factors have had a long-term influence on European house price growth:

1. A greater concentration of economic activity in a number of countries in a narrow range of growth regions. The more geographically concentrated economic activity is, the less is the available existing housing stock and residential land supply able to satisfy increases in housing demand.
2. One of the major problems of housing markets in Europe is that an already low supply responsiveness to housing market upturns is generally becoming worse. Some countries, such as Denmark, the Netherlands and Sweden, for a variety of reasons have relatively high construction costs. Most, to varying degrees, have tightening land-use policies that limit the supply of building land, particularly in the regions where it is in greatest demand.

The UK is renowned for the cap on suburban housing growth in southern England imposed by its planning system, and recent central and local government announcements about land supply indicate that the problem will grow (Barker 2004). Attempts to deal with the Irish housing boom have also focused on tardy land supply and the need for more infrastructure facilities to open up additional development sites (NESC 2004). Municipalities in Spain were blamed for delaying land release for several years, although housebuilding has picked up strongly in recent years – though less so in the major cities. In the Netherlands, in the second half of the 1990s, a stricter land development policy was introduced at a time when housing demand was extremely strong. Belgium is also experiencing severe land shortages. Even Sweden, which once could claim to have low land costs, now faces problems of growing development land shortages (Ball 2005b).

Some element of current house price surges, therefore, may be that market actors are anticipating the implications of a more restricted European housing supply.

Shifts in real wealth and impacts on labour mobility and general inflation

The real price of housing has risen by substantial amounts in a number of European countries. This can be seen in Table 3.1 where, by 2003, house prices have risen since the mid-1980s by over threefold in Spain; over twofold in Belgium, Ireland, the Netherlands and the UK; and by 20 to 60% in France, Italy and the Nordic countries.

This substantial wealth increase creates 'affordability' problems for new entrants to housing markets who are hit by high entry costs.[7] It also generates substantial shifts in wealth within societies between property owners (landlords as well as owner occupiers) and non-property owners. Such substantial distributional changes run counter to frequent claims within Europe of a greater concern with distributional issues than exists in less 'socially concerned' countries elsewhere in the world.

Furthermore, high housing entry costs restrict labour mobility identified by many as so important to European countries' growth prospects. It is paradoxical that a country like the UK can be proud of its labour market flexibility, contrasting its characteristics in that respect to countries such as Germany,[8] while at the same time negating the possibility of mobility for many by the existence of barriers in the housing market, which contemporarily exist far less in a 'rigid labour market' country like Germany.

It is interesting to note that many of the highest house inflation countries in Europe have also been the most general price inflation prone ones over the last five years, including Ireland, the Netherlands and Spain. In part, this has been due to the stimulus to consumer demand of house wealth and equity withdrawal, but there has been a labour market route for housing-related influences as well, particularly when collective bargaining is an important element of wage setting as it is in a number of European countries, such as the aforementioned countries Ireland, the Netherlands and Spain.

Are there world residential price cycles?

With many advanced economies and some lesser developed ones experiencing marked increases in real house prices over the last decade, many observers argue that there has been a world house price upswing over the period that, writing early in 2005, has yet to end.[9] Much debate focuses on whether these rises represent 'price bubble' features and what consequences are likely to arise. Within that debate, commentators and experts are divided on the lines of a two-by-two matrix; the rows of which separate those with a 'hard' view of a severe price crash or a 'soft' view of price stagnation after the boom and the columns divide those that think the impact of the end of the housing boom for individual countries' economies or the world economy will be substantial or limited.

One major problem with the notion of a world residential price cycle is that it relies on a one-sided interpretation of the available empirical evidence. The most notable counter-evidence is that the world's second and third largest economies – Japan and Germany, plus some of its richest – like Austria and Switzerland, rather than seeing rapid house price rises over the last decade, have experienced long periods of stagnant or falling house prices. Moreover, even for the countries with rises in prices, neither the timing of recent house price upswings nor their scale are actually that well correlated. Empirical generalisations about world property markets, thus, fall foul of widespread real diversity in housing market behaviour.

In addition, there are theoretical problems with the world housing market view. The question has to be asked as to what transmission mechanisms generate world, rather than country or region specific, residential price booms. People tend to live and move only within one country or even regions and cities within them. International migration is relatively small in housing market terms and, even though it may stimulate housing demand in the recipient nation, it is simultaneously depressed in the country of origin. In any case, the majority of migrants tend not to have incomes as high as incumbent households. The same conundrum is true of economic growth as a housing demand stimulus – booming national or regional economies may be offset by declining or stagnant ones elsewhere.

Real economic variables, however, rarely appear in generalisations about world house prices. The suggested causes focus overwhelmingly on monetary and financial factors. The three most cited concern the behaviour of the price level (inflation has fallen markedly over the last decade), interest rates (they are at historic lows) and asset allocation strategies (investors in an era of easy credit are frustrated in the aftermath of post-dot.com and bond price booms and have diverted funds into housing). Such monetary factors obviously affect housing markets but so do many other variables. No credible housing market model, in fact, is a purely monetary one; instead they identify arrays of real and monetary factors influencing demand and supply.

The timing of housing market cycles, moreover, depends on *local* demand and supply circumstances. Demand is determined by local demographics, migration, taxation and subsidy policies plus institutional and structural economic change, as well as the general pattern of income, interest rate and other macroeconomic change. Supply responsiveness varies considerably as well, so that regional housing market behaviour in any individual country varies in the timing of its cycles. The same lack of synchronisation holds when comparing countries as well.

Conclusions and policy implications

A diversity of housing market experiences has been identified across Europe and across time. The length and irregularity of housing market cycles has important policy implications.

First, changes in the phases of cycles are extremely hard to identify when they are occurring. Measures to moderate fluctuations, such as interest rate adjustments or demand stimulation measures, consequently face severe problems of identifying when to intervene. France shows this problem starkly. In the late 1990s and early 2000s, a series of housing market demand stimuli were introduced in the, what turned out to be false, belief that demand needed boosting – whereas, in fact, it needed to be dampened.

The second major problem facing attempts to intervene in housing markets is that general economic activity and housing market demand do not necessarily correlate well. It is easy to identify, after the event, situations when both move strongly in parallel. Yet there are probably more cases when they do not. Demand management clearly should be focused on performance in the macro-economy, rather than on the housing market. Dragging the housing market into such an arena, therefore, is often not helpful, especially as the relationship between house price and aggregate demand changes does not seem to be that stable.

It may be wisest to conclude that housing market fluctuations are an inevitable part of economic life. With that in mind, it is unadvisable to intervene and to regulate housing markets too strongly, because to do so loses substantial efficiency gains from market activity and builds up entrenched economic interest groups, whose rationale for state largesse becomes progressively diminished over time. Housing is a classic pressure group interest. Tax breaks and subsidies abound and, perhaps most important, special interest groups now have strong influences in restricting the supply of housing land in many European countries. Rather than over-reacting to housing market cycles, governments would be better advised to deal with the structural issues in housing of excessive tax breaks and subsidies, too much regulation (particularly in rental markets), poor productivity, weak infrastructure and insufficient land supply. Housing booms go away, these politically tricky structural issues do not.

Notes

1   An overview of these housing markets in provided in M. Ball *RICS European Housing Review 2005*, Ch. 3 [http://www.rics.org].
2   According to BIS data.
3   Japan has much self 'building' by owners, so that land prices proxy house prices. This makes for poor comparisons across time as the quality and size of dwellings built on land plots are likely to improve significantly over time, especially in Japan where land plots often arise from existing dwelling demolitions. Japanese 'house' price fluctuations, therefore, are likely to be substantially exaggerated relative to other countries' house price indices. This index number problem arises for several European countries where owner-organised building is prevalent, such as Belgium, Germany, France and Italy – see later – though the result might be to smooth price indices in some countries, such as Germany.
4   The average housing market cycle, from trough to trough, in Europe was estimated there to be around 12 years.
5   The same is true of housebuilding, over which there is a much larger historical literature than for house prices, see Ball *et al.* (1996).
6   German average house price indices are dominated by purchases and sales of flats, where owner-occupiers are competing with landlords. This may have an influential effect on the smoothness of German house price indices.
7   This does not mean that house price rises are necessarily bad news for new owner-occupiers because, as long as prices continue to rise, they receive large capital gains on their own highly geared capital.
8   This theme has been a frequent one of recent EU-related speeches by the current UK Chancellor of the Exchequer, Gordon Brown.

9   This view has been expressed most succinctly by researchers at the IMF, though other leading international banking organisations and many national central banks have also followed suit. More journalistic international publications, such as *The Economist*, have also promoted the world property boom view and issued dire warnings of the disastrous impacts of its aftermath.

4

Improving housing markets

Introduction

The last chapter examined housing markets in an affluent part of the world – western Europe. This chapter broadens the focus and concentrates on housing in countries where markets do not work so well. This is particularly the case in many parts of the Third World and in transitional economies that have been moving over the last fifteen years or so away from central planning and widespread state ownership and control. This chapter focuses on some general principles and the following one looks at the experience of Central and Eastern Europe in more detail.

An aim is to highlight why market processes are generally the best way to deal with housing problems and explore the conditions necessary to make markets work properly. Markets, it should be stated at the outset, are no panacea for housing problems. This is because many housing problems have root causes that lie outside of the market process itself in such features as poverty, the fact that many people cluster together in a few large cities and compete for scarce space, and the scale of the resources needed to provide adequate housing for all. The argument is that holding back the market makes matters far worse than they would otherwise be.

Housing markets are explored, first, by highlighting the high cost of housing and the need to spread those costs over long periods of time. Solutions to this time factor lead to the various housing tenures that exist, divided along the fault line of owner occupation and renting. Next, a high proportion of the world's population lives in 'informal' housing that does not have full legal title – yet this does not put it beyond the market. There is strong evidence from the informal sector that markets spontaneously arise whenever someone needs accommodation and others have the means to make money by assisting with that need. Then, the underlying causes of housing shortages are examined, and the following sections present the argument of why a market approach is best and the issues that need to be addressed if housing markets are to be improved.

It is argued that housing markets are the main way forward for housing provision, because of: the sheer cost of housing, the greater choice they offer, the better response to people's preferences and the efficiency gains of competition. The principal way to gain the benefits of market mechanisms is to create the appropriate institutional frameworks and to persuade governments to adopt market-friendly policies.

Housing is a basic necessity of life. Though many people in the world live in adequate accommodation, there are hundreds of millions who do not. The numbers are staggering. The United Nations Centre for Human Settlements estimates that 21 million new housing units are required annually in developing countries to accommodate household growth during the first decade of the twenty-first century. Moreover, over a billion people currently live in inadequate conditions in urban areas, and slums will grow to 3 billion by 2050 on current trends (UN-Habitat 2005), although some commentators suggest that extrapolating recent trends may be somewhat alarmist (Satterthwaite 2005). Nonetheless, the numbers are substantial even now. India alone lacks 20 million dwellings, 12% of its existing stock, and Mexico has a deficit of 6 million dwellings. Many homes lack basic services, such as sanitation and fresh drinking water. In addition, they may be located long distances from potential workplaces, with poor transport facilities.

Until a little over a decade ago, comments about poor housing provision would have led many expert commentators, politicians and ordinary people to conclude that housing was too important a feature of social life to be left to the market. Sustained intervention into housing markets – or their complete removal in some tenures – became a hallmark of virtually all countries' policies in the 1950s and 1960s. By then, for over 100 years, governments had been progressively conditioned to exerting ever greater intervention as one housing problem arose on top of others that previous policies had failed to resolve. Textbooks about countries' housing policy histories are weighty documents as they go through all the variations in subsidies, tax breaks, regulation, rent control and attempts to socialise ownership. Yet, by the late 1980s, the huge expense and the obvious failures of previous interventionist approaches meant that the policy pendulum was again swinging strongly in the direction of 'enabling housing markets to work'. That phrase has been the guiding theme of the World Bank programme aimed at raising interest in housing markets in development policy since the early 1990s (World Bank 1993). This programme has helped to change the policy debate. The extent to which such debate has been translated into actual policy practice has been more muted, because political barriers remain strong.

The high cost of housing

Housing is an expensive commodity. Typically, open market rents constitute between a fifth and a quarter of incomes, though in countries in transition from former socialist command systems, rents remain low at only a twentieth of incomes on average (Table 4.1). The poor often cannot afford to spend such proportions of their incomes on housing and so face particularly daunting housing prospects. Some developed countries subsidise housing for low-income groups; elsewhere, the poor have to cope as best as they can.

It is not in renting, however, but in owner occupation that market forces in housing have been recognised as most successful in recent decades. The majority of households in advanced economies are now homeowners and surveys show that most are relatively contented with their lot. Homeowner averages of around two-thirds of all households in the industrialised world contrast with the far lower shares of 50 years ago when the vast majority of households in such countries rented. This 'stake in the system' has made market processes more acceptable and understandable to the majority of developed countries' populations in ways that were infeasible in earlier periods.

Many developing countries also have strong owner-occupied sectors. Yet, there is a big difference. Typically, house prices in advanced economies are around four times household incomes, so that the finances, savings and asset holdings of many households are centred around their homes. Outside of the industrialised world, formal homeownership is often a far more expensive proposition. House price to income ratios are typically 7–9 times average incomes in Africa, the Arab States and Asia. In countries, such as Taiwan and Korea, household surveys show that people in their twenties and thirties often save a third of their income in order to try to buy a home. High house prices in South East Asian countries may, in fact, be an explanation of the phenomenally high personal savings rates there, because such saving is necessary to gain a foothold on the homeownership ladder (Deaton & Laroque 2001). In transitional economies, such as those emerging out of the former Soviet Union, house prices are even more daunting prospects for ordinary people with average prices 13 times incomes!

Table 4.1 Housing, infrastructure and finance: a world view.

Urban areas in:	House prices to incomes ratio (%)	Rents to incomes ratio (%)	Infrastructure expenditure per head ($)	Mortgage to credit ratio (%)	New houses per 1000 population
Africa	6.9	25	23	8	7.5
Arab States	6.5	19	71	10	5.6
Asia	8.4	23	21	5	9.6
Industrialised	4.3	21	589	38	4.6
Latin America	3.7	20	138	21	7.3
Transitional	12.7	5	82	10	2.5

Source: UN-Habitat.

Another barrier to homeownership is mortgage availability, which is limited outside of industrialised countries. In most of the world, residential mortgages represent 10% or less of the total credit advanced by countries' financial sectors. Recourse to borrowing for housing, when it is possible, relies instead on family sources or traditional, expensive money lenders.

That housing markets are no longer predominantly associated with private landlords has made them more politically acceptable to some, but at the cost in recent policy debate of underplaying the tenure that has been a traditional source of accommodation for those unable to afford direct ownership. Some, as a result, have criticised the World Bank's housing market policies for an over-emphasis on owner occupation (Gilbert 1997; UN-Habitat 2002).

Market-unfriendly housing policies

UN-Habitat estimates that 30–50% of households in developing countries are tenants. However, many countries' housing policies continue to discriminate against the tenure. Rent control was introduced in many countries decades ago, such as during the immediate post-colonial era in Africa and, most surprisingly, in Central Europe in the 1990s while other aspects of economic life were being hauled into the market sphere. The disastrous effects of rent control on the long-term supply of housing and housing choices can be seen throughout the world, as uneconomically low rents cut off new supply, the existing stock deteriorates with no incentive to maintain it and an important living option for households is closed off.

In 1960s Brazil, for example, two-thirds of new private housing was built to rent: now hardly any is constructed (De Soto 2001). Private rental sectors, nevertheless, are still large: for example, they are home to 34% of urban families in Colombia and to 4 million households in Mexico City alone (Gilbert & Varley 1991). Detailed studies have identified the debilitating effects of rent controls in cities in countries such as Ghana and Nigeria (Malpezzi & Sa-Aadu 1996; Ikejiofor 1998).

Rental housing provides opportunities for migrants to move to cities and is interlinked with owner occupation in two important ways via housing life-cycles. First, many tenants eventually become homeowners and, second, once they have built up small amounts of capital may well invest some of it in rental housing. This provides house-owning families with steady, secure rental incomes, which supplement other sources in contexts where regular savings through financial intermediaries for pensions and the like are non-existent and, simultaneously, inject much needed investment in housing. This life-cycle pattern, for example, was discovered in recent surveys of two Indian cities (Kumar 1996; 2001; 2002). Kumar has also pointed out that most rental housing remains 'opaque': hidden from the official gaze for fear of rental controls and punitive property taxation.

Market-unfriendly regulations, in fact, are endemic in housing provision throughout the world. Onerous, excessively slow and unnecessary building, plot-ratio and other planning controls, for instance, are common (Gilbert & Varley 1991). Many sub-Saharan African countries ban traditional building materials from neighbourhoods despite their cheapness and environmental benefits (Agbola 1987; Rakodi 1991; Wells *et al.* 1998).

Housing policies in developing countries tended to copy the practice in the developed world after 1945 by the setting up of public housing bodies for working-class housing and specialist housing finance institutions for middle-class and public-sector households to embark upon owner occupation. Public housing drained public-sector budgets, but had only limited effects on housing shortages, and became marked by inefficiency, high cost and poor quality throughout Latin America and Africa. In market-oriented societies, outside of Europe, public housing became a significant source of housing supply only in the unique environment of Hong Kong.

In the command economies of Eastern Europe, the former Soviet Union and China, though homeownership always remained significant, especially in rural areas, state housing became the major source of supply. It often came along with a job, as it was provided directly by state-owned large enterprises. Rents were kept very low, but so were housing and neighbourhood standards, and shortages remained persistently high.

The rise of informal housing

Faced with the prospect of no housing that they afford or obtain in formal housing markets, households live instead in the 'informal' sector. In many Third World cities, half or more of housing is in the informal sector. According to UN-Habitat, in Latin America around 70% of new housing is created in it.

For a variety of reasons, governments throughout the developing world have tolerated and even encouraged the phenomenal growth of informal sector housing over the last 50 years. After a number of years of occupation, states have also allowed the formalisation of parts of it. In contrast, countries that industrialised prior to 1950 were far more draconian with attempts to create squatter housing neighbourhoods. Statutes and strenuous court action from as early as Elisabeth I's reign, for example, made widespread squatting impossible in England.

With informal housing, property rights are unclear and many districts grow up from land invasions. Yet, it gives many households some degree of control over their housing needs. Its informal nature, moreover, means that dwellings can be built gradually over time as household resources permit.

Informal housing neighbourhoods, however, are characterised by very poor infrastructure facilities. This can be seen in the data provided in Table 4.1. Twenty-two times as much is spent on infrastructure per capita in industrialised countries as in developing Africa and Asia. Informal housing is both a cause and an effect of such low expenditure levels. Informal housing also inhibits labour market mobility, normal city growth and urban planning, which can all constrain overall economic growth prospects and long-term living standards.

The division between formal and informal housing, however, does not mean that markets exist only in formal housing sectors. Informal housing, instead, shows how pervasive markets are as people negotiate, buy and sell, and pay for accommodation. Builders, for example, may be hired to help with construction of the more substantial structures; money changes hands for connections to electricity cables; the right to live in a dwelling can be transferred via a series of quasi-legal devices; and the renting of rooms or whole dwellings is common. A survey of squatter settlements in Nairobi, for example, found extensive renting with some landlords letting out over thirty rooms (Amis 1984). Another study about Istanbul showed that informal building itself may be driven by the profit motive rather than directly by housing need. It was found that much illegal housing in the 1990s was erected on public land for financially speculative reasons by people or groups operating in the knowledge that the new homes would be made legal quite quickly by the populist local government. Invading a land site in this rapidly expanding city, consequently, offered the prospect of substantial capital gains from the new informal housing created when it was subsequently granted title (Turel 2002).

The division between home and work is frequently blurred in the informal sector. Housing is often integrated with income-generating work, with workshops built into homes. Studies, therefore, have found that upgrading homes can simultaneously lead to higher earnings from home-based activities (CUDS 2000).

Though by no means out of the market, informal housing, nevertheless, imposes considerable constraints on market relations. Its illegality makes buying, selling and renting both risky and inefficient. Dwellings cannot be used as collateral for loans. Mobility and household wealth, therefore, are much diminished. (It has been argued forcibly – and perhaps too strongly – that economic development in the Third World has been severely constrained by an absence of legal rights that stops capital, particularly from informal housing, being used as collateral in the financial system (De Soto 2001).)

Subsequent legalisation to achieve legality – recognised by many governments as the cheaper and politically preferable option to mass expulsions – is often cumbersome and costly. It is also hugely expensive to install infrastructure into such districts and basic building safety and urban planning criteria are absent. The fragmented spatial organisation of Third World cities makes traditional city planning tools well nigh impossible (Balbo 1993). Such features depress property values as well as environmental and living conditions.

The paradox, consequently, arises that the very benefits of easier access to housing via the informal sector impose long-term costs. Those centre on improving housing and living conditions within informal housing neighbourhoods once they have been established. Their existence, furthermore, significantly lowers access by large sectors of society to financial systems and wealth creation and, possibly, constrains general economic growth itself. Informal housing is now here to stay, but its limitations need to be addressed if developing countries are to achieve their economic and social goals. Many of those limitations exist, moreover, because of the constraints on market processes and incentives implicit in this type of housing.

What causes housing shortages?

The principal causes of housing shortages in developing countries are poverty, the sheer scale of population growth and the huge rates of urbanisation that have occurred in recent decades as the movement of people from the countryside into the cities (Satterthwaite 2005). Even with the most efficient of housing systems, it would be extremely difficult to cope with such poverty and change, especially in countries that already are very poor. The fundamental problem may be more a question of poverty than housing (UN-Habitat 2005). Much also depends on what happens to growth in China and India, which has been high in recent years, because a third of the world's poor live in those two countries. This growth has brought many out of poverty and increased the available resources to invest in areas like housing. Furthermore, some commentators suggest that the current ways of measuring poverty may underestimate the speed at which world poverty is being reduced (Deaton 2005).

Neighbourhoods and houses take time to build and only a limited proportion of national income can be devoted to housebuilding. Advanced economies typically devote 3–5% of their national incomes to housing production. Developing countries tend to build more and, so, their housing investment ratios are somewhat higher, but such large allocations mean less for other consumption and investment goods. This resource crowding out creates greater hardship in other aspects of personal consumption and may slow down economic growth.

With economic development, history shows that crude housing shortages are gradually overcome. Photographs of New York in the mid-nineteenth century, for example, show that what is now Central Park was covered in temporary 'squatter settlements'. Unfortunately, such long-term predictions are of little help to those in need of housing now. In the past, this 'now' predicament encouraged politicians to go for the apparent 'quick-fixes' of rent control and public housebuilding only to see them frequently leech away the mobilisation of large-scale private resources into housing, so that more 'action' leads to less 'result'.

Housing problems, moreover, are never completely eradicated, no matter the level of economic development. Extra housing is always needed as populations and household numbers change. Houses, furthermore, deteriorate and need replacement and modernisation. Economic inequality is expressed in housing, so the poor populations of rich countries often have relatively poor housing as one characteristic of their less fortunate economic state. Like all consumption goods, furthermore, the demand for housing is nearly inexhaustible. The higher incomes rise, the more housing people want to consume and the nicer is the location that they want to live in.

The locational aspect is important in making housing problems permanent fixtures of social and political life. Demand pressures at highly desired locations are inevitably greater than the available supply. The locational aspect is often neglected in debates over housing policy. People do not want any sort of housing, but accommodation that is in an attractive place, convenient for work and other aspects of life. Housing shortages, in part, are thus expressions of the fact that many people want to live at the same locations. Markets help to sort out such locational preferences through willingness-to-pay. Alternative social criteria on which to base policy when choosing between one person and another to live somewhere are by no means self-evident. They evolve by custom and practice when they occur in countries with bureaucratically allocated housing tenures and often seem fair only to their beneficiaries and their supporters, not to those who lose out.

Even so, the ways in which resources are directed to housing can make a great deal of difference: by affecting the amount of housing than can be created from a given set of inputs and by influencing the uses to which the existing housing stock is put and the extent to which housing is maintained and periodically refurbished. The market tends to be superior in these respects, as with most goods and services. The profit-motive and people's desire to better themselves can mobilise large amounts of resources into housing in ways that taxation and government direction cannot. More choice is available in the market and there are better and more rapid responses to people's changing preferences and needs. Market-based competition, in addition, forces home producers and providers to be efficient and cost-effective. The desire for financial gain encourages less wasteful use of the existing stock and also its continued maintenance and improvement. Locational desires are tested against willingness-to-pay, so that preferred locations are not simply the gain of a politically privileged few.

Important environments for well-functioning housing markets

Macroeconomic stability

Crises in housing markets are invariably associated with more general economic crises. The immediate transmission mechanism is generally via financial markets, which is not surprising as housing is such an expensive asset, but macroeconomic imbalances are usually the root cause. Economic crises may lead to high rates of interest, for example, and rising unemployment causes widespread loan defaults. Sharp bursts of inflation push up interest rates and create havoc with mortgage lending. The fate of many traditional mortgage lending institutions in Latin America, for instance, was inflation-induced insolvency.

Unsustainable real estate booms are typically lengthy subsequent periods of painful readjustment (Renaud 2002). Recovery can be extremely drawn out, as can be seen in the exceptional case of Japan where the housing market did not bottom out until 2001, more than ten years after the 1980s house price bubble. Japanese housing plot prices, for example, were worth 18% less in 2001 than seven years earlier[1] and in the more desirable parts of the major cities, like Tokyo, only small fractions of their heady 1980s values.

It is, of course, impossible to remove economic cycles completely and, to an extent, established housing systems are designed to cope with quite substantial market fluctuations. Marked economic crises, nevertheless, have disproportionate effects on housing because of its long-term characteristics. One of the criteria for improving the operation of housing markets, therefore, is to strengthen institutions so that they can withstand such shocks, as well as to manage economies so that sharp economic fluctuations do not wipe out housing institutions.

Functioning capital and credit markets

One of the reasons why mortgages are so little used outside of the advanced economies is that private capital markets are limited in scope and governments regulate and direct many capital flows. This is often done so that the public sector can gain a larger share of the available savings pool, but it is especially detrimental to housing, which relies on long-term savings and capital accumulation for its existence. Typically, in an advanced economy, housing represents about 50% of a nation's fixed capital stock.

Appropriate institutional structures for well-functioning housing markets

Complex webs of institutions are necessary for housing markets to work. When they function well, the average housing consumer hardly recognises its significance. Yet, when one or more is missing or performing badly, the result can be substantial costs and delays, and a far lower level of market activity than is feasible. The whole thrust of the current raft of policy initiatives aimed at enabling housing markets to work is precisely to create housing institutions – though there are inevitably differences in emphasis as to which are the most important. The World Bank, because of its position and objectives, has particularly been pushing the importance of mortgage providers. Others have been arguing most strongly for clearer property rights. Such differences, however, are questions of degrees of emphasis, because in practice all aspects are required. Reforms, however desirable, are likely to be piecemeal. So, is it better to put in place institutions that have a continuing interest in improving housing-related property rights and regulation or to fix the latter first, so that institutions can emerge? The issue is one of tactics, not strategy.

A subsidiary institutional factor is a need to create competitive environments to encourage organisations to be as efficient as they can. It is not always possible to have competition – in legal structures and depositories for documents about properties, for example. Then, there need to be mechanisms by which pressure can be exerted to ensure their efficiency and effectiveness. The lack of feedback loops – complaints procedures, legal redress, etc. – is one reason why bureaucracies can perform so badly.

Institutional procedures do not simply have to be in place, simultaneously there must be widespread knowledge of them and a skill-base to operate them. Both of these are frequently lacking.

Making demand and supply effective

Fixing property rights

Property law in the most well-defined and clearest of systems is a complex business as even the briefest glance at the bookshelves of a legal library demonstrates. Without clear property rights and means of enforcing them, it is hard for housing markets to function effectively. Buying and selling becomes problematic. Recourse to the courts is difficult. However, in many countries property law is frequently hazy and simultaneously based on a conflicting variety of systems. In such contexts, it may be impossible to prove full title to a dwelling or piece of land. Foreclosure laws are often weak as well, which discourages mortgage lending because there is little likelihood of being able to call in loan securities at times of default.

Legal transactions can also be lengthy, costly and arduous, involving repeated long queues to obtain successive pieces of paper, authorisation signatures and official stamps. It takes, for instance, 13 to 25 years to formalise informal property in the Philippines; 6 to 11 years in Egypt to build a legal dwelling on former agricultural land; and almost 7 years to obtain permission to build a home on public land in Peru (De Soto 2001).

Open and transparent markets

In most advanced countries, house selling and buying is a straight-forward business of advertising and searching in which professional agents are used to facilitate transactions and to assess the condition and value of properties. Anyone can buy and sell and laws are specifically enacted to stop unreasonable discrimination by sellers and mortgage lenders. Extensive information also exists about prices and the relative attractiveness and facilities of particular locations. Trends in house prices are well-publicised and are widely discussed. Rental information is also easy to come by. For little effort and cost, therefore, most home-owners have a good idea of what their property is worth, if they are selling, and, if they are buying, how much to pay and how much can be borrowed at what cost. Landlords and renters are pretty much in the same abundant information setting. Such general knowledge is an important by-product of open and transparent markets, but is frequently missing in many countries' housing systems.

In addition, in several countries, not everyone is allowed to operate in markets. Only people with permission to live in particular towns or from particular ethnic or religious backgrounds may act as buyers, sellers or renters. As well as being discriminatory, such practices severely distort market processes, which may end up hurting even the groups that the measures are supposed to privilege.

Transaction costs

Being active in the housing market is associated with high costs. Many of these costs are non-monetary: the time, for instance, that it requires to search for a home. Others, however, involve payment to agents or officials and as taxes, stamp duties and bribes. High transaction costs can limit market activity dramatically. In India, for example, a plethora of agencies exist from which approvals must be sought and they help to push trans-action costs up to 17% of property values in some states.

Mortgage finance

Borrowing enables households to fund owner occupation over a long time-period, in line with their income receipts, and makes it possible for landlords to raise finance for housing to rent. Not only is finance required for purchase, but also to fund builders when they acquire land and construct dwellings. All developed countries' housing markets, consequently, operate on the basis of extensive mortgage and other residential lending facilities and have done so since the early days of industrialisation. Mortgages in the developed world as a proportion of total house prices, moreover, have also risen significantly in recent years with liberalisation, greater competition and an increasing financial sophistication of homeowners.

Residential mortgage markets also represent good savings mediums for investors. Individuals can deposit their savings in retail mortgage institution accounts at good rates of interest in competitive mortgage markets. Alternatively, individuals, corporate or institutional investors can purchase mortgage bonds from specialist mortgage banks and buy mortgage-backed securities in the capital markets – again all at competitive rates if those markets are allowed to operate freely. Consequently, there is generally no funding shortage in private housing markets as long as borrowers are prepared to pay prevailing rates of interest. This contrasts with situations of financial rationing, where households cannot actually borrow the sums of money they need and are capable of repaying.

Mortgage markets also have to be structured to enable them to prosper in a risky environment. Mortgages are risky investments for many reasons: default risk, interest rate risk and prepayment risk. To cater for these risks, a variety of institutions and procedures have developed to provide liquidity and ensure solvency. Some of them have direct government or statutory backing, such as in retail savings deposit insurance or the charters of mortgage banks, or indirect public support – as with US secondary mortgage market institutions.

A successful mortgage finance industry, thus, requires considerably more than simply setting up mortgage issuing bodies. In addition, those bodies have to be embedded into a network of institutional rules and procedures, so that risks are contained and borrowers and investors have faith in them. Competition is also important to keep down intermediation costs and to enable financial innovation and associated technical changes to be absorbed rapidly and efficiently.

In developing countries, mortgage markets are often weak, monopolistic and limited in their scope (Buckley 1996). As a result, they represent far smaller proportions of credit systems, as was shown earlier in Table 4.1. Mortgages from private sector institutions are generally available only to higher income groups and, even then, frequently on less favourable terms than enjoyed by consumers in advanced economies.

Many countries have state-sponsored or owned mortgage bodies targeted at specific middle to higher income groups – public sector or formal sector factory workers, for example. Sometimes compulsory housing savings out of wages are channelled through such bodies. Such institutions are often forced to lend uneconomically and are prone to collapse (for example, in Brazil in the 1980s). Their monopoly powers, furthermore, inhibit the growth of other mortgage lending institutions. Low-income households, particularly those in the informal housing sector, are completely denied the advantages of mortgage finance.

Without finance to oil the wheels of commerce, housing markets inevitably function less effectively. Market transactions and consumption are both lowered, as consumers cannot so easily spread their housing costs across time. New housing is curtailed and moves are less frequent, so that households cannot switch to dwellings and locations that are better for them. This, in turn, hampers labour mobility and raises unemployment. There is less liquidity in the market and prices are likely to be more volatile and uncertain as a result.

Major efforts, none the less, have been made in recent years to improve mortgage finance, although it will be many years before residential mortgages are as important as in developed countries. Mortgage banks, for example, are being developed in several central European countries, including the Czech Republic, Hungary, Poland and the Slovak Republic (Black *et al.* 2000). A National Mortgage Bank has been set up in Mexico; secondary mortgage market institutions have emerged in Jordan and Malaysia. The World Bank has been instrumental in setting up mortgage corporations in Hong Kong, Korea and Colombia with hybrid mortgage origination and capital market functions. According to the Asian Development Bank, mortgage lending in India has been growing by 50% year-on-year in recent years. Though data are poor, a similar pattern of exponential mortgage growth has taken place in China.

A good example of such a development is Cagamas Berhad, the Malaysian National Mortgage Corporation, which has been in existence as a secondary mortgage market facility since 1986. Its aim is to improve access to capital finance for the country's mortgage finance system, which cuts mortgage costs through lowering both the liquidity and interest rate risks of originators. Cagamas does this by purchasing originators' mortgages and issuing mortgage-backed securities (mortgage payment risk remains with originators). By 1997, after only ten years of operation, it owned almost a third of Malaysia's residential mortgage debt and its securities represented 45% of all outstanding private credit sector securities. Its financial structure, furthermore, allowed it to weather the financial crisis of 1998 (Chiquier 1999).

The World Bank has been instrumental across a large number of countries in funding programmes aimed at reform and institution building in residential mortgage intermediation. The aim is to improve household access to bank financing for home purchase, building or renovation. For example, one recent project was aimed at creating a well-functioning mortgage loan market in Algeria. Its programme included: (1) legal and administrative measures to improve property rights, mortgage lien efficiency and a property titling and registration system; (2) strategic assistance to financial institutions; and (3) training of operational staff in mortgage lending.

Mortgage finance has little effect on those on low incomes because they do not have the means to repay loans, so that formal mortgage finance systems can only benefit the middle and higher income strata in developing countries. Moreover, about 70% of housing investment in developing countries takes place through incremental building, which is not financed by conventional mortgage financing institutions.

Shelter micro finance has answered this need in recent years, but its scale is still small in many countries (Smets 1997; UN-Habitat 2005). The micro component is twofold. First, small loans are generally required by low-income households but they involve unprofitably high transaction costs for formal lenders. Second, small lending institutions are needed, so that they are embedded in local social networks and able to provide adequate scrutiny of borrowers' ability to repay loans.

Micro loans have either evolved in housing through the extension of existing facilities aimed at small business enterprises or through the direct formation of housing sector bodies. Micro loans are used to fund construction works or housing improvement in the informal sector – though, to date, they have had little impact on land acquisition. Such micro initiatives are widespread. Examples include the Homeless People's Fund, South Africa; the Community Infrastructure Lending Programme, Guatemala; the Centre for Agricultural and Rural Development, San Pablo City, Philippines; the SEWA bank, India; and the Grameen Bank, Bangladesh (CUDS 2000).

Mortgage lending is only likely to develop at a rapid pace when markets are formal and efficiently functioning. This is because mortgages have to have unequivocal first-call on housing as an asset, which requires that a property's title is equally clear-cut. Moreover, lenders need to have information systems that enable quick evaluation of borrower risk and speedy, cheap recourse to foreclosure when payers default. Without the 'stick' of foreclosure, severe 'moral hazard' problems can emerge when borrowers know that it is hard to force them to pay and, so, are tempted to take out loans that they only have a low probability of repaying. Yet, in many countries, foreclosure is an expensive and time-consuming process. This is the case in India, for example, and the process of achieving the appropriate reform is proving politically difficult.

Mortgage lending, furthermore, can contribute to general financial crises if inappropriate controls are put in place. Residential lending can contribute to real estate bubbles that threaten the economy as a whole. This was evident in several South East Asian economies in the aftermath of the 1998 financial crisis. Similarly, in the run-up to the 'second' Mexican financial crisis in 1996 many middle-class homeowners took out mortgages they could not cope with at crisis interest-rate levels and, hence, defaulted in large numbers. The linkage between real estate bubbles and general financial and economic crises, of course, is by no means limited to the developing world. Some of the most spectacular real estate bubbles of the last two decades have occurred in the richest of the advanced economies – including the USA's Saving and Loan Institution collapse of the mid-1980s and the Scandinavian housing market bubbles of the late 1980s/early 1990s (Hilbers *et al.* 2001). Getting the appropriate rules for mortgage institutions, consequently, is a difficult exercise in which the targets are often moving as the world's financial systems evolve.

Housebuilding and materials

Housebuilding in most countries is an industry that is small scale and easy to enter. This means that building 'firms' are almost ubiquitous. Yet, builders need more than rudimentary building skills to operate in housing markets that themselves operate in more than a rudimentary fashion. Land development, for instance, is a difficult process to master proficiently – in terms of acquiring land, negotiating the necessary permits, designing sensible and marketable schemes, raising finance and coping with market fluctuations.

Self-building may have the idealised image of pre-industrial craft directness – housing's equivalent of directly from farm to table – but in reality the product is often of poorer quality and more costly than the mass home-builder equivalent. Home builders exist in most advanced economies because they offer a far broader range of cheaper dwellings at better quality than alternative ways of building, including self-managed construction (see Chapters 9 and 10).

Many developing countries, furthermore, are characterised by a generally low level of education and skill amongst their workforces. This is reflected in the skills base of their construction industries, which constrains the sophistication of the houses built, the nature of the techniques used to build them and the fittings contained within them. Building quality becomes a major problem in low skill contexts.

Import substitution industrialisation was a common development strategy in Africa and Latin America up to the 1980s. One effect of it was to champion monopoly domestic suppliers of building materials and components. The command economies produced similar monopolies. The consequences were invariably building materials of poor quality, limited choice and high prices. Revitalising materials industries and procurement processes, thus, are vital parts of improving housing markets.

Land supply

It is important to make the obvious, but frequently forgotten or misunderstood, point that housing markets cannot function without land on which to put residences (Hannah *et al.* 1993). It, moreover, has to be at locations and of environmental qualities that are appropriate. Inevitably, such land is going to be in high demand for other uses and those opposed to residential development will object by highlighting in an exaggerated form the costs of such development, while being silent about its benefits.

Land supply constraints are rife around the world and they are often tied up with building regulations that further constrain what can be built. There is now an extensive literature identifying such issues (Hannah *et al.* 1993; Yuing & Somerville 2001; Bertaud & Brueckner 2005).

The role of government

It is important to stress that a market approach strategy is not one based on some notion of *laissez-faire* – let whatever happens occur with minimal state intervention. It may be the case that in any reasoned analysis of housing policies in the world, a series of instances can be highlighted of where government policies have helped to distort housing markets severely, as shown in this chapter. Yet it is also possible to indicate situations where a lack of government action has been a major contributory factor. Housing markets, in other words, cannot function effectively without the guiding hand of government. Policy, however, needs to be based on a clear understanding of why and when market principles are superior.

Housing markets, as was noted earlier, are unlikely to solve all housing problems. Even so, they are still the most cost-effective and efficient tools for delivering housing to the mass of the world's population. One advantage of all the non-market housing experiments undertaken during the twentieth century is that many countries have gone through enormous exercises to see whether there are better ways of providing housing. Social experiments with regard to housing provision have been done. Their huge expense, lack of unequivocally superior outcomes and the abundant list of failures arising from them all suggest that once maligned market mechanisms usually are not so bad after all.

One problem is getting governments to focus upon market-friendly policies. Many lobbying groups have vested interests in sustaining widespread state intervention into housing markets and imposing constraints on market behaviour. Short-term populism can always win votes by claiming miracle cures for housing shortages or offering benefits to specific groups via housing policies.

Of course, merely changing the direction of policy towards a greater emphasis on markets does not remove interest group lobbying, opportunistic political responses and special interest politics. In fact, one of the dangers of a change in direction towards market-oriented housing policies is that such programmes are used in inappropriate ways. For instance, they may be tacked on to traditional political structures, which themselves have not been reformed. The outcome is an inappropriate relationship between the state and the market. UN-Habitat, for example, has been critical of switching resources to low or zero user cost infrastructure provision in place of direct housing expenditure in situations where the benefit goes to more prosperous localities rather than to providing access to basic amenities for low-income groups. Another problem is that the benefits of markets come through widespread competitive interaction, whereas institution building is often far easier when only a limited number of enterprises are created. The issue then arises of how to introduce and sustain competition.

Genuine mistakes can also be made in situations of substantial institutional change with uncertain outcomes. Policy makers, for instance, are more likely than not to be bombarded with conflicting advice and have insufficient information and analysis to hand with which to discriminate between the proposals made. Path-dependency then sets in once an inappropriate programme is mistakenly put in place and the costs of admitting mistakes in political, economic and credibility terms loom large. Correcting previous policy errors is likely to occur only with a change of government but, then, policy enters the realm of party political conflict rather than consensus. Repeated switches in policy with changes in governments is destabilising and unlikely to create housing institutions with credibility.

This inadvertent process of policy change is unfortunately a common one, as the discussion of developments in Central and Eastern Europe in the next chapter demonstrates. The trick, therefore, is to translate general principles into good policy action. The political economy of housing policy – explaining which housing policies exist, why they do and how to change them – is unfortunately far harder than comprehending which of humanity's less than perfect economic systems is likely to deliver the best housing to the world's varied population.

Note

1   Source: http://web-japan.org

5

Restructuring housing provision in Central and Eastern Europe

Introduction

The places where real estate institutions have changed most abruptly in living memory are the countries that were formally 'socialist' centrally planned economies (CPE). They are obviously good examples of the importance of a markets and institutions approach to understanding real estate. The objective will be to highlight the major changes in housing institutions and to identify the resulting impacts on housing provision and wider economic and social factors.

This chapter will concentrate on events in those seven Central and Eastern European (CEE) countries that joined the European Union in 2004: the Czech Republic, Estonia, Hungary, Latvia, Lithuania, Poland and the Slovak Republic. Although there has been some work on the commercial side (McGreal *et al.* 2002), most emphasis in the burgeoning literature has been placed on reforms to housing.

These countries have a diversity of housing systems and standards and a general enthusiasm for market-based solutions to housing provision. The market emphasis is hedged around, however, with a strong keenness of governments to influence housing outcomes via their policies.

Housing systems

Comparative housing standards

It is always dangerous to classify countries and their housing systems into broad categories, because of the myriad of differences that always exist comparatively. Yet, generalisation does seem pertinent with respect to housing in these CEE countries.

With the addition of these countries, the population of the EU increased by a fifth but economic output rose by only 5%. This indicates the much lower prevailing standards of living.

All have lower standards of living than are usual in Western Europe (Figure 5.1), but they have high hopes of catching up with the rest of the former EU15. With the exception of Cyprus, Slovenia and Malta, the ten countries that joined the EU in 2005 have noticeably lower GDPs per head than did Greece and Spain when they joined the then EU9.

The speed of catch-up inevitably varies significantly between countries as they grow, depending on such factors as economic structures and public policies – Greece, for example, is taking much longer to converge than Spain. Whatever, catch-up inevitably takes many years or, in fact, decades. The OECD estimated in 2004 that it would take Hungary 29 years, Poland 37 years and the Slovak Republic 40 years to halve their income gaps with Western Europe, based on their growth rates over the last decade. Even if these countries manage to introduce reforms that speed up their growth rates, full convergence to Western European standards of living is likely to take two generations or more.

Such dynamics provide a background against which to judge housing provision in the new accession countries. Because they have lower living standards and housing is an important element in determining them, it is to be expected that housing conditions, prices and costs should be far lower than in Western Europe. Dynamically, if it is going to take a very long time for incomes to catch up, it is to be expected that housing will take an equally long time to reach Western European standards as well. Any comments on the housing market outcomes of institutional change need to bear this issue of relative living standards in mind.

Whilst average income levels may be a good indicator of general hous-ing standards, there are several reasons why the gap between housing conditions at least on some scores, such as space per person, in these CEE countries can be expected to be closer to those in Western Europe than is the case with incomes. Over time, typically, there is a U-shaped hous-ing consumption pattern in relation to changing average income levels. In order to meet basic shelter needs, a high share of housing expenditure exists at relatively low levels of income; then a falling share at some-what higher levels; followed by a rising share of income at much higher

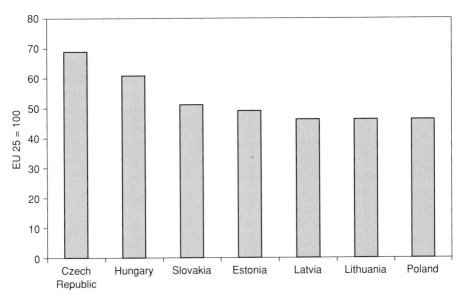

Figure 5.1   CEE GDP per capita (at purchasing power parity prices) 2003.
Source: Eurostat.

income levels as the status and luxury characteristics of housing kick in (World Bank 1993). So, as housing often remains at the consumption level of a basic necessity in the CEE countries, expenditure on housing is likely to represent a relatively high proportion of incomes. In the old CPE system, this expenditure was generally borne by the state in urban areas, so that out-of-pocket costs were usually very low by market standards.

Along with this basic consumption good characteristic usually go high levels of national investment on housing. As incomes rise, the share of housing investment in national income then tends to fall, even though the absolute level of expenditure is likely to rise. This predicted broad-brush pattern of high investment is historically observable in the new accession states, though not from the 1990s (see later).

Moreover, faster-growing countries also tend to invest proportionately more in housing because of rising consumption, migration and the needs of expanding workforces in the major growth regions. This characteristic has been seen strongly in such European countries as Greece, Ireland, Portugal and Spain over the last decade (Ball 2005b).

Furthermore, the past histories of CEE countries made housing investment especially important within them. Housing played particular roles in CPE frameworks. They tended to build lots of dwellings, especially during the 1970s and 1980s. What was constructed was generally standardised, industrialised-building apartment blocks containing dwellings of limited quality and size. Housebuilding became as much a component of the command economy, with five-year plan targets to be met, as being aimed at satisfying consumer needs.

In addition, housing was built in rural areas and small towns by owners in piecemeal ways, using the available building materials, which were not always the most appropriate or of good quality. The legacy is a rural housing stock that has a relatively high absence of basic amenities and poor build quality.

In Poland, overall housebuilding did not manage to keep up with rising household numbers, so that it has been facing an absolute shortage of about 1 to 1.5 million dwellings for a long time, despite relatively high building rates during the 1970s and 1980s. The Slovak Republic and Lithuania also faced shortages. The speed of change has also varied and some countries have been criticised for holding on to their centralised systems, despite high levels of privatisation, and, sometimes, for the directions that reform has taken (UNECE 1999; Buckley & Tsenkova 2001).

Overall, the pre-1990 housebuilding legacy has left unique housing stocks in the CEE7 of relatively young, but often rundown, homes – with limited internal and neighbourhood amenities and poor insulation. Dwelling sizes are also notably smaller than in Western Europe. In the old EU15, dwellings have an average of 4.4 rooms and 84 square metres of living space, whereas in the new CEE7 members, they have only 3.2 rooms and 58 square metres of living space. In East Germany, around a million of the apartments-in-industrialised-block types of dwellings have been abandoned since reunification (Ball 2005a) but in CEE states they remain central elements of urban housing provision. So, in much of the CEE, housing issues relate to the quality of the existing stock as well as its general availability. Moreover, these dwellings are often not physically adaptable for serious upgrading to provide better sizes, nor is it often worthwhile modernising many of them. This suggests the need for very high levels of dwelling replacement over the long term.

The significance of maintenance issues can be seen in Central Statistics Office survey data in Hungary. Only a quarter of the country's dwellings require no repairs, around two-fifths need partial restoration and another fifth need full restoration. For the remaining 13%, it is uneconomic to do any work to them. The situation is even worse in Budapest, where only 10% of dwellings require no works and 38% full restoration or demolition.

Another unique feature of the housing systems of old CPE countries is that the land market traditionally did not play the role that it does elsewhere in influencing urban densities and the distribution of housing opportunities over space. The urban structure of CEE cities, consequently, is differentiated far less than it is further west and relates more to subtle gradations in social status than to accessibility and urban history. In many neighbourhoods, there is also not that much of the costly urban infrastructure as is commonplace further west. As the land market takes on a greater role in these countries in the future, given such histories, the cities of many of these countries may develop widely decentralised, spread out urban structures, more in keeping with US models than the emphasis on historic city centres more common in Western Europe. There will be less of the pull factor of pre-existing infrastructure and neighbourhoods of high environmental quality in central city locations that intensifies the pull of city centres in Western Europe. As a result, activities may well push towards the fringe if planning controls permit such movement in order to search out the cheaper locations, lower congestion and higher amenities of the fringe.

Another factor to remember when examining CEE housing markets is that many of the countries have quite small populations. Poland with a population of almost 40 million is the only relatively large country. The Czech Republic, Hungary and the Slovak Republic are in the 5–10 million band and the Baltic countries are much smaller. Housing markets outside of Poland consequently tended to be dominated by one, or at most two, major urban locations. Consequently, they are likely to have few of the regional smoothing effects on national data that take place in larger countries and will look relatively more volatile as a result.

Housing tenures

One of the most noticeable features of the CEE7's housing systems is the high levels of owner occupation. They are far higher than the old EU15 average of 65% of all dwellings (Figure 5.2). Only the Czech Republic has a relatively small share of owner occupation yet it has a co-operative sector where rights can be bought and sold, which accounts for 17% of the stock. Adding this in, it brings the share of owner occupation to 64% and very close to the old EU15 average.

Owner occupation did exist in the CEE7 prior to the 1990s. In Hungary, for example, in the 1980s the homeownership rate was around 35% and private ownership was as high as 48% in Poland in 1988. Nonetheless,

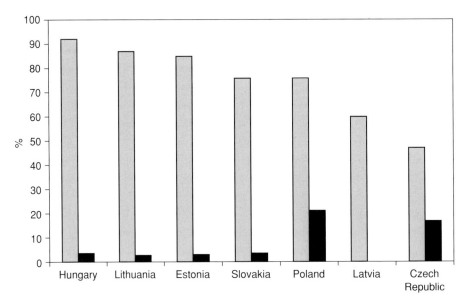

Figure 5.2   CEE tenure shares.

Note: various years, usually 2000–2002.

Source: National Statistical Offices, *Housing Developments in European Countries*, 2003, Department of the Environment, Dublin.

most urban housing was rented at very low rents in either of the municipal, state or co-operative-owned rental forms. Tenant rights-to-buy also existed in formal terms from the 1970s or earlier in a number of countries.

With the switch to market-based economies, however, there was a major shift to the tenure with thousands of flats sold off to sitting tenants at knock-down prices (20% of market-value or less was common), with resulting monthly payments, including heating, less, and sometimes far less, than equivalent rent levels. In some countries, the buildings as well as individual flats passed into the private sector; whereas in others, like Poland, privatisation has been taking place through the sale of individual flats in building structures owned by municipalities, employers and co-operatives (Węcławowicz 2005). In Budapest, the number of local authority owned dwellings fell from 150 000 in 1996 to only 63 000 towards the end of 2000; yet, the number of residential buildings owned by local authorities fell by only 1500 to 16 000 over the same period.[1]

Bulgaria and Romania have even higher home ownership rates than the current new EU countries, with virtually all their housing now in owner occupation. Albania, Russia, Slovenia, the Ukraine and other post-Soviet states have also had mass sell-off policies, as to a smaller degree has China

(Renaud 1995). In Russia, for example, private housing is up from a third of the stock in 1990 to 59% in 2004 (UNECE 2004). In member countries of the Commonwealth of Independent States and China, what to do with state housing still remains a major issue (Zhang 1998). Privatisation initially proceeded rapidly in Russia with 55% of housing in private hands by 1996, but then reform ground to a halt. Housing stocks actually declined during the 1990s in 14 out of 18 former socialist countries – a world record in peacetime.

The speed of the tenure transfer and its precise details, especially who owns and manages the building in which privatised flats exist, has varied from country to country. Nevertheless, this shift to owner occupation has been undoubtedly the most consistent and dramatic housing policy in the CEE7 – and in Europe as a whole – for a long time and it is not entirely over yet.

The justification for this homeownership-only policy was based partly on a desire to meet personal aspirations and provide households with the freedoms of homeownership and a wealth asset. However, there were other significant political influences, which are outlined below.

1. *Financial* With a switch to market-based systems and extensive privatisation of industry, traditional CPE public finances were no longer viable. Governments were now bereft of surpluses from state enterprises, had weak tax bases, and requirements for more transparent public accounting. Therefore, they had no means by which to continue to subsidise so heavily such large proportions of their housing stocks. Importantly, they also subsidised high heating costs in winter.
2. *A reluctance to charge market rents* One way to cover costs would have been to raise rents significantly on the grounds of moving towards a market-based rental system. However, this would have met with substantial tenant resistance, especially as real incomes plummeted in the early years of transition in the face of high inflation. The inflationary consequences of government policies in other areas consequently closed off options in housing. This also helps to explain the mistaken imposition of rent controls. In addition, there is no ingrained cultural acceptance of paying 'fair' market costs, adding to consumer resistance to higher rents. (This characteristic may also turn out to be a problem in mortgage markets as well.)
3. *Political composition* As important parts of the old political apparatus, municipal housing bodies and co-operatives were often not viewed favourably by the new reform-minded political elites. In Poland, housing co-operatives can be huge organisations of up to 100 000 members.

Nominally, their boards are voted for by members, but turnout is low and typically little notice is taken of memberships in the larger organisations. There is consequently periodic political pressure to break co-operatives up into smaller, more manageable and accountable organisations (Węcławowicz 2005).

4. *Other reform options regarded as infeasible* Another privatisation option is to sell off social housing estates to the highest bidder. This has been the programme adopted in Germany in recent years. There, investors, many of foreign origin, either hold on to the whole housing stock they purchase or renovate parts and sell as much as possible on to sitting tenants or others. This did not occur in the CEE7 privatisation processes, probably for political fear of the rents that would be charged and potential criticisms of new landlords. In such an ideological framework, any economic rationality took second place to perceived political imperatives. In such a constrained environment, handing them over to tenants was the only politically feasible way out.

In the main, the privatisations have been popular, though not without their policy critics (Pichler-Milanovich 2001). There has been no overwhelming political pressure to roll back the clock and reintroduce the old systems. Some countries, such as the Czech Republic, have recently put moratoria on further social housing sales, though others are still keen to extend the process further. However, in most countries issues other than housing and urban policy are politically more pressing. Out of the glare of political controversy, governments may be more likely to be responsive to special interest group lobbying.

Institutional gaps in CEE housing markets

Many of the institutional arrangements associated with developed owner-occupied housing markets still have to be put in place across the CEE7. Considerable efforts to overcome these problems have been made and more are currently under way. However, the results may take years to become fully embedded into the framework of housing markets and, unfortunately, as with any machine, all the interconnected bits have to work for a housing market to function well.

Several examples illustrate the point.

- *Well-defined and enforceable property rights* These have implications in many aspects of real estate provision, so a few examples will have to suffice. For instance, many of the CEE7 and other countries, like

Germany, still have prolonged legal disputes over the legality of property nationalisations in the aftermath of the declaration of socialist states. Although this tends to affect only a relatively small number of properties in historic centres, it contributes to an aura of legal confusion. Not all property rights, furthermore, relate to ownership but to issues like security of tenure. Many building renovations in Warsaw, for example, have failed to conform to prevailing regulations – up to 60%, according to some informed but informal estimates. Some renewal, for example, has led to the illegal eviction of existing tenants. However, there is little prospect of restitution for them or for any of the previous property owners who would have commanded much higher market prices if the affected properties had been sold with vacant possession.

- *Clear and effective public regulations* For housing markets to function effectively, building regulations and planning guidelines have to be clear, subject to informed debate and scrutiny, and fairly enforced. Yet often, such practices are still opaque, ambiguous and obscure. With the discrediting of old systems, continuing bureaucratic cultures and limited staffing lead to important remaining state functions becoming weakened. In Poland, for example, the introduction of a new planning regime for major cities made pre-existing land-use plans redundant as they no longer had any legal status. However, several years later new plans are yet to be formulated for most areas (only 13% of Warsaw had new plans in 2004, for instance). All development was technically frozen until the new plans were drawn up and ratified. Therefore, in many localities no land-use change could legally proceed without special dispensation from the local authority, which takes time and involves substantial transaction costs for developers.
- *Easy transfer of property* While some of the smaller countries have managed to introduce comprehensive central land and property registers, other countries have not. Poland's new land registry system, for example, will only be fully implemented by 2009 (Ball 2005b).
- *Comprehensive market information and marketing* Newspaper and web-based advertisements are increasingly common but real estate sales intermediaries tend to operate only in sections of the higher end of the market. In some cities, like Prague, there are now quite a number of agents, whereas Budapest, a city with almost 2 million inhabitants, had only two or three significant estate agencies in 2004, and these mainly dealt with foreign investors.[2] Information deficiencies and mispricing can be substantial, with a lack of widespread sales intermediation and, therefore, markets are likely to function less efficiently and effectively then they could do.
- *Various types of insurance are often lacking* Insurance protects buyers against unforeseen liabilities. It can also induce positive market outcomes

by encouraging suppliers to conform to insurance requirements for fear of being blacklisted by insurance providers with disastrous implications for sales. For example, in the UK, housebuilders try to signal the quality of their products by submitting them to independent inspection in an industry-wide quality survey and insurance scheme (see Chapter 9). In most of the CEE, building defects insurance is unavailable, so that new house purchasers may find themselves facing large unrecoverable costs. Superior builders also cannot easily distinguish themselves from others who erect shoddy structures. This is especially problematic given the variable build quality of many new homes.

The fundamental point beyond the array of institutional detail is hopefully clear. Markets only work effectively within specific and complete institutional contexts. As a result, country-specific structures of housing provision may suffer severely if:

- there are important gaps in the 'full service' market framework;
- only a narrow range of consumers, such as higher income groups or foreign investors, can enjoy the benefits of well-equipped market processes;
- markets violate the principles required for effective competition.

It is hard to conclude that the CEE7 to date score 10 out of 10 on market mechanisms. Moreover, 'infant' market arguments, after a decade and a half, may be beginning to wear thin.

The collapse of housing investment

Nowhere are the problems of housing market relations in the CEE brought more sharply into focus than in the low measured housing investment that exists throughout the region. The CEE7 at present, therefore, are confounding the generalisation, noted earlier, that lower-income countries tend to invest proportionately more in housing than higher-income ones. Instead, for large parts of the 1990s and into the 2000s, housebuilding virtually ground to a halt.

The situation has improved somewhat in recent years but building rates are still comparatively very low by international and historic standards. This is true even compared with the low housing construction rate countries in Western Europe, while the high growth countries in the old EU15, such as Ireland and Spain, have much higher housebuilding rates (Table 5.1). Most new building in the CEE, moreover, is targeted at the

Table 5.1 Dwellings built per 1000 inhabitants, EU countries compared.

Estonia	0.6
Latvia	0.4
Lithuania	1.1
Hungary	2.2
Poland	2.3
Slovak Republic	2.4
Czech Republic	2.5
France	5.1
Germany	3.5
UK	3.1
Ireland	14.1
Spain	13.8

Note: 2000–2002 depending on latest available figures.

Source: National Statistics Offices (Norris & Shiels 2004).

most affluent segments of society. Some renovation and repair is taking place in existing housing stocks but this is insufficient to have much impact on the huge backlog of necessary work.

Supply-side difficulties can be illustrated by the example of the Baltic States, which were experiencing the highest, and double-digit, house price inflation in the region during 2004–5. There was a sharp upswing in housebuilding in 2004–5 but from extremely low bases. Even then, these countries with ostensibly market-friendly policies still could not even match the per capita building rates of Hungary and Poland, let alone those of countries in Western Europe (compare Figure 5.3 and Table 5.1).

Deficiencies in housing investment mean that the housing stocks of most of the CEE7 at current building rates will take many years to change. Unless the supply-side improves significantly, convergence with Western European housing standards is unlikely for generations.

Boosting mortgage finance

Great policy attention in the CEE7 has been focused on creating new institutions in mortgage finance. Mortgage borrowing has been seen as the keystone in the transition to a normal financial and market-based housing system. Much advice has been offered, institution building undertaken and public money spent. Many CEE governments also provide mortgage interest tax relief to consumers (in contexts where marginal tax rates are often high) and subsidise long-term housing savings schemes.

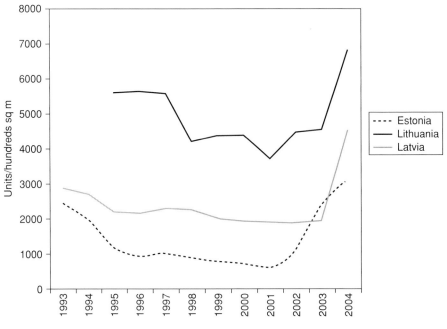

Figure 5.3 Housebuilding in the Baltic States 1993–2004.

Source: National Statistics Offices.

Hungary offers open-ended interest rate subsidies over the life of mort-gages. It and others subsidise the activities of German Bausparen-style saving-and-lending institutions and those of mortgage banks. In Poland, enabling legislation permits complex indexation of mortgage loans. Secondary market mortgage activity has been introduced in a number of places, with Hungary and Bulgaria being pioneers. Foreign banks have entered and tried their hand at mortgage lending, though national players heavily predominate.

There have been some notable increases in the use of mortgages. Com-petition between lenders has often been intense, leading to sharp reductions in mortgage interest rates and borrowing terms as inflation has fallen. In 2004, in Estonia, for example, typical mortgage interest rates had fallen below 4% and 100% loan-to-value ratios were on offer. Borrowing in foreign currencies, especially Euros, is popular, though it is often associated with notable exchange rate risk for the borrower.

In general, the amount of outstanding mortgage debt, though growing fast, remains at much lower levels than in Western Europe. It is also questionable how far mortgage borrowing can extend down the income distribution: an important issue in contexts where owner occupation ratios are so high.

In some respects, it is easy to see why mortgage finance faces constraints. The interest rate spreads required by lending institutions to cover their risks and other costs are generally much higher than in countries with more established financial systems. With regard to origination and screening, there is little credit history to go on. Macroeconomic performance has also frequently not been conducive to long-term lending.

Subsidy focus on owner occupation

As part of the common policy of encouraging mortgage finance, the tax-relief and subsidy regimes in CEE have been overwhelmingly shifted away from social renting to owner occupation. Part of that subsidy effort leaks out to benefit mortgage and other providers and it also raises the value of existing dwellings and development land. The prime intended beneficiaries, none the less, are the better-off owner occupiers who can avail themselves of savings accounts and mortgage interest tax-reliefs.

Some tax write-offs of mortgage costs and subsidies to the required down-payments aim at specific target groups. In some countries the range of special treatments is wide, including those for people under 35, those with children, first-time buyers, those buying new dwellings and those purchasing existing ones. There may be caps on the mortgage values eligible for subsidy or similar restrictions on the prices of the dwellings being bought. The array of subsidies can be seen to be complex and often regressive.

The impact of demand subsidies and mortgage finance in the context of poor supply

The introduction of a personal mortgage finance system where none existed before considerably stimulates housing demand by enabling purchasers to spread buying costs over a long period of time. The result is that the market will move to a significantly higher turnover level. What the impact is on prices crucially depends on the response of supply to the demand stimulus. Housing supply takes time to come on stream, so there is likely to be an initial surge in prices prior to extra supply. So, the important questions are the speed of adjustment to the long run and the scale of those long-term effects.

If supply is highly elastic in the long run and responds quickly to price rises, most of the demand increase in a relatively short time leads to extra housebuilding. The result is an expanded housing stock and relatively little long-run change in house prices. Moreover, because house prices rise little in the elastic supply case, most of any mortgage subsidy remains with its direct recipients. There is an additional pay-off to households unable to afford mortgage borrowing, because many of those taking out mortgages to buy new dwellings vacate parts of the existing housing stock into which others can move. Gradually, the worst of the present stock can be abandoned, or demolished and replaced, and everyone's housing is slowly upgraded through filtering processes (Rothenburg *et al.* 1991).

In this scenario, the introduction of a mortgage system has positive economic benefits in the long run and leads to improvements in overall housing conditions. The speed of the supply response, moreover, should mean that there are few transitional effects associated with temporary price overshooting as new supply comes on stream. Historically, for example, such situations occurred in the UK in the 1920s and 1930s and in the USA in the 1940s and 1950s. These were two societies during two specific periods when owner occupation grew rapidly on the basis of substantial new housing supply to near universal acclaim.

Alternatively, if supply only responds weakly, or not at all, the extra demand induced by mortgage borrowing predominantly leads to higher prices in the existing stock. The owners of the existing housing that is attractive to the purchasers with new-fangled mortgages experience significant rises in their property prices. If there are marked quality differences in the stock, as there are currently in CEE countries, a dual housing market could easily arise with limited substitutability between the 'luxury', mortgage financed, sector and the rest of the stock. In the parts of the stock that the new mortgage borrowers shunned, prices would hardly be affected by the introduction of the mortgage market and, so, market segmentation would grow. Between the two segments, marked differences in prices and qualities would exist. A 'luxury' sector with an array of market institutions would emerge, alongside a more poorly traded, credit-risky, mass sector of affordable but unfungible housing. Furthermore, as new housing is scarce, it would be concentrated in the luxury sector because the returns on building 'luxury' houses are likely to be so much greater than those for producing more basic ones.

It should be noted that, in this two-sector model, it is the lack of new supply that generates the market segmentation, because the differential characteristics of the existing stock then become important; whereas, with plentiful new supply, segmentation does not arise because new building would be spread more evenly though the housing market and because of filtering as the worse of the existing stock is displaced.

Micro-managing demand-side policies in tight supply situations would have little positive impact. Any attempts to stimulate production in the affordable sector through selective subsidies, for example, could feasibly help only a few households before the costs become too onerous for government to bear. By swallowing up scarce supply, moreover, such programmes would crowd out demand in the luxury segment and, so, raise prices in the mortgage-using sector. Housing costs and shortages would simultaneously grow and seem insuperable problems.

The housing market implications of introducing mortgages into housing markets with an extremely unresponsive supply are consequently adverse for most, with the principal gainers being the original owners of the dwellings in demand plus the providers of the new mortgages and the politicians (and their advisors) who gained votes from implementing such policies. Regressive distributional effects would also be substantial and opaque. For instance, mortgage subsidies may appear to benefit the higher-income households able to afford borrowing but even they would not actually gain much, because the weaker the supply price elasticity the greater is the capitalisation of the benefits of mortgages and mortgage subsidies into the house prices that they have to pay. With higher house prices, moreover, affordability barriers grow, pricing more households out of the market. In addition, all citizens would be paying through the tax system for any existing mortgage subsidies and the financial institution supports deemed necessary to help with the high cost of housing.

Furthermore, any housing demand shocks would be transmitted wholly through prices (probably with lagged effects), so that cycles of boom and bust in the luxury sector may ensue. Such instability could end up threatening the financial viability of mortgage finance institutions, affecting the operation of monetary policy and undermining general macroeconomic stability.

In a world of tight supply, it can be concluded, introduction of a mortgage finance system to a market where it did not already exist can be seriously bad news. The policy would be regressive, even when it is not associated with financial capacity building subsidies and mortgage interest tax reliefs. It mainly benefits a relatively few, predominantly already better-housed families and several housing market institutions. It would not improve general housing conditions, because only additional supply can do that. Finally, it would impose greater risks on monetary and economic stability.

Fixing the supply side, if it is currently uncompetitive or unable to respond to price signals for other reasons, is thus a pre-requisite if positive effects are to be had from mortgage finance reform. The supply-side, however, is a rare perspective in the voluminous literature on mortgage finance in developing and transitional economies in recent years.

That housing stocks can expand rapidly through new building can be seen in recent experience in Germany, where the housing stock rose by over 10% in a little over five years and in Ireland where it rose by over 40% in less than a decade (Ball 2005b). However, in contrast, the CEE countries exhibit characteristics of severely unresponsive housing supply. For one thing, as noted earlier, housebuilding has been very low since market liberalisation. The experience of CEE countries subsequent to the introduction of mortgage finance and owner-occupied fiscal breaks would therefore seem to correspond more closely to the adverse tight supply scenario just described than to the positive elastic supply one.

Problems with housing supply

An embryonic industry

Housebuilding and development industries in CEE typically lack the broad array of formal and informal institutions common elsewhere. Housebuilding industries in market-oriented developed economies are characterised by extensive flexibility and entrepreneurship (see Chapter 9). Institutions are important in terms of: subcontracting networks; good sources of working capital; competitive markets in materials with extensive networks of traders in building materials able to extend credit; similar networks of construction equipment providers where machinery can be hired flexibly; skilled workers used to operating in market contexts with limited supervision and training systems geared up accordingly; arrays of professionals, valuers and measurers and other market-makers; plus many others.

These complex networks evolve over many years. In contrast, under CPE regimes a handful of giant housebuilding firms and materials producers, employing a relatively narrow range of directly employed workers, were geared up to meet housing targets through inadequate industrialised processes. They were consequently the antithesis of the supply-side institutions existing in well-functioning market-oriented construction markets. As Dowall has noted, it is extremely difficult quickly to switch from the old CPE type of building regime to a market one (Dowall 1992).

A mass of small housing producers and developers do not seem to have emerged in the surge of market liberalisation in CEE countries. They may exist in the traditional owner-occupied 'self-build' and repair markets but few seem to provide speculative housing. In Warsaw, for example, the general market sector is dominated by five firms: two local developers and a handful of subsidies of large Western European construction firms (Ball 2005b).

Building regulations and land supply constraints

Though little hard evidence exists, the general impression is that there are strong hangovers of state regulation. They effect land supply, development processes and housebuilding and, hence, militate against rapid, market responsive building. Restrictive building regulations and planning controls are rife: the problems of planning in Warsaw have already been discussed. Moreover, mobilising local authorities and utility providers to facilitate service provision in new areas of urban expansion seems difficult. Speculative land holding behaviour is encouraged in such a regulatory environment and it can be highly destabilising (Renaud 2002).

Labour market regulation

Another reason for the limited emergence of small-scale housebuilders is the labour laws, which do not correspond to general housebuilding industry practices and distorted relative costs. Poland, for example, has the unfortunate combination of a relatively high minimum wage, a fifth of its workforce unemployed, an estimated lack of a million homes and labour-driven building costs that are too high to allow ordinary Poles to afford even the most modest new housing.

Resource crowding out

Excessively low levels of housing investment may also arise because other activities are absorbing national resources. A clear candidate in central Europe currently is government and the scale of its deficits.

Experience elsewhere

Historical experience in other countries also highlights the significance of the supply side. In Greece, Italy, Spain and Portugal the widespread use of mortgages evolved long after the evolution of market-oriented housebuilding and the emergence of a modern development industry. In fact, in Greece and Italy mortgages are still limited in scope. Piecemeal additions to housing is a common characteristic of investment in Greece.

Turkey is another example. It has much lower GDP per head than the CEE7 and a history of public sector deficits and economic instability. It is also only introducing a mortgage finance system in 2006 and has a relatively limited array of standard advanced country housing market institutions. Nonetheless, it has vibrant development and housebuilding industries, few constraints on suburban development and significantly higher housing investment levels than the CEE countries. Over the period 2000–2002, at 3.1 dwellings per 1000 population, it produced almost a third more dwellings than Hungary and Poland and considerably more than the Baltic States.

A lack of support for market renting

In contrast to the strongly positive stance towards the expansion of owner occupation in the CEE, rental institutions have faced substantial constraints on making investment worthwhile for them. Severe rent controls in the private rental sector frequently exist – many of them arising in the 1990s when market liberalisation was supposed to be at its peak – while security of tenure provisions are strong. Both of these controls deter investment.

In addition, social housing institutions have often been unable for political reasons to raise rents to levels that make breaking even and additional investment feasible for them. However, repair and heating costs are more likely to be covered by rents in recent years than in earlier ones.

An example of contradictory political aims in relation to rents concerns the reform of rents in non-profit sectors in Poland. They were supposed to move from the mid-1990s towards more realistic levels. This would have led to a more efficient use of space and provided higher incomes to housing institutions, enabling them to spend considerably more money on improving poor existing housing conditions and removing the need for continued municipal subsidy of loss-making organisations. Laws were passed that enabled rents to rise toward a maximum annual level of 3% of replacement costs for municipal and co-operative housing. However, political pressures, especially in the recessionary years between 2000 and 2003, have meant that co-operative and municipal rents remain low and far below those levels (Muziol-Weclawowicz & Oracz 2004).

Apart from borrowing as an owner, renting is the only other option available to people for smoothing over time the capital costs associated with living in a dwelling. This is one way of looking at rent: it is paying some-one else in order to use their capital to enable habitation of a dwelling. This contrasts with repaying interest and amortisation on a capital loan to a mortgage institution as a homeowner does, yet is essentially the same principle of spreading housing costs over a long period of time by using someone else's money.

Renting might even be a cheaper option, tax rules permitting, if landlords are prepared to take lower spreads on their money when they rent out property than financial institutions are prepared to when they directly lend to home owners. For example, they might have lower administration costs or, perhaps, lower defaults on rental payments than mortgage lenders do because of their closer monitoring of tenant payment behaviour. The rental approach is typically constrained by controls in the CEE countries that make private landlordism unattractive, so private rental markets are either already small or declining rapidly.

The only growing rental sectors, undoubtedly, are the informal ones that escape the tax, regulatory and statistical nets. Almost, by definition, it is impossible to guess their size though housing surveys suggest that they might be small.

In recent years, a paradox has arisen. The lack of affordable housing is encouraging a number of new accession countries to start subsiding social housebuilding again, after a decade or more of heavily privatising such rental housing on the grounds of its unpopularity, inflexibility, expense and inefficiency. The wheel may seem to have turned, but this should not necessarily be regarded as vindication of previously discredited poli-cies. Inevitably, the subsidies are of a scale that is unlikely to have much impact on housing shortages. Their consequences are likely to be far more noticeable on already stretched government budgets. There is also scant evidence that the institutional problems of this tenure have been resolved over the intervening years.

Weak markets

A characteristic of an insufficient depth of housing market institutions in the CEE is the fact that formal market processes, though growing in higher-priced sectors, become less observable further down the market range. Transactions become more informal and less transparent, not only in terms of hidden renting but also in terms of sales transactions and maintenance.

Often most households cannot afford to purchase, especially if they fall outside of the screening criteria of mortgage lenders, and many owners cannot find anyone to sell to and, so, they cannot move either. New households, unless they have been lucky in the job market, may find their housing options extremely limited. Many new owner-occupied households, especially if they are not working, have very low incomes and, so, have been able to do little with their properties. Apart from the implications for those households, this has frozen housing transactions in wide parts of the stock, which in any case were generally low, and has created difficulties in renovating rundown buildings.

Paradoxically, private ownership has thus frequently constrained mobility, which was in any case already low. In Hungary, for example, a typical person moves 2.7 times in their life compared with 6 or 7 times for a person in Western Europe. Such significant effects on labour mobility are particularly problematic in countries where structural change and economic flexibility in the face of shocks are vital for much needed economic growth.

Conclusion

This chapter has examined housing developments in the CEE since the early 1990s and the trends towards creating well-functioning housing markets and institutions. Such a shift over such a short time is virtually unprecedented, outside of other old 'socialist' economies, and has generally gone further in the CEE than elsewhere. Great strides have been made towards creating functioning market systems in the unfavourable contexts of housing shortages and quality problems and frequently unfavourable economic environments.

Much variation exists across the seven countries, about which the generalisations of a brief survey like this may not do justice. However, there are a number of common features. The two most important are: (1) the scale of owner occupation (and the concomitant neglect of renting) and (2) the efforts put into creating mortgage finance markets. There have also been significant, though incomplete, developments in the area of transactions, such as the formalisation of property rights and the creation of land registries. Nevertheless, there seems to be a common lack of emphasis on housing supply and a current degree of regulation and control that is stifling rental markets and housing supply. Problems in housing supply can create severe feedback effects and threaten the potential efficiency gains hoped for in the withdrawal of direct state control over housing provision.

Events in the CEE will undoubtedly induce further institutional changes. Nevertheless, the experience of reform in this region of the world helps to illustrate the maxim put forward in the conclusion to the previous chapter – that it is easier to identify the benefits of market processes in housing in principle than to apply them in practice.

Notes

1   Hungarian Central Statistics Office.
2   On the benefits of real estate brokers, see Chapter 6.

6

International comparisons of estate agency/real estate brokerage services

Introduction

This chapter and the following two examine the role of firms that act as go-betweens in the buying and selling of real estate. One purpose is to highlight major differences in their organisation between countries. Even terminology varies widely. In the UK, such intermediaries are known as estate agents in residential, and commercial property agents in commercial real estate. There are no legal registration or examination requirements at present and, so, no real distinctions in status. Some will be members of the Royal Institution of Chartered Surveyors, especially on the commercial side, but there are no formal requirements and anyone can set up as an agent without telling anyone but potential clients. In the USA, real estate brokerage is the appropriate term and a real estate broker is generally a person who has attended prescribed courses, passed some exams and registered with the appropriate state body, though there are variations in state practices. In the USA, an estate agent is a less-qualified person than a broker. Non-English speaking countries obviously have their own terms but, in addition, their own rules of practice. This chapter will use the English terminology on the somewhat weak grounds that 'estate agent' is a shorter phrase than 'real estate broker'.

The ways in which estate agency operates in different countries vary substantially. The differences are primarily caused by a mix of housing market, estate agency industry and public policy factors. In order to understand how each country's estate agency system operates, it is useful initially in this chapter to explain at a general, rather than country-specific, level why problems might arise in the relationship between estate agents and their clients. This is because they help to explain why the industry has evolved in the way it has – such as in the functional and ownership separation in many countries between those firms that undertake residential and those that undertake commercial work (see Chapter 7). Government has also played key roles, because most estate agency industry structures have been influenced by divergent country-specific public policy responses to those potential problems. However, it is not true to say that observed differences are purely a matter of divergent policy histories. Path dependency has played an important role. Furthermore, the interest (or the lack of it) by other related industries, especially the finance industries, in the agency business has had a substantial effect on the structure of this industry in a number of countries.

In what follows in this chapter, first the matching, selling and advisory functions undertaken by estate agents are outlined and problems clients have with monitoring them are raised. Then, market and public policy responses to these client–agent issues are examined. This is followed by an analysis of fee structures and estate agents' incentives; after which, the implications of the growth of the Internet are examined. Emphasis is put on the residential sector, as that is where most research interest has been focused, although many of the principles can be directly transferred to the commercial sector.

Estate agency functions and the client relationship

The matching function

An important benefit of estate agents is that they bring together home-buyers and sellers in more effective and efficient ways than would exist without them. In particular, by creating a list of properties for sale, estate agents greatly extend the number of potential buyers that are aware a property is for sale. As a result, the number of buyer–seller matches is raised and the fit between sellers' offers and buyers' requirements is improved. When successful, estate agents become a central institution in local home sales. By facilitating easy comparisons between properties, providing knowledge of relative prices in a locality and being a means through which offers to purchase can be made, estate agents make housing markets work. They, consequently, add value by either making sellers better off than they would otherwise be or buyers more satisfied with the home that they purchase and its price (though buyers only pay for this service directly when they directly hire an agent to find a property for them). Estate agents' existence in housing markets, in summary, reduces the amount of resources spent on search by buyers and sellers and makes searching far more worthwhile than in the absence of such an information network. (This is discussed in detail in Yavas (1994).)

Matching benefits arise because estate agents create a pool of properties for sale. So, as the size of the pool gets larger, the matching benefits increase. This principle has encouraged agents to pool their properties into a multi-listing service (MLS) in a number of countries, though until recently this did not occur to any extent in England and Wales. MLSs are the most common way in which estate agents operate in the USA. There, agents compete over selling properties on a local MLS list and one such list is often the prime provider of information of homes for sale in a particular area. MLSs exist also in the Netherlands and Scotland, but in those countries agents only post their sales on a list and other member agents cannot try to sell them.

Large lists, however, create the risks of monopoly abuse (Wachter 1987). In many Dutch, Scottish and US cities, for example, one agency network conducts most of the sales transactions. A successful agency list has the characteristics of a natural monopoly in that, once the network is in place, it is hard for others to contest the housing market in which it exists because their lists will initially be vastly inferior in terms of the number of properties listed on them.

Franchising has grown considerably in many countries' estate agency markets in recent years to gain networking economies and to secure increasingly important branding benefits. The franchiser provides a wide range of marketing services, which members pay for via an initial entry fee and a percentage of sales revenues (or a flat monthly fee). In addition, agency groups have been consolidated into wider ownership structures. In doing so, other specialisms involved in the house purchase chain have sometimes merged with estate agents or directly entered their market. In Scotland, for example, solicitors through their local Solicitors' Property Centres have managed to gain a large market share. Elsewhere, including in England and Wales, financial institutions may be major players in estate agency (see Chapter 8).

Changes in estate agency markets in recent decades have been profound. Aggregate data still show large numbers of agency firms in all countries and widespread entry and exit from the industry. Yet, in terms of specific housing markets, large agencies now have significant market shares in many countries. However, scale and scope economies in the residential sector in many aspects of activity may be limited, as the work of Zumpano and his colleagues in the USA has indicated (Zumpano *et al.* 1993; Zumpano & Elder 1994).

In the traditional small-scale agency business, overhead costs tended to be low but they arise for firms with many branches, each of which consequently needs to generate larger transaction volumes to remain competitive. Salaries are a fixed cost but the agency business usually works by paying large bonuses for sales. This both lowers fixed costs and incentivises agent sales effort. Many agents in some countries are also part-time, a typical feature of the traditional US industry.

In part, the precise trajectory of cross-country organisational change has been driven by common factors, such as sharply rising house prices over the past decade and technological changes that are giving larger networks competitive edges in the matching function, including postings on the Internet via costly Web pages. The institutional structure of a country's owner-occupied housing system and the ways in which housing transactions take place have also been influential. The particular policy stances of governments have been important as well.

A mapping of the changes in real estate markets and some of the influences on those changes are consequently important elements in understanding some of the current differences between countries and this is the aim of the following two chapters.

Potential problems in agents' selling and advisory functions

When agreeing to act as an agent for someone wanting to sell their home, estate agents formally commit themselves to using the best of their abilities to sell the dwelling. In doing so, they generally actively 'sell' properties on their lists to prospective buyers, rather than passively remain solely the holder of the list.

Most agents' time is spent either viewing the homes of potential house-seller clients in attempts to win business, or in showing properties to prospective buyers. Yet, the amount of time spent on showing a particular dwelling for sale is not simply a result of its popularity with buyers; it also depends on how much an agent wants to push a property on to buyers' agendas. The latter depends on the agents' calculations of the costs and returns of putting their effort into specific dwellings. What decisions agents come to with regard to effort will not be fully known to the client, so the agent–client relationship is based on asymmetrical information.

In the house-selling process, agents have superior information on the general market and on the real effort they intend to put into any specific sale with regard to house sellers and buyers. Two potential problems arise. The sellers' problems are that they do not know how much effort agents actually put into selling their homes nor whether they have given the appropriate valuation for their property. They can do some monitoring but cannot observe the actual effort being undertaken to promote a sale. Buyers, in addition, have to trust agents when they are being given information and sales pitches about properties. Furthermore, it is not uncommon for agents who are keen to clinch a sale to disclose information to potential buyers that is against a seller's interest. During negotiations over purchase, for example, to make a quick sale the agent may inform potential buyers that a seller would accept a discounted price, even though the seller may not want this revealed at such an early stage of the bargaining.

Another strategy might be for an agent to over-value a property in order to induce the seller to list it with them, accepting that it will subsequently take longer to sell. Many sellers may believe such estimates are credible and, particularly when fee charges are similar, select agents offering seemingly the best price. This may subsequently create grievances about agents' sales efforts or valuations amongst sellers when such optimistic prices are not realised. This strategy is more likely in single agent listing institutional arrangements than in MLS because in the latter it is easier for sellers to compare their property with other equivalent ones.

Although such potential opportunistic behaviour by estate agents forms the focus of study in much of the academic literature, the findings so far have been mainly theoretical. In contrast, there is little empirical evidence on the actual extent of the failure of agents to devote the optimal amount of effort to client interests because of the difficulty of designing studies with the data available. One recent US study, however, did suggest that the effect could be significant. Using a unique data set that included sales made by agents of their own properties as well as of clients' houses, this study concluded that agents typically make 2% more on the prices of their homes than on equivalent homes owned by others (Levitt & Syerson 2002).

Buying agents are uncommon in Australia, Ireland and the UK but they are more widely used in the USA and the Netherlands. Similar information problems to those outlined for client sellers can arise in such agent–buyer relationships. There are high risks of dispute with buying clients, particularly when agents are given powers by buyers to purchase houses on their behalf, because there is wide scope for disagreement over the precise instructions given to the agent by the purchaser and the extent to which the agent carried out those wishes and interpreted them reasonably.

Estate agents are also not simply co-ordinating and sales people, they also act as advisors. Their advice may be part of their services to a client house seller, such as making a valuation of the property and recommending the best way to sell it. Alternatively, they might advise buyers on financial products, lawyers and surveyors' services for which they usually earn a broking fee. Again, agents will have superior information over the buyer and the seller in this context most importantly, about their competences and honesty in such situations.

Fee structures and estate agents' incentives

The relationship between a client and an estate agent is specified in the contract made between them. The contract should be designed consequently to ensure that agents put in the optimal amount of effort. Contracts between clients and estate agents in England are relatively simple; whereas, in some other countries, they are complex documents that try to lay out behaviour across a wide range of issues. Whatever the complexity of contracts, clients will still not fully know the agent effort and whether their interests are being properly looked after. A good attribute of a commission structure, therefore, should be to provide estate agents with incentives that closely ally their interests with those of their clients. Unfortunately, commission structures in estate agency are not good at doing this.

The problem of how good agents are at representing sellers' interests is complex as there are so many potential variables to consider. Sellers' strategies as well as agent ones, for example, can affect the final sales price (Anglin *et al.* 2003). Homeowners might also simply wish to test the market with no real desire to move and under the typical 'no sale–no fee' arrangement agents may spend much effort creating a sale that is never actually going to happen.

To complicate matters further, the incentives are altered by how long contracts are made for and whether the seller can dismiss an agent at short notice. With a short-notice contract, for example, the agent has an incentive to sell the property quickly but that might not be for the best obtainable price. Alternatively under such arrangements, if after judging the prospects of a quick sale as poor, agents might well opt for a low-involvement strategy because there is a strong risk that they will reap no return (Skyes 1993).

There is a large literature exploring the nature of estate agent fee commissions (Jud & Winkler 1994; Yavas 1994). The standard assumption in it is that the more effort an agent puts into selling a house, the higher is the price achieved and the shorter the selling time. This forms the basis of the theoretical studies of the 'principal–agent' relationship between house sellers and estate agents (Arnold 1992). The actual shape of agents' response functions is important in determining the precise empirical consequences of these factors but they are impossible to measure in aggregate (Sappington 1991). Most of the literature originates from the USA and so refers to the estate agency system there.

One clear conclusion of the literature is that the normal contract arrangements between house sellers and estate agents do not perfectly match the interests of the two parties. For this reason, if no other, it is to be expected that house sellers will often be critical of estate agents' behaviour and that frequent non-negotiable disputes between the two groups will arise. This helps to explain why estate agency is a consumer-complaint prone industry – a feature that exists around the world.

The problems with the seller–agent relationship can be seen with the standard percentage of house price fee. In it, the interests of the agent and the seller are not perfectly aligned because, although both gain from a higher price, the incremental gain to an agent is only a small part of the increase. On a 2% commission, for instance, the seller gets 98% of any higher price and consequently has a far greater interest in obtaining a better price than the agent (Zorn & Larsen 1986; Larsen & Zorn 2000). Disappointment at the results of using agents may well arise as a result of such incentive disparities.

The main alternative form of fee structure to the percentage commission is the flat rate fee. This also does not bring agents' interests fully into line with sellers either, because the agent solely has an incentive to sell the property as quickly as possible, whereas the seller may prefer the best price, which takes longer to achieve. This type of fee structure is used far less than the percentage rate one, presumably for this reason.

Despite the drawbacks of the two main types of fee structure, other fee commission options are rare in estate agency markets. One option used for many other goods and services is the 100% commission. Shops when selling manufacturers' goods effectively take a 100% commission by purchasing such goods and selling them for a higher price. The same is true of second-hand car dealers. Such an approach is rare in housing, however, because of the high costs of holding a stock of houses and the uncertainties of sales in the housing market.

Another fee option would be to split the percentage fee on the basis of components of the expected price. In such a framework, a small percentage fee would be paid for an agreed price at which both parties believe it would be easy to sell the property. Then, graduated higher percentage fees would be set for prices achieved above that amount. The agent would then have a good incentive to achieve the best price, especially if the incremental percentages were set at high levels. These types of fee contract rarely exist, however, perhaps because they are too difficult to negotiate due to house price uncertainty and information disparities between estate agents and sellers.

The standard form of contract, thus, remains a fixed percentage fee of the whole house price. The percentage rate adopted, furthermore, is usually a standard market one that rarely changes. The fee in the USA, for example, has been around 6% for decades, whereas in the UK it has fallen to around 1–2%. This creates three puzzles.

1. *The persistence of variable sales returns* With a fixed percentage fee, agents can earn far more from selling more expensive homes than cheaper ones. Yet the difference in effort required to complete a sale is not so great. Why is there not a revolt of owners of expensive homes, who generally are not the meekest of individuals in society?
2. *The persistence of customary fee levels* There is some evidence of fees changing over the course of the housing market cycle and that the Internet is squeezing margins in some areas of activity. The practice of client–agent negotiation over fee levels, nevertheless, is rare in most countries.
3. *Why do some countries have higher fee levels than others?* Such differences cannot be accounted for solely through variations in house prices and living standards. (The former influence actual returns for any percentage level of fee and the latter affect agent earnings and, hence, costs in this labour intensive industry).

Fixed fee rates create significant anomalies, because it rarely costs an agent as much extra to sell a more expensive dwelling than a cheaper one as the increase in commission obtained. As a result, on the one hand, owners of higher priced houses end up paying more for their estate agency services than those owning less expensive properties. On the other, the much lower fee for cheaper properties may result in agents devoting limited effort to them, so that their owners might do better by agreeing to pay a higher fee. Whatever the market position of the seller, such percentage uniformity heightens the disparity between fee structures and optimal estate agency incentives.

In some other countries, fee rates do vary depending on a property's price, as in Australia, but the variation still does not lead to a close match between agent effort and their returns. Another market-driven option is for agents to specialise in market segments, so that they are not dealing with a widely diverse range of property prices, which again does occur but only to a limited extent. In general, the fixed rate fee may be an uncomfortable compromise between the concern of the seller at agent effort – a cheaper fee may lead to disproportionately less selling effort and a more expensive one might not induce much extra either – and a desire to incentivise agents to put more effort into selling higher value properties.

The second puzzle is the longevity of fee levels. Such longevity in fee percentages seems odd when competition between estate agents is generally regarded as intense. It also could be argued that fee levels should vary significantly depending on whether the housing market is booming or in recession. During a boom, agents need less effort to sell a property and find many homeowners eager to sell; in a falling market, sales are harder to achieve and business is more difficult to come by. These cost and demand elasticity factors would suggest that commission rates should vary a great deal over time, but observation shows only limited variance.

Some commentators argue that the persistence of customary fee structures indicates that estate agency is not a competitive industry after all, pointing to the existence of the rules of property listing systems as important barriers to entry (Bartlett 1981; Schroeter 1987). Most explanations, however, search for other causes because the universally observed ease of entry and exit from estate agency suggests that it would be hard to sustain a monopoly.

One hypothesis concerning the homogeneity of fees is that a common rate gives some indication to individual sellers that agents are putting as much effort into selling their properties as they are with other homes on their lists. This has been suggested by Levmore (1993). However, this is unlikely to be the sole reason. It could also be argued that sellers might wish to choose from a range of agent offers on cost and effort but agents generally are reluctant to reveal that they actually vary their effort levels and, so, a market failure is created. Alternatively, it could be argued that the 'customary' fee acts as a signal for the appropriate level of charges to sellers, who would have only a limited idea of what the service should cost in the absence of such customary amounts because they use estate agency services infrequently. 'Price leadership', therefore, exists – even when there are no dominant market participants.

One recent study has argued that customary-based fees produce considerable welfare losses to society and provide evidence from the USA that seems to support their claims (Hsieh & Moretti 2002). The argument is that when agents can move freely between local housing markets, agents will move into cities as long as their real earnings are at least as good as elsewhere. With fixed commissions, cities with higher house prices will generate greater agent revenues from each house sale than other cities with lower prices. The higher commissions, however, will not be reflected in long-term higher individual agent or firm income because more agents will move to the higher priced cities, until agents earnings are equalised across all cities. This means that higher house price cities have more estate agents per 1000 dwellings than lower priced ones, but real estate agents' earnings are similar between the cities. In the higher priced city, there are more estate agents chasing homeowners wanting to sell their properties and, so each agent will deal with fewer properties in a year than in the cheaper city, which is how earnings come to be equalised.

The essence of this argument is that customarily fixed commissions lead to a wasteful use of resources in which competition does not weed out excess capacity but rather creates it. Estate agency ends up in a free market context as an industry with far more capacity than is socially optimal: because agent productivity is far lower than it could be. By extension, this argument also gives a reason why commission rates vary so little. Agents' income does not vary in line with fees, the number of agents instead does. So, agents have no incentive to cut rates but they do have to move to another locality or quit the business when a housing market turns sour and earnings fall there.

Whether this argument will survive critical commentary intact is at present unclear. The policy response is also difficult to envisage as restricting entry to estate agency may have considerable implications for monopolistic abuse. Whatever the outcome, it illustrates the fact that policy issues in estate agency are extremely complex and not as straightforward as they may seem.

With regard to the marked differences in fee levels between countries, a number of observations can be made. First, as Table 6.1 shows, the variations in absolute fee levels are substantial. These calculations have to be qualified by the fact that they depend on prevailing phases of the house price cycle, which makes southern England look particularly high in 2002, and exchange rates, which enhance the US figures compared with, say, 2005.

Table 6.1   Average estate agency chargeable fees per dwelling, approximate international comparisons 2002.

	£ (at 2002 ex. rates)	% fee
Scotland	727	1
Wales	1667	2
Ireland	1890	1.5
Netherlands	2133	1.6
England	2679	2
Melbourne	3012	2.5
S. E. England	3526	2
Sydney	3568	2.5
Denmark	4953	3.5
US Mid West	5095	6
US South	5518	6
USA	5922	6
US North East	6146	6
US West	8009	6

Note: Published fee rates do not exist, as they would violate competition law in most countries, so % fee levels are those reported to the author by country experts (see Ball 2004a).

House price sources: OPDM, Permanent tsb, NVM, Aus. REI, Realkreditraadet, NAR.

Furthermore, in some countries there is significant cross-selling of other services – as in Scotland – which artificially depresses agency returns. Nevertheless, the scale of some of the differences is so great that they are likely to be giving some indication of major long-term differences in agent returns. Second, there is virtually no comparative literature on the issue. This suggests that even the experts have limited knowledge of cross-country data and, so, it is hard to expect the information to have a significant influence on individual country's agency markets. Third, until recently estate agency services were almost entirely a national industry. This is now changing in the commercial sector but it generally remains the case in residential agency services (see Chapter 7). In the absence of trade in this service sector, international competition cannot take advantage of arbitrage opportunities and, hence, the law of one price fails to operate.

Finally, from the available evidence, though limited, it seems that both the degree of regulation and consolidation within agency services are cor-related with higher fee levels (Ball 2004a). As the USA is one of the most regulated industries and has had long-term local monopolies in the institu-tional arrangements of its MLS, it is perhaps unsurprising that it has the highest level of fees. There is some anecdotal evidence that service levels are higher in the USA than elsewhere, though even if that were true it is unlikely to justify the scale of the fee difference from some other countries.

Furthermore, such non-price competition is characteristic of monopolistic industry structures where full-price competition is impossible.

Channelling agent behaviour in the client interest

Previous sections outlined areas where the selling and advisory functions of estate agents contain risks of agents abusing their informational advantages. These cannot be that widespread in practice, otherwise so many buyers and sellers would be reluctant to use agents' services that they would not be able to perform their core listing and matching functions. If using an agency was such a 'lemon', the agency market would thus fail to exist. The reason why the potentially negative aspects of the client–agent relationship do not overwhelm the market is that there are countervailing forces in operation that bring agents' interests more into line with their clients'. The first, and probably the most important, is the self-discipline that agents impose on their own behaviour because of their own beliefs about conducting business in a proper manner, peer group pressure and the regulations under which they operate. In addition, professional bodies and public policy create a combined regulatory framework determining how estate agents operate.

In a setting where information is not easily available on behaviour and competence, reputation becomes an important discriminator for clients. Agents that are dishonest or misleading, or firms that employ them, will become known and the most notorious will be shunned by buyers and sellers. The longevity of the agency will, therefore, be an important signal of its probity, because long-established smaller local enterprises face the threat of rumours on local information grapevines if they exploit clients. In areas with highly mobile populations, however, such informal regulatory devices will be weak in their effect.

Part of the moves towards branding and chains that has occurred in estate agency in recent years is associated with trying to enhance firm reputations at a large spatial scale, so that even mobile or newly formed households can have some assurance of probity. Larger firms face high costs in terms of lost profits and dented brand images if buyers and sellers come to regard them as disreputable. As a result, they are more likely to put in the appropriate training and management procedures to limit individual agent abuses.

Another market-based strategy, which governments have generally encouraged, is for agents to co-operate and form a 'club' or professional association. Such bodies lay down membership conditions, related to matters such as educational attainment and practical experience, and formulate rules of conduct that preclude opportunistic behaviour (see Chapter 11). The existence of professions, their strength and the degree to which governments co-operate with them all influence the way in which regulation of estate agency takes place in individual countries.

The degree to which the professional approach has been adopted varies across countries considerably. There are high levels of professional body membership in some countries, such as Denmark, the Netherlands and the USA. In contrast, in England and Wales less than a quarter of estate agents are members of the two main professional bodies. The National Association of Estate Agents (NAEA), with 10 000 members in the UK, is the largest one and its members are claimed to be in more than 60% of UK estate agency offices. The Royal Institution of Chartered Surveyors is the other professional body, which represents surveyors in a wide range of areas as well as residential estate agency, and it has far higher educational requirements than the NAEA. Both publish rules and set up disciplinary procedures in relation to them.[1]

Professional bodies representing estate agents differ widely in their rules and conditions for membership, within countries as well as between them. The two British professional bodies, for example, recently were in negotiations to merge but agreement was not reached because of differences in the educational attainment required for accreditation by each of them.

The other route to regulating estate agency is via public policy and legislation. Most countries have general consumer, as well as standard contract, laws through which consumers can take estate agents to court or to special tribunals. Most, furthermore, have specific consumer laws related to estate agency.[2] The latter highlights both the intensity of consumer problems in this area and their political significance. Many countries also legislate on who can act as an agent. This may be done by proscribing activities, such as mixing law or banking and estate agency, or, in many countries, by requiring that estate agents be registered with either the courts or specialist public or private bodies. To achieve such registration, prospective agents must meet a variety of educational and good character criteria and demonstrate financial capabilities, such as financial guarantees or liability insurance. England and Wales are two of the few places where currently some form of registration does not exist.

Not all complaints by consumers about estate agents, of course, are reasonable. There is a difficult balancing act for policy-makers of creating market and associated regulatory situations that protect both the interests of consumers and those of agents. They also have to make sure that excessive regulation does not stifle agent enterprise, competition and market functioning. Regulation is also expensive both in terms of the institutions that need to be set up and in terms of the consequences for the costs of market transactions.

Regulation also varies in its effectiveness. The pay-off for breaking the rules might be far higher than the cost of being caught, especially if the probabilities of detection and punishment are low. Merely requiring a person to obtain a qualification does not guarantee honesty. Regulation, in addition, imposes costs on all. It is equivalent to an insurance premium on transactions, even though most would never need to claim. Different judgements have been made in individual countries about these issues, so that a range of regulatory regimes can be observed – ranging from the permissive to the highly regulated.

The Internet

Earlier, it was argued that one of the most important market functions was in the matching of buyers and sellers through the creation of information sites about properties in a locality. In recent years, this function of the estate agent's shop – or office – and press advertising is being contested by Websites.

The advent of Internet advertising has been beneficial to consumers by expanding the range of information and the ease of search. Other innovations include text messaging and e-mail shots detailing information of properties to relevant potential buyers. The consequences of the Web for estate agents are not fully worked through but are already profound. Developments have varied across countries, yet all are driving significant industry change.

One view is that cheap Websites, where sellers pay only a small fee to list their property, will eventually supersede the current matching role of estate agents and that agency services will gradually disappear without this core role. Estate agencies are clearly worried about such eventualities as they are highly reluctant to allow others to post information on their sites or permit their listings to be displayed elsewhere. There is strong evidence, in particular, that agents acting for buyers are suffering a marked loss of business as a result of the ease of searching for properties on the Web.

An alternative hypothesis about estate agents and the Web seems more likely. Use of the Web has benefited agents by arousing more interest in the properties they have for sale. Most property Websites to date are proprietary ones and there is some evidence that they have generated more buyer interest in properties agents have for sale. The experience of using the Web as a means of undertaking for-sale-by-owner – including showing round intrusive house viewers and amateur sales pitches – might convince many sellers of the superiority of the selling skills of a professional, especially in the modern world of extensive housing transaction regulation. Empirical studies of the impact of the Internet are rare. Tse & Webb (2002), using data from Hong Kong, found that the Web increased per staff transactions and commissions in agencies, which suggests that to date the Web has been favourable to agents.

Websites also seem to be encouraging the trend towards larger agency networks, because there are high set-up costs and the need for daily updates. The network effects of a real estate Website, furthermore, are increased, the greater the proportion of the sales in a locality are listed. For MLS, this feature already existed prior to the Internet. In contrast, for single-listing institutional arrangements, the impact of the Web has been profound, as it has generated bandwagon effects for the largest listings. For example, the largest residential Website in the UK already claims to list 60% of sales in England. An MLS is gradually coming by default to the UK and to other countries but without the sales pooling character typical of MLSs in the USA.

Conclusions

The analysis in this chapter has ranged over a wide number of issues related to the relationship between residential estate agents and the consumer. It has highlighted that, although the current literature provides many insights, there are no easy off-the-shelf answers to many of the problems in estate agency. As with all policy matters, some problems are irresolvable. Finding a fee structure that perfectly aligns client and agent interests is one.

Notes

1   The National Association of Estate Agents (1997) *Residential Estate Agency – Code of Practice*; the National Association of Estate Agents (1998) Rules of Conduct; Ombudsman for Estate Agents (2001) Code of Practice; the Royal Institution of Chartered Surveyors (2003) Rules of Conduct.
2   In England and Wales, they are the Estate Agency Act 1979 and the Estate Agents' (Provision of Information) Regulation 1991.

7

Spatial reach in commercial and residential real estate brokerage

Introduction

Chapter 6 examined some economic issues in relation to estate agency/real estate brokerage services[1] and it made some comments on international institutional differences. This chapter takes a somewhat different perspective. It compares the recent dynamics of the commercial and residential sectors. A notable divergence in industry structure can be seen. On the one side, firms in commercial markets have tended to become much more multi-functional real estate service providers in recent decades; with the largest rapidly gaining market share and a global reach. On the other side, residential firms have all remained national and, even, local in character, focused on brokerage, and there is generally a much lower level of concentration. The question asked here is why does this division in the spatial reach of commercial and residential brokers exist? Answering provides some insights into the nature of the property services and sales brokerage industries.

The scope of real estate brokerage and services firms

To start with it is useful to recap and expand upon the description of brokerage activities given in Chapter 6. Real estate brokers are the sales intermediaries between buyers and sellers in the markets for commercial and residential buildings. They are involved in 80% or more of building sales transactions in most advanced economies. Table 7.1 summarises the typical activities undertaken by real estate brokers (Yavas 1994).

Table 7.1 The activities of real estate service companies.

Real estate brokerage encompasses four core activities:
- Provide market information
- Transaction agent role in the buying and selling of real estate
- Transaction agent role in finding tenants and rent setting
- Valuation of buildings and land

They may be associated with several other real estate service functions:
- Consultancy advice on real estate projects and markets
- Research on markets and other aspects of real estate
- Property management and related services
- Intermediary between property owners and financial community
- Intermediary between property owners and other real estate professionals
- May operate as real estate investment fund managers

To elaborate on the four core brokerage functions:

1. They *provide market information* for buyers and sellers in terms of the properties that are currently available, their characteristics and price.
2. They *act as transactions agents for owners* wishing to buy or sell real estate. Brokers acting for buyers are less common than those acting for sellers, because selling agents provide much of the information that buyers require. Buying brokers, therefore, have to justify their existence in the face of such competition. They typically do this primarily by having access to private information not available in the public domain that they claim provides a superior information set for decision-making (e.g. detailed up-to-date knowledge of comparable commercial market rents or superior knowledge of houses on the market). Alternatively, they may claim to provide better overall brokerage services to clients, not tainted by any threats of self-interested behaviour that may arise when they are simultaneously acting as sellers' agents.
3. Another core function of real estate brokers as transactions agents takes place *in rental markets*, whereby brokers find tenants for building owners or, again less commonly, act as agents for those looking to rent commercial or residential accommodation.
4. They undertake *valuations of properties*. The valuation may be an initial assessment of market price for a potential property seller; alternatively, it may be a valuation required by a mortgage provider; or, finally, it may be the actual pricing basis on which a deal is struck. The latter is common in most commercial real estate transactions, because the heterogeneous nature of buildings and local legal requirements mean that most commercial buildings are transacted on agreed specialist valuations of their worth rather than through direct price setting by buyers and sellers. Real estate brokers in such contexts are, therefore, literally price-makers.

Alongside these core functions, real estate brokers often are associated with other real estate services, especially the larger commercial ones. If they undertake all of them, they are often called full real estate service providers.

5. *Consultancy advice on real estate projects and markets* is given to clients of other services provided by the firm or to third parties interested in real estate markets, such as financial institutions and large investors. This has been one of the most rapidly growing spheres in recent years for real estate service providers operating in commercial real estate markets.

6. They provide *research on markets and other aspects of real estate;* firms' own information on transactions, valuations and other real estate matters provides a basis for undertaking real estate research. This is generally practically oriented, rather than academic in nature, and is frequently associated directly with consultancy. Yet it may represent stand alone market analysis or forecasting undertaken and publicised, say, as a means of enhancing a firm's brand image or client reach.

7. *Property management and related services* are undertaken by most firms, especially on behalf of landlords with tenants in their properties.

8. *Intermediary roles between property owners and the finance community* differ between the residential and commercial sides of the brokerage business. Many residential brokers will have arrangements with mortgage and insurance companies to sell their products to clients; whereas on the commercial side brokerage firms will often be active in helping developers and investors to formulate, often complex, financing arrangements and tax positions.

9. *Intermediary between property owners and other real estate professionals* as a first port-of-call for many clients who have only infrequent dealings with real estate. Real estate brokers are ideally placed to offer advice and to direct clients towards other real estate specialisms that they may need.

10. As *real estate investment fund managers*, some firms directly set up and manage their own real estate funds for private investors or, alternatively, run them as publicly listed vehicles for general investors.

Economies of specialisation and scope

There is a clear, though imperfect, distinction between the real estate brokers that specialise in commercial and those that specialise in residential property. The principal reason for the divide is to derive the benefits of specialisation.

There are several key differences between the two areas that explain the tendency to specialise in one or the other.

1. The two spheres of activity have distinct types of clients – business people and housing consumers.
2. They deal with buildings with different characteristics and problems.
3. Usually the branch offices of these firms exist at distinct spatial locations – characterised by the city centre–commercial hub versus the suburb.
4. Finally, the production functions of these two activities are becoming increasingly divergent, so that there are distinctive opportunities for scale and scope economies in the two spheres.

Specialising in one of the two markets enables an appropriate division of labour to develop within a brokerage firm and facilitates the generation of deep market knowledge and specialist skills by staff. Firms then become known for their particular skill base and, hence, attract clients for the particular types of property in which they specialise. On the commercial side, in particular, firms will tend to specialise in particular market segments: offices, warehousing, retail, etc. and, possibly, sub-groups within them.

When brokerage firms undertake business in more than one type of property, all but the smallest enterprises typically evolve multi-divisional structures, with separate divisions specialising in particular building types. Though the requirements of commercial and housing markets often mean that they do not exist in the same organisation, there are exceptions. As a general rule, the greater the common characteristics between residential and commercial markets, the more likely firms are to specialise in both types of property because there may be complementary benefits from doing so. The higher ends of housing markets have similar international characteristics to commercial ones, for example. Smaller office and retail properties are likely to benefit from a similar local knowledge to residential ones. Small, remote markets tend to have brokerage firms that undertake all types of building sales because the benefits of greater specialisation are limited by the extent of such local markets. Elsewhere, institutional arrangements may encourage multi-function brokerage firms, such as with the national organisational arrangements for qualified brokers in the Netherlands. So, many Dutch firms straddle the residential–commercial divide.

Where no particular organisational form has a competitive edge, the local history of real estate brokers may play an important part in explaining current firm structures. In New Zealand, for example, most towns including the smallest will have a branch of the UK-listed firm, DTZ Holdings, because one of New Zealand's traditional residential brokerage firms ended up in the DTZ fold; whereas in the UK this company is known as one of the largest commercial real estate service providers and its residential division operates in specialist niches only, avoiding the general market.

At the same time as there are benefits from specialisation, real estate brokers also gain from diversification, as was seen in the typical list of brokerage functions described above. Diversification, however, is into related areas only, because that is where brokerage characteristics may provide a competitive edge with one aspect of an activity usefully employed in others. A client-base for properties, for example, easily spills over into finding client-bases for real estate-related financial products or property management operations. Similarly, confidential information gathered as part of brokerage and valuation activities can form part of a propriety information base for consultancy and research.

There is a clear tension between diversification and specialisation. Too much diversification negates specialisation and firms are in danger of losing their edge in all the markets they serve. Because brokerage firms diversify into related areas of activity, there is less of a risk-pooling effect on overall returns than gained by firms that spread across less closely cor-related activities. Sharp downturns in real estate markets may consequently affect all parts of a real estate service providers' business simultaneously, although spatial diversification may limit the effect if the markets chosen are weakly correlated in their cycles.

Divergent trends in real estate brokerage

Up until the 1970s, real estate brokers were primarily nationally or regionally oriented and were focused predominantly on acting as agents in property transactions and in undertaking valuations. Since then, on the commercial side, there has been substantial expansion in the range of real estate service functions and firms have become international in market spread and organisational form. The largest enterprises are now mega-organisations with connections across the globe, either of direct ownership or in interlinked formal arrangements of independent brokers, although even the largest still tend to have far greater market shares in particular lines of business and locations than in others.

Residential sales and lettings brokerage shows a complete contrast. Although there has been some consolidation with national chains emerg-ing, the nature of the business is still resolutely national and, even in many cases, highly local. Moreover, although some property management, mortgage origination and other financial service activity may occur, the prime functions of residential brokers have remained in transactions and valuation.[2]

The principal reasons for this divergence in growth trajectories between the two main branches of real estate brokerage would seem to lie in a number of key economic differences between the two lines of business. The hypothesis being suggested here is that scale and scope economies have become far greater in commercial real estate brokerage in recent decades and those economies are often international in character, whilst in residential brokerage any improvements in scale and scope economies have been far smaller and have remained nationally or locally oriented.

Good empirical evidence on scale and scope economies is sparse. Zumpano and colleagues found some evidence of both in residential brokerage using data from the 1980s, though they seemed to level off at relatively small firm sizes (Zumpano *et al.* 1993; Zumpano & Elder 1994). More recently, it has been suggested that a trend towards larger residential brokerage firms in the USA has arisen because of economies in brand advertising and in back office functions, like training and accounting, and because of a more business-like approach by such firms, which has enabled the returns of brokers and agents in larger firms to be higher than in smaller ones (Becker 2005).[3] However, in depth cost function studies of commercial firms are particularly hard to come by.[4] So, reliance is necessary on conjecture from the available information on firm change in the commercial and residential sectors.

Evidence for the divergent growth trends in the commercial and residential sectors can be found by looking at recent developments in the UK. The UK is particularly apposite as a case study as its commercial brokers have long undertaken international business and they have been at the centre of recent globalisation trends in commercial brokerage. Table 7.2 shows the top six UK commercial real estate service providers in 2004, ranked by global turnover, and Table 7.3 identifies the top fifteen residential ones, ranked by number of UK branch offices.

The first point to note is that the top six commercial brokers probably[5] have a larger share of UK commercial market transactions (sales and new leases) than the top fifteen residential real estate brokers do of residential transactions. Commercial brokerage, in other words, is probably significantly more concentrated than residential.

Table 7.2 The top six UK commercial agents, 2004.

	US owned or partnership*	Global turnover (£)	Own offices	Global offices including most affiliates
CB Richard Ellis	Owned	978	192	325
Jones Lang LaSalle	Owned	581	106	106
C&W Healey & Baker	Owned	484	82	160
DTZ Holdings	Partnership	364	56	195
Savills	Partnership	302	160	244
Knight Frank	Partnership	158	211	211

Source: *Estates Gazette.*

* Partnership defined as a formal linkage with a US-based property services company.

Table 7.3 The fifteen largest UK residential estate agency groups, 2004.

Rank by offices	Group	Residential sales branches	Parent grouping
1	Countrywide	842	Independent R.E. & insurance brokerage (spin off from Hambro Investment Bank, life insurance arm separated off in 2004)
2	TEAM Association	570	Franchise of independent agents
3	Connells Estate Agents	487	Owned by Skipton Group (mutual building society) mortgages/insurance/personal investment products
4	Halifax Estate Agency	360	HBOS One of largest 'retail' financial groups in UK
5	Bradford & Bingley Estate Agents	307	Bradford & Bingley Bank (previously a mutual building society)
6	Your Move	291	Independent, though owned by AVIVA (insurance) until 2004
7	Spicerhaart	236	Spicerhaart Group. Independent R.E. & insurance brokerage
8	Reeds Rains	136	Independent
9	Arun Estates	120	Independent, bought from Prudential Group (insurance) in 1991
10	Kinleigh Folkard & Hayward	66	Independent
11	Winkworth	58	Independent
12	Hamptons International	55	Independent
13	Chancellors	52	Independent
14	Andrews Estate Agents	50	Independent
15	Savills	46	Independent

Source: *Estates Gazette* and company Websites.

The second notable feature is that only one of the commercial brokers is also listed amongst the largest residential firms, namely Savills, and, even then, it is relatively small at only the fifteenth largest. Most of the commercial brokers do have residential arms but they tend to be comparatively limited parts of their businesses and they also specialise narrowly within the housing market. Typically, in terms of sales and rental they specialise in up-market housing where they have a competitive edge and that has by far the largest share of international clientele for UK residential property. Within that luxury segment, they further specialise – either geographically, say into large country properties in southern England, and/or by sub-market, such as new housing. They consequently avoid the mass-agency market in either owner occupation or private renting, because in that line of business pure residential real estate brokers are more likely to have a competitive edge.

The third feature to note is that commercial firms have a much smaller number of offices relative to turnover than do residential firms. They are also tightly concentrated in the city centres of major conurbations. Residential offices, in contrast, are widely dispersed.

This is partly because commercial real estate is lumpier, with each typical sale equivalent in value to many residential properties, so that agents are more willing to travel to meet client needs. In addition, the commercial market is more geographically concentrated. In the UK, for instance, London alone encompasses around 70% of the country's office stock by value and in most other cities city centre locations are the most important. Housing is obviously not so spatially concentrated but, instead, more spread throughout a country – though its value is greatest in the most affluent urban areas.

Furthermore, there is a demand side factor to the different locational choices of commercial and residential firms. Commercial clients are more likely to be willing to deal with, and travel to, the regional or national offices of their brokers than are the owners of housing, who are far more likely to prefer dealing with local neighbourhood offices. Only in parts of the upper market for residential property does clients' geographic spread of interest extend beyond the local, making them more willing to travel or deal with distant offices in search of a home or a buyer. This further reinforces the upper end of the residential market as being the locus of any residential trading activity undertaken by predominantly commercial firms, as noted above. Commercial real estate oriented property services companies through their management services operations may be involved in the management of residential properties, especially large city centre apartment blocks.

The next feature to note is that all of the fifteen residential real estate brokers listed in Table 7.3 are UK owned. There has been some consolidation in residential brokerage over the last twenty years with national brands and franchises emerging and they are the larger firms listed in Table 7.3. Yet the industry remains predominantly a local one, with some marked differences in organisational structure across the UK, particularly in Scotland as compared with the rest of the UK (see later). Few residential brokers, furthermore, undertake much business outside of the UK, apart from in some localities in Southern Europe where the British tend nowadays to buy second and retirement homes.

Some of the residential brokers, furthermore, are owned by financial enterprises but none of the major commercial firms are. Financial enterprises moved into UK residential estate agency in the 1980s, with the aim of being able to sell more of their own financial products through branch offices. Many were unsuccessful and have since quit the sector, although several remain, as can be seen from the information provided in Table 7.2 (Chapter 8 provides more details). Such cross-selling opportunities do not exist on the commercial side and many real estate investors would be put off by financial firm ownership of commercial real estate service providers, because they will often be their direct competitors, which may explain the lack of financial enterprise ownership in the commercial sector.

The globalisation of commercial real estate service provision

Another difference between the two sectors is in changes in the ownership of firms. In contrast to the pure UK ownership of residential brokers, all of the major UK commercial firms are now either owned by US real estate service providers or they are in formal alliances with one of them (Table 7.2). Moreover, these developments have only happened in the last decade in a rapid phase of cross-Atlantic consolidation.

Earlier, the period from the 1970s to the 1990s was characterised by the formation of large national enterprises in both the UK and USA. During this era there were a series of mergers. Moreover, at the same time, traditional partnership corporate structures were often replaced by publicly-listed, limited liability company ones. It was these new national leaders that in a few years in the late 1990s and early 2000s became global in their business activities through the merger of US and UK enterprises.

The UK market is obviously far smaller than the American one, although up to the late 1990s the UK firms had further increased their size by expanding overseas, building up strong presences in international markets, especially in Europe but also in Asia and Australasia, as well as in other places with strong British cultural links. By purchasing UK firms consequently large US real estate service corporations bought firms that, as well as being leading enterprises in the large UK market, also had strong international presences, some of them even in the USA.

These takeovers all took place during 1998 and 1999, at a time when stock prices were rising rapidly in the USA, which formed an opportune basis on which to make international deals. In this way, the world's current three largest real estate service enterprises were formed, as listed in Table 7.2. From these initial mergers, the new real estate service giants subsequently purchased other firms worldwide to consolidate their positions in the global marketplace. The three second-tier firms listed in Table 7.2 still remain UK-owned or quoted on the London Stock Exchange at the time of writing, but they have all formed alliances with US counterparts.

It is illustrative to describe the ownership changes that have occurred in each of the top three firms as case studies to help understand the causes of the shift to global market reaches in the commercial sector.[6]

1. *CB Richard Ellis* is the largest firm by turnover. It was formed in 1998 when the USA's CB Commercial Real Estate Services Group purchased the UK firm, REI International, which owned all of the UK firm Richard Ellis's international operations. CB Commercial Real Estate Services Group had originated in San Francisco early in the twentieth century. During the 1960s and 1970s, the company expanded its functions and geographic spread to become a full real estate service provider US-wide. After a management buy-out in the late 1980s, the firm then acquired US-based capital markets, investment management, mortgage banking, and property and corporate facilities management companies during the 1990s and it began to compete world-wide, leading to the Richard Ellis acquisition amongst a series of complex manoeuvres.

   Soon after the Richard Ellis purchase it also bought Hillier Parker May & Rowden, another large UK property services firm. It then went private in 2001 as CB Richard Ellis Group Inc. Subsequently, this company then acquired Insignia Financial Group, another major US real estate company, which earlier in 1998 had acquired the UK operations of Richard Ellis. By 2004, turnover was $2.4 billion and in that year an initial public offering of common stock in CB Richard Ellis was made.

2. *Jones Lang LaSalle* was founded through the merger in 1999 of London-based Jones Lang Wootton with Chicago-based LaSalle Partners Inc. Both firms already had significant international interests. In particular, LaSalle had previously, earlier in the 1990s, acquired a number of other

companies involved in various aspects of the provision of real estate services in the USA and UK and it had completed its initial public offering of common stock in 1997. Jones Lang Wootton earlier had expanded into Europe from its UK origins and it had been active in New York since the mid-1970s, channelling British, Middle Eastern and Asian investment funds into that market.

3. *Cushman and Wakefield Healey and Baker* emerged when Cushman and Wakefield based in New York merged with London's Healey and Baker in 1998. This followed an earlier alliance between them that lasted for ten years. After the formation of Cushman and Wakefield Healey and Baker, further acquisitions took place in Asia, South America and Mexico.

   Cushman and Wakefield have been operating in the New York region since the First World War. They expanded their range of services and geographical area in the USA from the 1960s to the 1980s. In the mid-1970s, the Rockefeller Group acquired the firm and then in 1989 the Mitsubishi Estate Co. Ltd. became the majority shareholder of the Rockefeller Group.

   Healey & Baker had started in 1820 and a hundred years later was concentrating on commercial property in London. Its business, especially in valuations, grew rapidly post-1950. By the 1970s, the firm was expanding into the rest of Europe with offices in Amsterdam, Brussels and Paris. European-wide growth continued during the 1980s and 1990s.

All the main UK firms consequently are now US owned having been bought by US firms intent on expanding globally. The purchase of the UK firms was encouraged by the common bond of language, the pre-eminence of London as a world real estate market and because the UK firms were already quasi-international themselves. Furthermore, all three companies are now full service providers, although they do still have some differences in strategic market emphasis by type of commercial property, geographically and real estate service function. The three 'partnership' firms listed in Table 7.2 are similar in nature to these top three, although of a somewhat smaller scale.

It is interesting to note that the investment by Mitsubishi Estate indirectly in Cushman and Wakefield, at the peak of the Japanese 1980s real estate boom, is the only case of a Japanese firm being involved in the global changes in real estate service providers. It is possible to speculate that this lack of major international engagement may have something to do with the ownership of Japanese real estate, which is more likely to be owner occupied than in the UK or USA, and also on the impact of the long subsequent recession in the Japanese real estate market, which has put Japanese real estate firms in a relatively weak international position. A greater role for direct ownership is also common in other major economic powers, like France and Germany, which also have no major international commercial real estate service providers. These two countries' commercial markets were already being dominated by London-based firms in the 1960s and 70s. US firms, by taking over London-based ones, consequently currently now face little major international competition from firms in other countries.

Drivers of change in commercial real estate brokerage

The evolution of large global commercial real estate service companies embracing the full range of services can be attributed to a variety of interactions between demand and supply changes. A variety of likely influences is considered below. It is worth noting that most of the reasons are relevant only to commercial brokerage and not to residential, which helps to explain why the two spheres have had divergent development paths over the last few decades.

A changing product market

The role of offices, retail outlets and other commercial real estate has changed significantly in the world's economies over the last fifty years. Economies have become more service oriented in their activities, replacing earlier agricultural or manufacturing emphases. In addition, modern service industries have spread out from the initial narrow range of economically developed economies to encompass most of the world's economies. This has greatly increased the demand for commercial buildings, because the earlier predominant manufacturing, extractive and agricultural industries tended not to be extensive users of complex built structures.

Within the service sector, moreover, there has been a relative growth in the importance of industries that use commercial real estate particularly intensively and, often, at high value locations, such as the financial and business service industries. This bias in the direction of service industry expansion has increased the importance of commercial real estate as an intermediate capital good.

A greater functional role in the economy as a whole for commercial buildings obviously means that the market for them has both widened geographically and deepened in many urban areas as economic growth has proceeded. Far more commercial buildings are now built, bought and sold, and need valuing than was the case half a century ago and their increased number has stimulated the need for other types of real estate services, such as property management. The demand for real estate service providers' activities has consequently grown at a faster rate than economic growth as a whole, creating an ideal marketplace over many years and a fertile environment in which large real estate service providers could emerge.

The growing importance of activities within economic life that use commercial buildings has meant that the geographic spread of commercial real estate markets has increased enormously. In the 1960s, only a handful of world cities – such as Chicago, London, New York and San Francisco – had significant stocks of tradable commercial real estate, especially offices. Nowadays, substantial agglomerations of office buildings exist at many locations in the long-established advanced economies, in rapidly-growing Asia and in most other developing countries. Moreover, offices have been joined by new types of structures used in retailing and distribution – such as shopping malls and warehousing complexes – not to mentioned the science parks, regeneration schemes and mixed use projects that have blossomed in many places. Large hotels and other types of business and leisure operations have also spread around the world. The globalisation of real estate service providers has consequently gone hand-in-hand with an evolution and globalisation of modern office, retail, warehousing and other commercial space.

It is perhaps no surprise that today's giant real estate service provider firms have all originated from locations that had the earliest demands for significant commercial brokerage and valuation services – London and the three traditionally largest US cities. Those markets bequeathed to such firms' endowments that gave them a significant competitive edge as commercial real estate markets evolved in scale, functionality and geography. When they entered new markets, those firms could use their prior expertise, knowledge bases, reputations and contacts to win clients, thereby putting the smaller brokerage firms that already operated in those markets and other potential entrants at a disadvantage.

The production technologies used in service industries have also been changing and at an especially rapid pace during the current era when information and communication technologies are transforming many activities. This is accelerating the rate at which firms need to change the premises from which they undertake their businesses. Unsurprisingly, as a result, the expected life of a commercial building has declined due to accelerating technological obsolescence (Ball 2003). This greater turnover of commercial buildings has further increased real estate service providers' market turn-over and, at the same time, stimulated the need for additional specialist advice on matters such as building use, design parameters and replacement.

Furthermore, increasing scale economies in many service industries and the technologies that go along with them have raised the demand for larger and more complex real estate structures – large office blocks and shopping malls being two classic examples. Clients are now also expecting higher quality structures with 'smart building' characteristics. Building technologies have improved greatly making more complex structures both possible and significantly cheaper over time. Real estate service providers have consequently had to develop the expertise and professional net-works to cope with these technical changes in buildings and client-needs. Traditional, simple, small commercial structures required far less real estate service provider expertise and networking, so, could be more easily dealt with by small local firms than is the case with contemporary structures.

Changes in the real estate product markets in a variety of ways have con-sequently created a fertile environment for the growth of large real estate service providers. This enabled them to exploit scale and scope economies and to diversify into markets that made them more able to withstand adverse shocks to particular parts of their businesses.

New types of client and accommodation needs

Not only have commercial real estate products been changing, so have commercial clients and their space needs. There are now many firms in service industries with accommodation needs that are significantly greater than their forbears. This is perhaps most obvious in retailing with the growth of large national chains. The greater international orientation of large companies, the quintessential signifier of globalisation, has also increased the need for the simultaneous provision by them of branch offices in many countries and cities. Many of these modern firms have large space demands at particular locations, stimulating the demand for large-scale, expensive commercial space (Gibson & Lizieri 2001).

Firms are now also more footloose in their locations. Globalisation is a factor in this trend but it arises partly because demand patterns alter more frequently and, as noted earlier, technical change is accelerating. This desire for greater accommodation flexibility has increased, along with taxation and financial influences, the likelihood that commercial building users prefer to be tenants rather than the owner occupiers of buildings. (Although overall commercial owner occupation rates are still high – 50%

in the USA, for example, according to one estimate (Deng & Gyourko 2002).) Such trends have consequently encouraged the expansion of landlord– tenant relations in commercial building provision at the expense of direct owner occupation. Although accurate data are scarce, there seems to be a long-term decline in owner occupier rates in commercial accommodation (Johnson 1993).

A world in which a significant proportion of commercial space is rented is obviously a different one from where most buildings are owner occupied. Specifically, rental markets offer a substantial increase in the demand for real estate services. Real estate service providers have three distinct client bases within rental markets: users, developers and long-term investors, whereas in owner markets those aspects could all be embodied in one agency. Furthermore, in modern rental markets there is likely to be a greater reliance on loan finance than in earlier owner occupied ones. Capital market and monetary enterprises, like banks, may be lending finance to either of the three parties typically associated with new rental buildings and, as part of their screening and monitoring of loans, will require input from real estate service providers. So, financiers could be added to commercial real estate service provider client lists. Each type of client requires somewhat different advice, moreover, further adding to real estate service provider market turnover and the scope of their operations. Such a mixed client-base, in addition, raises the likelihood that at least a part of it will be international in character, either as tenants, developers, investors or financiers, thereby encouraging real estate service providers to have similar international profiles themselves.

Expanding real estate service functions

The complexity of the commercial real estate markets has greatly increased over time, partly due to external influences, such as general financial innovations, and because of evolutions within those markets themselves, such as improved information and investment evaluation. This greater complexity has led to those markets becoming more efficient.

One of the factors influencing this growth in market complexity and efficiency has been innovations in the content and range of activities undertaken by real estate service providers. Some of the change has been supply led and some client driven. No longer are many clients content solely with brokerage and valuation functions but expect a full range of real estate services from the agencies they use. Growing market complexity, as a result, has encouraged increases in the size, functional range and geographic scope of real estate service providers.

For example, the corporate real estate service provider business has increased as the outsourcing of real estate ownership and management has become more common. Corporate real estate service providers act as advisors and intermediaries between firms wishing to outsource their building needs and investors in real estate. They also manage properties or, alternatively, can put building owners in contact with other property management service providers and negotiate on their behalf over the fees for such services.

Real estate finance has also become vastly more complex than it was 30 years ago, so that real estate service providers have to provide more in-house expertise and act as conduits between clients and the wider financial community. In addition, greater financial sophistication has encouraged more frequent building valuations. Other pressures for more frequent valuations arise from such issues as tightening accounting rules and firms becoming more interested in deriving the full value from their assets.

Some investors are reluctant to invest directly into real estate because of their lack of experience of property ownership, finance, taxation and management. Additional investment disincentives include lumpiness, asset specificity, illiquidity and property specific risks. An alternative to purchasing is to invest in real estate investment funds that hold a portfolio of properties, which enable greater risk pooling, less investment lumpiness and improved liquidity in comparison to direct investment (Ball 1998). Furthermore, risk pooling is enhanced by holding properties in different countries, because of the weak long-term international correlation between real estate market performances. Real estate service providers, especially those with good international profiles, are in ideal positions to set up such funds for either private clients or publicly listed ones, by trading on their reputations and skill base.

All types of client, tenants, developers, investors and financiers, moreover, are demanding higher levels of information and advice about real estate markets and associated issues. This has driven a significant expansion of research and consultancy across a wide range of real estate issues. As a result, research and consultancy divisions have grown from small beginnings to become more important parts of real estate service provider functions over the last two decades. These knowledge-based activities have also helped the largest firms to expand their global profiles and activities.

Reducing client transaction costs

Clients of real estate service providers face significant costs when hiring one or more of the functions of real estate service providers. They also face significant principal–agent issues in relation to virtually all the functions of real estate service providers. For example, how do they know that a specific real estate service provider is producing the ideal valuation on properties they own or the true market valuation when they buy? How do they know that their agents are putting the greatest effort into selling their properties or giving them the best advice? Using more than one agent as a cross-check is one option but it is costly and the heterogeneity of real estate makes it difficult to provide exact comparisons. Moreover, much transactions and valuation information in commercial real estate is private and remains confidential to individual brokers, valuers, etc. It is consequently difficult for clients to be able to access adequate external information sources to monitor broker performance. Monitoring, moreover, becomes especially difficult when trying to source accommodation in a foreign country, because the firm or its procurement operation may have little information or experience when selecting or monitoring local real estate service providers. A high reliance, therefore, has to be put on trust and reputation.

One strategic option for clients is to use brokerage firms with an international spread when acquiring accommodation in new countries. They are then more likely to have experience of their services. Another related possibility, particularly advantageous for large international clients, is for firms to commission one agency for all of their estate service needs. They can thereby use the market power of offering a high value, long-term relationship to lower agency fees, other transactions costs and performance monitoring expenses.

Transactions costs are likely to fall as a result of the need to make only one agency contract for, say, many building acquisitions and/or sales, instead of separate ones for each real estate transaction. The effort of monitoring and assessing the performance of brokers' skills and success are also likely to be lowered: initially by the incentives given to real estate service providers to promote themselves in sales pitches by revealing confidential information to a prized client and, subsequently, through the client having only one periodic ongoing performance review to undertake. Finally, fear of the loss of a major client is likely to increase the chance that the chosen real estate service provider more closely aligns its interests with those of the client than when a client is only a small part of a real estate service providers' business. For instance, according to industry sources, it is now common practice for real estate service providers to invest in seconding one or more of their staff to work in major clients' offices for a specified period of time. Despite such efforts, there are still potential agency problems for clients when they use real estate service providers as a means of outsourcing their real estate requirements.

There has thus been a trend in recent years towards single real estate service provider sourcing by large clients. This has encouraged the growth of large, global real estate service providers because such firms have the resources to match such clients' needs.[7]

Increasing scale and scope economies

So far, most emphasis has been put on changes in demand for real estate services, because they have been key drivers of change in commercial real estate service provision. These probably have gone hand-in-hand with significant supply-side increases in scale and scope economies within real estate service provision, although it is difficult to measure such economies and no rigorous up-to-date assessments seem to exist. The two are, of course, interlinked for, as Adam Smith noted over two centuries ago, potential specialisation benefits (i.e. scale economies) are limited by the extent of the market and the extent of real estate service providers' markets has increased enormously in recent decades.

Such economies are probably greatest in such areas as personnel, information, reputation and marketing. The benefits of size to reputation and marketing are fairly standard ones common to other industries. Personnel is more industry-specific, given the skill acquisition required to operate effectively in real estate services. The largest firms can afford to employ the best staff and incentivise them with appropriate salary packages and bonuses. Those personnel also tend to embody the corporate culture and can pass it and their own specialist skills on to others. Information is especially important given its private nature. Firms can build up databases on specific real estate markets through their brokerage and valuation functions that can be used across their divergent areas of business. Even in the relatively few countries where commercial real estate prices are in the public domain, large firms still have important information edges through the timeliness of their information and the fact that they have detailed information on building characteristics and quality, unavailable in public registers.

Commercial real estate information also has network characteristics, which derive from firm size and geographic spread. The more joint real estate information is available to specific real estate service providers on the world's commercial property centres, the greater is likely to be the value of that information to themselves and their clients.

Scale and scope benefits have also been driven by technical change. For example, over the last few decades the benefits of within firm information storage and gathering capabilities have increased exponentially. As information and communication technologies have improved, the ability to access, retrieve, analyse and utilise market and other real estate information has risen enormously, enabling the largest firms to offer a range of interlinked services beyond the capabilities of their smaller rivals.

Firm strategies

Although many efficiency arguments can be made for the growth of giant commercial real estate service providers, such firms may also have narrower profit-making motives that do not translate into wider economic efficiencies and may even limit them, say, through resultant reductions in competition. Large firms, for example, may be able to gain market dominance in specific localities and be able to deter competitive threats from others through a variety of strategies – pricing, monopolising information, etc. Similarly, it could be argued that US majors took over foreign firms that charge far lower fee percentages than typical in the USA in order to avoid the threat of potential low cost entrants to their own home markets rather than for any true worldwide efficiency gains.

While these strategic factors may be potential causes of increases in firm size, it would be hard to prove them empirically to be the prime drivers. Moreover, given the arguments made above about the possibility of significant efficiency gains in commercial real estate brokerage, the weight of judgement probably lies on the side of efficiency rather than market power causes of the growth of large firms.

Conclusions

Commercial and residential real estate brokerage have undergone distinct changes in recent decades. On the one hand, in the commercial sector, brokerage is now associated with a wide range of services and some huge global firms, although there are still many smaller national, local and specialist firms as well. On the other hand, in the residential sector, globalisation has not occurred and the industry in most countries remains dominated by small firms and localised units. Several reasons were suggested for the differences, associated with variations in client needs and scale and scope economies in the two sectors.

Notes

1 In this chapter, the terminology of real estate brokerage will be used instead of estate agency to reflect more clearly some important functional separations.
2 Property management has been a growing area in countries, such as the UK, where a free-market private rental sector has come into existence in recent years.
3 For evidence from the UK and elsewhere, see Office of Fair Trading – OFT (2004).
4 Access to relevant firm data is the prime constraint on rigorous studies of scale and scope economies.
5 There is no definitive data on total turnovers in these markets.
6 These corporate histories are derived from the firms' Websites.
7 See, for example, CB Richard Ellis' *Annual Report 2004* [http://www.cbre.com].

8

Financial services, mortgage markets and real estate brokerage: an international survey

Introduction

The barriers between different areas of financial services have been strongly eroded in recent decades. Universal banking, extensive international competition and cross-national ownership are now commonplace. Where permitted by bank regulators, mortgage markets have followed this trend with widespread mortgage origination and financing activity now undertaken by banks and frequent bank ownership of specialist mortgage lenders. The questions to be addressed here relate to whether the expansion of financial service ownership will extend to residential real estate brokerage and what are likely to be the competitive effects on the real estate brokerage industry.

When buying or selling their home, consumers commonly renegotiate and reassess some of their largest financial products, including mortgages, insurance and their overall asset holdings. It seems obvious, therefore, that financial institutions should have an interest in the housing transaction process as a place for the selling of their own products. Many real estate brokerage firms are already key conduits for the cross selling of mortgages and other financial services. Therefore, a reasonable hypothesis is that direct ownership could enhance the likelihood of financial enterprises gaining a competitive advantage by moving into real estate transaction services. As will be shown later, this hypothesis has been put to extensive and expensive real-world testing with banks setting up real estate agency chains in some countries.

In recent years, there has been much controversy in the USA about the possible entry of banks into residential real estate brokerage.[1] Critics have argued that bank entry would lead to unfair competition, exacerbate excess capacity, lead to moral hazard problems when a range of finance and real estate services are jointly supplied, and generate greater than optimal firm sizes. The overall result, they argue, would be that consumers would end up paying a higher price for home selling and buying services and have less choice of brokers, with no offsetting benefits in terms of retail financial services.[2] Proponents of bank entry counter with the opposite conclusions, by emphasising that the entry of banks would lead to greater competition in real estate brokerage and noting that, in any case, many brokers already jointly provide real estate and financial services.[3]

When looked at from the perspective of only one country, debates about the potential impacts of future regulatory changes can only be informed conjecture about likely outcomes with the policy in place. A variety of effects might arise and it is the way that they interact to produce new industry equilibriums that is generally at the centre of debate. Informed alternative views often use similar market theories and generally differ because they put different weights on likely empirical interactions and outcomes. Whether the weights assigned are correct can only be discovered once the change has actually occurred.

In relation to the integration of banking and residential real estate brokerage services, cross-country sources of evidence do exist. Other countries do not have the same regulatory barriers as the USA to the integration of banking and real estate brokerage enterprises. This may be because of recent liberalisation or because such barriers never existed. Their experience, consequently, provides some hard evidence of the effects of allowing banking and real estate brokerage integration and the significance of mortgage origination within it. International comparison is unfortunately by no means perfect, because the institutional frameworks of banking, mortgage origination and funding, and real estate brokerage vary considerably between countries. This means that it is necessary to interpret differences and outcomes with care. Nonetheless, some useful insights are possible.

The situation in five countries is examined here: Australia, Denmark, Ireland, the Netherlands and the UK. None has explicit barriers barring banks from entering into real estate brokerage. All have well-developed owner occupied housing and associated mortgage systems and extensive market turnovers of existing dwellings. Like the USA, furthermore, all have experienced significant increases in real house prices and outstanding residential mortgage debt over the last decade (Table 8.1).

Table 8.1   Cross-county mortgage and housing market characteristics.

	Residential mortgage debt as % GDP (2002)	Typical loan-to-value ratios	Typical mortgage interest rate	Share of owner occupation (2002)	Average annual real house price growth (1995–2002)
Australia	51	65	Variable	70	5.8
Denmark	74	80	Fixed	51	5.1
Ireland	34	66	Variable	77	10.1
Netherlands	79	90	Fixed	53	8.2
UK	64	69	Variable	69	8.2
USA	58	78	Fixed	68	3.8

Source: OECD, Ball (2004a).

Nevertheless, there are some general differences from the USA situation. Mortgage securitisation is generally more limited, with the prime conduits for mortgage finance occurring either via general banks and specialist mortgage lenders or via mortgage bond based systems. Three of the countries, furthermore, mainly have variable interest rate mortgages (Australia, Ireland and the UK); while Denmark and the Netherlands with their bond-based systems have fixed rate products more in line with US practice. In terms of specific market importance, the relative scale of the mortgage market is notably lower in Ireland than in the USA, though it is greater in some of the other countries when measured as a share of GDP. Home-ownership rates are less than the USA in Denmark and the Netherlands, but higher in Ireland (Table 8.1).

The five countries all have established housing and mortgage markets of a sufficient scale and longevity that institutional arrangements in each are stable. The USA apart, only one of the countries surveyed has extensive multiple listing services (MLS), namely the Netherlands, although they also do exist in some parts of the UK, notably Scotland. A comparative study of the UK and USA in the 1980s suggested that the UK might converge on US MLS practice in subsequent decades (Miceli 1988). This has not proved to be the case for England, Wales and the most populous region of Scotland.

Real estate brokerage is a service industry with common technological characteristics across countries. Unfortunately, there is little up-to-date information with which to investigate this industry's cost structures. In the journal literature, only one rigorous study is available (Zumpano *et al.* 1993; Zumpano & Elder 1994) based on cost structure data assembled by the National Association of Realtors up to the late 1990s. More up-to-date or other international information is hard to come by, partly because residential broker trade and professional bodies are reluctant to collect it, partly for fear of being accused of collusive practices by the competition regulators in their own countries.[4]

What information there is suggests that economies of scope exist across the range of functions typically associated with the industry – valuation, listing, showing properties, etc. Scope economies may also extend to other services related to house purchase, including mortgage origination and insurance. There are some scale economies but these are believed to tail off at quite low firm sizes. Such cost structures, however, do not indicate extensive pressure towards concentration; rather the industry is characterised by a large number of small firms. Small scale in context of easy entry and exit leads to an environment with considerable competition forces in play.

Recent years have seen the growth of Internet-based home sales marketing, which has changed cost profiles and the opportunities for cross selling. The growth of Web-based sales listings has raised both fixed costs and the ongoing costs of keeping the lists up to date. However, there is little hard evidence of the Internet's effects. Such trends are common to all the countries surveyed here, so the extent to which they have encouraged organisational change and cross-industry integration can be explored.

Although detailed cost and production function data may be unavailable, international comparison does provide data on industry structure outcomes. Assessments can consequently be made as to the likely degree of competition. Firm size hierarchies, moreover, are only compatible over the long run with underlying cost structures, so such information can provide indirect evidence of them. Furthermore, the existence or not of multi-function firms gives some indirect indication of potential scope economies.

The existence of scope economies between real estate buying and selling and financial services does not necessarily imply that the two industries should inevitably merge into multi-function firms. One consideration is that welfare losses could arise as a consequence of such mergers if monopolistic practices arose as a result that outweighed any scope economy gains. Alternatively, other forms of industrial structure may offer greater efficiency, such as independent brokerage arrangements in both types of consumer services. Independence, for example, may more effectively deal with certain principal–agent problems associated with broker effort in home sales and screening biases in mortgage origination and funding than internal firm governance procedures (Williamson 1996; Martin 2002).

The following sections examine each of the five countries. They are ordered to take account of important differences in residential brokerage and mortgage industry characteristics. First, Australia and Ireland are examined, followed by the UK, Denmark and the Netherlands. A final concluding section then draws the themes together.

Limited integration: Australia and Ireland

Both Australia and Ireland share similar residential brokerage arrangements and a common type of mortgage product, based on variable interest rates. There are no multiple-listing services, rather sellers of existing housing make contracts with brokers on a single agency basis for a fixed period of time, typically three months. Auctions are also a common alternative method of house selling, especially in Australia (Mather 1989). Mortgages are funded and sold by the major retail banks and specialist non-profit building societies, though the latter now have a small market share. Originations take place through branch networks or via mortgage brokers.

With regard to residential brokerage, there is ease of industry entry and exit with limited licensing requirements,[5] and the industry is characterised by a large number of relatively small firms. Given the traditional agrarian backgrounds of Australia and Ireland, it is unsurprising that many real estate brokers undertake a broad range of selling and auctioneering functions typical of a rural community, particularly those located in smaller towns. In such areas, the local market is insufficiently large to permit detailed functional specialisation. In the main cities, in contrast, a few major firms that have expanded rapidly in the strong housing markets of the last decade and some have significant market shares in particular localities. Franchises have also grown. A monopolistic competition market structure, therefore, is evident, similar to that in the USA (Frew 1987; Wachter 1987; Yavas 1994).

Brokers in these two countries frequently jointly undertake real estate dealing and related financial services, including selling mortgages. This suggests that there are scope economies to be derived from combining the two spheres of activity. The larger city-based firms have also formed alliances with international brokerage firms in order to facilitate commercial real estate sales. Yet, there has been little development of formal ownership arrangements and takeovers of real estate brokers by financial enterprises, despite the absence of regulatory controls on the practice. Most brokers, instead, are still run by owner proprietors.

In Australia, there are some instances of firm integration across the residential–banking divide. One of the country's largest brokerage firms, L. J. Hooker, was taken over by a Queensland state-owned bank, Suncorp, in 1989; this has since been privatised and merged with other financial institutions to become one of Australia's largest financial companies, Suncorp Metway. It has promoted a retail customer 'all finance' strategy and, since the late 1990s, has rapidly expanded its mortgage origination operations via Hooker's network of sales offices, securitising the resultant mortgage portfolios. In 2001, Westpac Bank also bought a 20% interest in McGrath, one of Sydney's largest and fastest growing brokers – though the broker remains an independent entity owned by its founder. Finally, Elders, the country's oldest residential broker set up in 1836, owns a bank and insurance arm as part of its large-scale rural interests.

Even so, these three examples are exceptions, rather than indicate that widespread integration between residential brokerage and banking is occurring in Australia. For the most part, the two industries remain separate. Although residential brokers originate mortgages and sell other financial products, they are not the only market conduits for such services, which also take place via independent financial service agencies, such as mortgage brokers, or directly through banks and other mortgage providers. The outcome is that different organisational forms co-exist, within these the integration of residential brokerage and finance is limited and a question of firm strategies rather than of competitive necessity. As most banks and other finance organisations have chosen not to adopt the integrationist strategy, this suggests that the benefits of it are limited.

The UK: strategic intervention by some financial enterprises into real estate brokerage

Most mortgages are of a traditional variable interest rate type funded by retail financial institutions, which can raise the finance in whichever way they choose, subject to capital adequacy and other regulatory requirements. Securitisation of mortgage portfolios does exist, although the decision to do so depends on the contemporary funding strategies of the issuer.

Under British practice, lenders' standard mortgage terms enable them to alter interest rates at any time with no caps on the rate changes. A wide variety of new mortgage products, however, have been introduced in the last decade, so that borrowers can choose whatever type of mortgage instrument they wish. The vast majority, however, choose either a pure

Table 8.2   The ten largest UK mortgage lenders, 2003.

Ranked by outstanding loans	£bn	%
HBOS	172	22
Abbey	88	12
Nationwide Building Society	71	9
Lloyds TSB	71	9
Barclays	62	8
The Royal Bank of Scotland	48	6
Northern Rock	37	5
Alliance & Leicester	26	3
HSBC Bank	25	3
Bradford & Bingley	23	3

Source: Council of Mortgage Lenders, London.

variable rate product or one with a rate fixed for a few years only after which it reverts to a variable one.

The UK mortgage system evolved during a hundred year period when non-profit building societies (similar to US Thrifts) predominated. Following the deregulation of financial services in the 1980s, retail banks took much larger shares of mortgage provision. New entrants now abound and most previous mutual building societies have converted to profit-making plc status. Traditional specialist mortgage lenders have also branched out into a wider range of retail banking functions and several have been taken over by major retail banks. The largest traditional mortgage lender, the Halifax, merged with the Bank of Scotland in 2001 to form HBOS. It has a 22% share of the residential mortgage market and the market shares of other providers fall rapidly down the size rank (Table 8.2). In 2004, a rare cross-border take-over occurred in EU mortgage markets when the Spanish company Banco Santander Central Hispano acquired Abbey, the second largest UK lender.

UK residential brokerage is predominantly organised in a similar way to that in Australia and Ireland: with sole agency housing transactions using brokers on a time limited, single listing basis. Over 90% of owner occupied house sales are believed to take place via brokers and, unlike in Australia and Ireland, auctions are rare. In addition, the UK is one of the few countries where there are no real estate broker qualification requirements at all, so that entry and exit from the industry is particularly widespread. Nevertheless, a small number of real estate brokers may still have significant market shares in any specific locality, with the market being shared between, say, four or five firms. However, those market shares are contested by new entrants, who keep fees low (typically 1–1.5% of transactions prices, according to OFT, 2004b).

Following liberalisation in the 1980s that permitted general banks and specialised mortgage lenders to diversify from their core activities, financial institutions began setting up residential brokerage chains and taking over existing ones. They now own several of the largest residential brokerage operations and three financial firms are joint owners (with an independent broker) of the largest national Internet-based property listing service, which claims to have over 30% of all the properties transacted in the UK on its Website.[6]

The experience of the UK consequently seems to justify fears that allowing banks to enter residential brokerage leads to domination by them. However, a more detailed analysis suggests that the situation is less straightforward. Only a handful of financial enterprises have actually entered the residential brokerage industry. Many others have not followed, yet there is no evidence that they have lost market share in housing-related financial products as a result.

The most typical entrant to residential brokerage was a 'building society', the traditional mutual provider of mortgages. They set up integrated brokerage chains during a housing boom in the late 1980s on the basis that they would be able to sell large volumes of mortgages and other financial products through their residential agency branches. The set-up costs proved to be far higher than anticipated and house sales turnover plummeted in the subsequent prolonged housing market downturn to an extent that losses forced most of them to exit the residential brokerage business only a few years after entering it. This experience may again be highlighting the U-shaped cost characteristics of residential brokerage, because the high overhead costs of these new financial entrants meant that they could not withstand the loss in margins caused by a housing market slowdown in ways that were possible for their smaller residential brokerage competitors that had lower cost bases and could be more flexible in terms of staff recruitment and marketing.

Following this disastrous experience, it was noticeable that there were no new major financial entrants into residential brokerage during the next housing market upturn that lasted from 1996 to 2004. Even so, a number of finance firms remain significant players in the residential brokerage business. They had entered in the 1980s and weathered the housing market downturn and remained as major players, often as part of even larger financial conglomerates than in the previous decade.

Nevertheless, the overall structure of the residential brokerage industry has not become dominated by financial institution affiliates. The leading

Table 8.3   The fifteen largest UK estate agency (residential brokerage) groups, 2004.

Rank by offices	Group	Residential sales branches	Parent grouping
1	Countrywide Assured	842	Independent R.E. & insurance brokerage (spin off from Hambro Investment Bank)
2	TEAM Association	570	Franchise of independent agents
3	Connells Estate Agents	487	Owned by Skipton Group (mutual building society) mortgages/ insurance/personal investment products
4	Halifax Estate Agency	360	HBOS One of the largest 'retail' financial groups in the UK
5	Bradford & Bingley Estate Agents	307	Bradford & Bingley Bank (previously a mutual building society)
6	Your Move	291	Independent (owned by AVIVA, large insurance group until 2004)
7	Spicerhaart	236	Spicerhaart Group. Independent R.E. & insurance brokerage
8	Reeds Rains	136	Independent
9	Arun Estates	120	Independent (bought from Prudential Group (insurance) in 1991)
10	Kinleigh Folkard & Hayward	66	Independent
11	Winkworth	58	Independent
12	Hamptons International	55	Independent
13	Chancellors	52	Independent
14	Andrews Estate Agents	50	Independent
15	FPD Savills	46	Independent

Source: *Estate Agency News*, 2004.

fifteen UK residential brokerage firms in 2004 are listed in Table 8.3.[7] Only three of them are owned by financial institutions, all of which were once traditional 'building societies'. Two of them converted to profit-making banks in the 1990s and one of them, the Halifax, is part of HBOS, one of the largest banking groups in the UK, as noted above.

The same experience has occurred with the UK franchise and affinity groups that have emerged in residential brokerage in recent years. Only one of them is owned by a financial enterprise: an operation run by a major insurance company with independently-owned franchisees.

The residential brokerage industry in the UK consequently has remained a predominantly small-firm, locally-based one, in competition with a relatively small layer of larger regional and national players. In 2004, only eight of the 11 000 firms believed to exist in England and Wales had more than 100 branch offices, as can be seen in Table 8.3, and only 17 firms altogether had 40 branch offices or more. The size range also diminishes rapidly with the top eight firms having 23% of all estimated offices in existence and the next nine firms adding only an extra 4%. Moreover, there are only nine franchises/affinity groups with a hundred or more branch offices, representing a potential 36% of all offices in existence.[8]

Three major residential brokerage firms, paradoxically, are the outcomes of acquisition attempts by insurance-centred institutions to set up integrated mortgage–insurance–real estate brokerage operations, but all were subsequently sold in management buyouts or to other investors and, so, have since become independent residential brokerage firms. The difficulty of financial institutions being able to make money out of residential brokerage is illustrated by the experience of the insurance company, the Royal & Sun Alliance, which until 2003 owned the fourth largest residential brokerage chain. That subsidiary had been loss making for a number of years, despite the strongest and longest upswing in the UK housing market, and it was sold to another broker (to Connells, owned by a mutual building society).

The number of failures of financial enterprises with strategies to set up real estate brokerage chains, in fact, has been greater than the number of successes. This suggests that it is not easy for banks to enter and dominate the real estate brokerage industry.

It is interesting to note that insurance companies have been less successful than traditional mortgage providers in the residential brokerage business. They did not have a tradition of high street branches like the mortgage providers did and, therefore, had less experience of operating a complex network of branch offices. In addition, they had tended to specialise in endowment mortgages, whereby life insurance, equity investment and mortgages were combined in once tax-efficient packages. However, the market for them has all but disappeared, taking with them any hopes of economies of scope. With endowment mortgages, borrowers sign up to a life insurance policy and make regular payments into managed investment funds in the expectation that the returns will be more than sufficient to cover the cost of repayment of the principal of the mortgage at the due date. The eclipse of endowment mortgages was caused by declining tax benefits and low stock market returns plus consumer reactions to revelations of high commissions and mis-selling.[9] In 1988, such products had represented 80% of all UK mortgages issued, yet, by 2003, they had fallen to only 4% of them.

Despite the lack of success of many financial institutions in residential brokerage, the impact of their entry has clearly been significant with three of the largest UK brokerage firms now under their ownership and the result has been intensified competition. Yet, there seems no likelihood of a full-scale takeover of the industry so that it becomes primarily one of a branch activity of mortgage providers. Instead, financial institutions have markedly failed to achieve an overwhelming preponderance within the industry, even in specific localities. There are an estimated 12 000 residential brokerage sales offices in England and Wales.[10] The sales branches of the financially-owned majors, therefore, are only around a tenth of the total and that is after 20 years or so of activity by them in the industry.

The predominant UK ownership form in residential brokerage is still the personal proprietor/family-owned enterprise. The scale and scope cost profile, indicated by the industry's firm structure, may well account for much of this experience. In addition, the industry is risky, especially over the full range of the housing market cycle, which has meant that many firms entering during market upswings are forced to exit during subsequent downturns.

Thus, the general UK experience has been that allowing financial institutions into residential brokerage has stimulated competition rather than led to an inexorable takeover of the sector by them. This is despite the fact that the mortgage-focused finance firms that have entered the industry have generally been successful in selling homes, mortgages and other financial products jointly. In one sense, therefore, the strategic rationale for entry into residential brokerage was correct. One building society owned residential brokerage firm, for example, claims its origination rate for mortgages is around 50% of the value of its house sales.[11] That situation, however, does not distinguish finance-firm owned brokers from others, because most residential brokerage firms derive significant fee income from selling financial products (particularly mortgages and insurance). A recent survey found that, on average, real estate brokers earned fees from financial products equivalent to 54% of their fee income from housing transactions.[12]

The fact that all types of residential brokers seem to have been equally successful in financial product sales suggests that any scope economies between the two areas are a consequence of the nature of the relationship between brokers and their clients, house sellers and buyers, rather than on what type of firm actually owns the brokerage. Furthermore, scope economies may, in any case, be limited or non-existent because many independent agencies and mortgage institutions originate mortgages without having any connection to residential brokerage. Many consumers may prefer to shop around or use an independent broker and there are no obvious cost benefits to them of solely using the residential broker route.

The finding that economies of scale and scope are exhausted at relatively small firm sizes seems to be borne out by the firm structure of the UK industry, in which many small firms seem to be able to survive and compete successfully in local markets against large, multi-branch ones.

However, the largest firms and franchise chains are growing in size, which may suggest that the biggest firms do gain some additional scale or scope benefits, possibly through marketing benefits, though the precise advantages of very large relative size cannot be discovered rigorously for lack of detailed cost information.

Why did some finance entrants survive and become established parts of the residential brokerage industry, whilst others failed? A number of competing arguments can be suggested. One is that the surviving ones may simply have been lucky, whereas other financial institution entrants were less fortunate. Another is to note that traditional mortgage lenders (or their new owners) have been more successful than other types of financial enterprise. This may indicate some specific scope benefits between residential brokerage and mortgage origination that exist when they are under single ownership, cannot be exploited when independent residential brokers sell financial products on an agency basis. A further alternative hypothesis would deny such a joint ownership effect. Instead, the survivors may have adopted superior management strategies that recognised the specialist and detailed attention required in relation to residential brokerage activity and as a result they have paradoxically limited full-integration of it with financial services activities. Chandler (1977), Williamson (1975) and others, for example, have suggested that large multi-product firms require a multi-divisional management hierarchy of separate operating divisions for each product or geographic market, with corporate management dealing only with strategic planning. Such a multi-divisional arrangement corresponds to the organisational structures adopted by the successful financial institutions in residential brokerage.

One final conclusion from the UK experience concerns the strategic behaviour of the mortgage providers that have entered residential brokerage. Some may have successfully entered, yet this outcome does not seem to be adequately explained by the hypothesis that they have used market power to stifle competition and gain excess returns. Instead, they may actually have reinvigorated competition through the lack of a clear advantage over other types of residential brokerage ownership forms. Nor do they seem to have gained a competitive edge over other mortgage providers, because the vast majority of the latter seem to feel no impelling reason to enter residential brokerage. The strategy of entry, therefore, ends up being more a study of the history of particular enterprises than an indication of the future of the residential brokerage and mortgage industries.

Scottish solicitor–estate agents

An exception to the typical UK residential brokerage structure exists in many parts of Scotland. Scottish property law is different from that in the rest of the UK. When there is more than one interested buyer, potential purchasers submit binding sealed bids and the highest one usually wins the auction (Gibb 1992). Solicitors (i.e. legal attorneys) process the paperwork required during and subsequent to the bidding process. This advantageous position has enabled them to become the main providers of residential brokerage services in much of Scotland, apart from the main region with a third of the country's population, which is centred on Glasgow. Elsewhere, there is a common solicitor's multiple listing service (MLS) of dwellings for sale, called a 'Solicitors Property Centre', of which there are twelve in all. In some cities, including Edinburgh, such property centres account for more than 90% of all residential transactions.[13] Few solicitors specialise in residential activity, offering instead a full range of legal services, and most are small-scale enterprises. Contrary to US practice, only listing agents can sell the properties they list (MMC 1997; Findlay & Gibb 1998), so the property centres predominantly act as marketing and information centres.

This type of institutional arrangement in residential brokerage effectively excludes external entry by anyone else but solicitors recognised to practise in Scotland. Regulatory rules permit solicitors to sell houses, but forbid any merging between financial and legal enterprises. Regulation, therefore, and the market power of the solicitors' MLS have meant that other competitors are effectively excluded from operating in the areas where they are strong.

Denmark: marked integration between finance and real estate brokerage

Traditional annuity mortgages have a 30-year redemption period with a pre-payment option and a maximum loan-to-value ratio of 80%. Such mortgage loans are financed by specialist mortgage banks matching their offer terms with bond sales on the capital market, secured by a first call

Table 8.4 Danish estate agency groups and their market shares,* 2002.

Group	Number of sales outlets	Owner/Affiliates
EDC	270	A co-operative with BRF and local commercial banks
Home	175	Danske Bank Group
Nybolig	170	Nykredit Group
Danbolig	130	Nordea Group
Estate+	40	Nykredit Group
Scheel & Orloff	32	Nykredit Group
Other and non-franchise	500	Links to Totalkredit and local commercial banks
Total	**1320**	

* Mortgage transactions based data from Association of Danish Mortgage Banks.
+ Formerly known as Ejendomsringen.

Source: P. Angelo, Home Group, Copenhagen.

on the mortgaged property (Frankel *et al.* 2004). The market is highly competitive and mortgage banks operate on a spread of 0.5% or less between the interest rate paid to bond holders and that paid by homeowners. High volumes of mortgage business consequently are necessary to sustain profitability and residential brokers are good conduits for originations. Concentration has increased greatly in the mortgage industry in recent years, so that now two banks have over 75% of the market (Table 8.4). The major mortgage banks, in turn, are owned by large financial conglomerates. There are four large mortgage banks: Nykredit (including Totalkredit), Realkredit Danmark (Danske Bank), Nordea (Nordea Bank) and BRF – accounting for 42, 32, 11 and 9% respectively of gross new mortgage loans – with seven other market makers in existence.[14]

In residential brokerage, there is a sole agency, sole seller system and the country has the most concentrated brokerage industry of all of those surveyed here. This was not always the case; instead concentration has rapidly taken place over the past decade or so via the development of six major owner/franchise groups. All but one of them, furthermore, are owned by major mortgage banks, which were allowed to enter residential brokerage following financial market liberalisation in the early 1990s.

Strong price rises in the housing market in recent years have helped to induce industry change and smoothed the process of transition within it. There is, however, a relatively high turnover of estate agents in the franchise chains as some proprietors exit voluntarily or are asked to leave when they do not perform as well as expected.

The approximate ranking by market share in 2002 of the top Danish residential brokers is given in Table 8.4, along with their linkages to financial service providers. EDC is the franchise with the largest number of outlets and a 25% market share of the 90 000 or so annual dwelling sales handled by all agents. Unlike the other chains, it is owned by its participating members.

Nonetheless, the group has formal links with a mortgage bank, BRF kredit (a private foundation, which cannot be taken over), to sell its products. All other franchises have direct ownership links with commercial banking groups. The Nykredit Group has 281 direct real estate brokerage subsidiaries and the Danske and Nordea bank groups own other franchises. Totalkredit, a mortgage bank, which was owned by regional and local banks until 2003 and then merged with Nykredit, also has formal links with brokerage chains and independent agencies.

The estate-agency market is now highly concentrated into bank subsidiary and bank controlled franchise groups in contrast to the previous small, independent firm structure. Thus, there is a marked contrast with the other countries surveyed here in that the real estate brokerage industry has actually been taken over by financial firms active in the mortgage market. Moreover, there is now a high degree of concentration in the residential brokerage industry, in contrast to the limited concentration recorded prior to their entry. The top two groups have a 50% market share of housing transactions involving a mortgage and the top four have an 82% share.

Consolidation in Denmark, therefore, has gone much further than elsewhere. Such levels of market concentration, however, are matched in many individual cities in other countries, so that the recorded national levels of market concentration may partly reflect the fact that Denmark is a relatively small country. Even so, the fears of the pessimists in the USA about allowing bank entry into residential brokerage seemed to have been borne out in the Danish case. However, there are special reasons associated with the institutional structure of the Danish mortgage market and housing transactions processes that may account for this market structure. Consequently, it may be difficult to generalise from the Danish situation.

In part, the keenness of Danish banks to get into the residential brokerage business is driven by the country's unique mortgage bond system, which makes estate agents key conduits for mortgage business. Furthermore, there are other market advantages. First-time buyers usually cover most of the 20% of the house price that cannot be funded via a mortgage loan through additional borrowing, so they tend to put down a deposit of only 5% of the purchase price. Finance may also be offered to cover transactions costs. When organising these top-up funds, residential brokers play a key role. Furthermore, given that the mortgage market itself is highly concentrated, when residential brokers are owned by the financial groups that own the mortgage banks then that market too is likely to be highly concentrated.

The distinctiveness of the Danish mortgage market, nevertheless, seems insufficient to explain why residential brokerages have become predominantly owned by banks, whereas this has generally not been the case elsewhere. The independent residential brokerage model with significant turnovers in housing-related financial products, common elsewhere, seems equally feasible within the institutional framework of Danish mortgage banking. Moreover, the potential pitfalls of financial institutions owning residential brokers were illustrated earlier in the UK case.

An added inducement to integrated ownership, however, may arise from government policy. A compulsory home seller's pack was introduced by law in 1993. This pack must provide all the information required for dwelling assessment, purchase and closure: such as details of the building and its contents, a structural survey, title and transfer documentation, and usually insurance to cover the twenty-year liability that the seller has for undeclared building defects. The existence of the home seller's pack greatly increases the marketing and co-ordination role of residential brokers in the house transactions process. Although the law does not specify how the pack should be assembled, it is obviously easiest for most home sellers to accept their residential broker's offer to undertake the process. The pack has consequently heightened the scope of the relationship between residential broker and house seller, thereby intensifying the marketing opportunities for brokers to sell them related products and services. This clearly makes the brokerage function of greater interest to the providers of those financial services, because residential brokerage can become a significant marketing tool for them.

This marketing feature is reinforced by an additional requirement of the home seller's pack. It has to include at least two potential pre-arranged mortgage finance packages that a buyer can chose from with all the terms laid out. The buyer does not have to take these up but, even so, this stipulation gives a mortgage bank an obvious advantage when it owns real estate brokerage firms, because it can then ensure that one of its products is an option presented to buyers. Other firms' mortgage products have to be offered as the second option, but the fact that buyers face no search costs when considering a mortgage product is a clear marketing benefit. The home seller's pack may consequently have been more important in influencing mortgage banks to enter and dominate the residential brokerage industry than the structure of the mortgage market itself.

What have the consequences been for competition? Whether the dominance of the mortgage market and residential brokerage by an oligopoly of banks has led to limited competition and an overall welfare loss is debatable. There is still extensive competition in the mortgage market, where spreads have narrowed rather than widened, for example. Competition is also fierce between the residential brokerage chains and between them and independents, which limits the possibility of monopolistic abuse. Moreover, the market is contestable. As elsewhere, the costs of setting up new brokerage operations are relatively low. If substantial monopolistic profits did arise, new entrants are likely to push them down again.

There is also extensive monitoring of the residential brokerage industry by government, a tripartite supervisory body designed to protect consumers' interests, and a powerful national consumers' organisation. The latter has not argued for renewed separation of residential brokerage and banking, nor expressed concerns about monopolistic abuse.[15] It, therefore, would seem that, even in a situation of considerable ownership of real estate brokers by banks, sufficient checks and balances exist so that any feared outcome of monopolistic abuse has not actually occurred.

The scope for strategic retaliation: the case of the Netherlands

There are a variety of mortgage lenders in the Netherlands. The most important are general commercial banks, such as ABN Amro and ING (including Postbank), followed by special mortgage banks and building funds ('bouwfondsen'), insurance companies and savings banks. In 2001, the commercial banks had a 44% market share, the insurance companies 12% and a variety of other lenders 44%.

Although fixed interest rates with a five-year review are the most common mortgage product (with over 95% of the market), consumers have a wide range of mortgage types to choose from. They often obtain mortgage packages, financed with a mix of first and second mortgages that contain various potential combinations of payback terms and fixed and variable interest rates.

Residential brokerage has a unique organisational form. It is dominated by one national level MLS called NVM,[16] which is co-operatively owned by

its 2300 member enterprises. This was set up with government encouragement in the 1980s to bring some of the benefits of the US model to the
then fragmented Dutch market. Approximately 65% of all dwelling sales
in the Netherlands now take place through a listing on NVM. Unlike in
the USA, however, only the listing brokerage firm can sell the properties
it lists, although it has become common practice for homebuyers to employ
a buyer broker to help them in their search.

There is also another MLS, though it is much smaller and specialises in
particular localities and house types. For many Dutch cities, the NVM list
is the only game in town. Given the potential for monopolistic abuse that
exists with such a dominant MLS, there is close government monitoring
and requirements for transparency to ensure that competition exists. There
is also relatively free ease of entry and exit for brokerage firms into the
co-operative.

There is no formal legislation forbidding banks and other financial institutions from entering residential brokerage. However, once again, there is
little indication that financial institutions have any interest in entering
the sector.

In the Dutch case, furthermore, entry may well be discouraged by the
existence of such a dominant player as the NVM, as well as by the factors
already mentioned earlier. Within an MLS arrangement, the members can
operate strategically in relation to actions of other participants. This potential type of behaviour, for example, has been suggested in the literature on
US MLS as a means of enforcing conformity on all participants of common
fee levels (Wachter 1987). If an external institution, like a bank, tried to
take over one or more members of a MLS in a move that other members saw
as detrimental to their own positions, they could then retaliate by turning
the co-operation inherent in an MLS against the interloper. Such retaliation
could use some powerful devices, such as under-cutting fee rates, refusing
to market their financial services, spreading unfavourable information and
so on. The ultimate sanction would be to dissolve the MLS altogether or,
where legally possible, to expel the undesired agency from the MLS.

Conclusions

Five countries that permit bank entry into real estate brokerage have been
surveyed here: Australia, Denmark, Ireland, the Netherlands and the UK.
The characteristics of their mortgage and residential brokerage markets have
been examined and the extent of cross-industry ownership investigated.

The situation with regard to financial industry ownership of brokerage firms is variable. Three countries have little or no cross-industry ownership, Australia, Ireland, the Netherlands; one has a moderate degree, the UK; finally, in Denmark, banks entered residential brokerage after deregulation and now own or have strategic links to the majority of firms.

Where entry has occurred the predominant impetus has been related to the mortgage market and the usefulness of real estate brokerage as a point of sale for mortgage products. The evidence for the consequences of allowing banks to enter residential brokerage is mixed, but it generally points to a limited impact with increased rather than diminished competition arising after entry.

From a cost structure perspective, residential brokerage industry structures point to the general existence of relatively low economies of scale, a result that corresponds to previous academic studies of the situation in the USA. This conclusion may need qualification for the largest firms, which seem to play significant roles in either major towns or across national markets. Their existence, plus the widespread role of franchises, may indicate scale economies at the largest sizes, especially with respect to the costs of e-business, branding and advertising. Yet, despite growing pressures for consolidation, apart from the special case of Denmark, the market shares of larger firms at national levels are still quite small.

The expansion of larger firms in recent years has also taken place during long upswings in housing markets and may not be sustainable during subsequent downturns in activity, when such firms may find that their higher overheads put them at a competitive disadvantage. This was the experience, for example, of many of the UK bank/insurance/building society owned chains set up in the 1980s, which withdrew after large losses during the subsequent downturn of the early 1990s.

There is also weak indirect evidence of economies of scope between residential brokerage and selling housing-related financial products, such as mortgages and insurance, because many real estate firms do sell significant volumes of the latter. The evidence is weak, however, because in all countries, most mortgage business takes place outside of the residential brokerage industry. This may be because of certain procedural issues, such as the potential moral hazard problem of third parties screening mortgage applicants, or because mortgage origination specialists themselves can gain alternative scale and scope advantages that have nothing to do with real estate brokerage. Residential brokerage, for example, is not an immediately obvious conduit for consumer re-mortgaging, which has been such an important element of mortgage business in all countries over the last decade. Even in Denmark, where cross-industry integration has been the greatest, not all mortgage banks have felt it necessary to enter residential brokerage.

The evidence from most of the countries surveyed is that different business models co-exist side by side. Thus, some residential brokerage enterprises have ownership linkages to financial services firms, but many of them do not. A proportion of housing-related finance products, therefore, are sold through residential brokerage, but the majority originate through finance specialist brokerages, banks or insurance companies. The lack of a clear competitive advantage to any one business model makes cross-industry strategic actions by firms feasible. So, some finance firms have decided to enter residential brokerage with mixed success and others have not. Only in Denmark does there seem a clear imperative to cross-link residential brokerage and mortgage finance and this seems to relate to housing policy issues more than the characteristics of the mortgage market.

Strategic actions, of course, are not the sole prerogative of potential entrants to real estate brokerage; incumbent firms can also adopt retaliatory strategies. Such retaliatory strategies probably have the greatest effect, and are least easy to detect, in the USA style institutional arrangements for MLS, whereby all participants of MLS can sell each others' properties listed. In such situations, agents can boycott the listings of a firm disapproved of, slowing its sales rates and, thereby, discouraging homeowners from listing with it.

There are important differences between countries' mortgage markets and there is little evidence of institutional convergence occurring across them. The area that this chapter has reported on – the role of real estate transactions agents in mortgage origination – clearly shows wide institutionally-influenced differences. It also highlights a similar lack of convergence in market practices between countries. This suggests that it is not simply regulatory barriers that keep separate the organisational frameworks of the residential brokerage and mortgage industries, but also economic factors that influence the institutional frameworks of markets.

Notes

1   Terminology varies between countries. Residential real estate brokerage is used here to identify the people and firms involved in the process of selling and buying residential property in all the countries surveyed.

2 See, for example, Zumpano (2002) and the National Association of Realtors (http://www.realtor.com).

3 As argued, for example, by the American Bankers Association (http://www.aba.com).

4 An exception is the work of Peter Risseeuw at the Free University, Amsterdam, which tends to confirm the results of Zumpano and his colleagues.

5 They are simply depositing a bond of relatively modest value and declaring personal propriety with a local court of law in Ireland, and registration after a brief training course and personal checks in most states of Australia.

6 See the Rightmove Website (www.rightmove.co.uk). It is owned by Connells, Countrywide Assured Group, Halifax Estate Agents and Royal & SunAlliance.

7 There are several large franchise operations not listed in Table 8.2. Apart from one run by an insurance company, Legal & General, and the Home Sale Network, owned by the US Cendant Group, they are independently or mutually owned by their members.

8 Calculations based on branch data from *Estate Agency News*, 2004 survey. The franchise/affinity group data contain double counting as many firms belong to more than one franchise/affinity group.

9 Financial Services Authority (2005).

10 The offices estimate is from *Estate Agents Market Report 2003*, Key Note, London and an estimate of 11 000 independent brokers is given in OFT (2004b). The two numbers, unfortunately, are not easy to reconcile, but both are clearly very large.

11 http://www.conells.co.uk

12 Calculated from data in OFT (2004b).

13 The exception is the Strathclyde region (centred on Glasgow) where the solicitors' MLS has not been very successful, so that real estate brokerage services are more similar to those in the rest of the UK.

14 http://www.Realkreditrådet.dk

15 In discussions with the author.

16 Nederlandse Vereniging van Makelaars o.g. en Vastgoeddeskundigen.

9

International differences in the housebuilding industry

Introduction

The housebuilding industry is the prime provider of new housing in most countries. Its characteristics as an industry can vary quite significantly from country to country in terms of the functions undertaken by firms and ownership structures. This chapter explores some of these differences and attempts to explain them. It concentrates on advanced economies and the impacts on such countries' housebuilding industries of market conditions, regulatory constraints, production characteristics, institutional structures and land supply.

Some cross-country differences are caused by relative input prices. Housebuilders in higher wage countries typically economise on labour and, so, adopt less labour intensive techniques than lower wage ones. For example, they exhibit a greater use of off-site fabrication and on-site equipment. The relative abundance of particular types of building material, especially those that are expensive to transport, also has an effect on production techniques. For example, those countries with abundant supplies of timber or clay are likely to have a greater prevalence of timber or brick-framed structures than those with lower endowments of such inputs. These choice-of-technique influences help, for example, to explain why high wage and timber rich North America and Scandinavia have housebuilding industries that rely on pre-manufactured timber-frame systems and extensively use pre-assembled modules of internal house fittings. In contrast, high wage but timber poor, the Netherlands and France have more commonly adopted concrete panel off-site fabrication for house structures.

Though influential, such choice-of-technique factors have only a limited role in explaining cross-country firm variations. For that task, a greater understanding of the operation of housebuilding markets and of cross-country institutional differences in them is required.

Housing output variations

Housebuilding is well known as a cyclical industry with variations in output and prices driven by cycles in the housing market as a whole. Such volatility is typical of consumer durable and investment goods industries, because users' existing stocks of such goods are far greater than current output. Relatively small changes in the overall demand for such goods consequently are transmitted into far larger variations in demand for the new product. As a low ratio of housebuilding to the existing housing stock is typical, changes in overall housing demand tend to induce large variations in the demand for newly built housing (Malpezzi & Wachter 2005). It takes a long time, moreover, to build sufficient houses to satisfy demand increases. So, when demand grows, prices rise in response to shortages and overshoot their long-term equilibrium levels as households try to find homes before supply has caught up.

Housing market cycles are an inevitable consequence, therefore, of housing supply mechanisms (Ball *et al.* 2000). The extent to which volatility occurs more in prices or in levels of housebuilding depends on the extent to which extra housing can be supplied when prices rise and the speed of that response. Furthermore, once cycles are under way, the wealth effects of rising house prices encourage further demand, so that cycles may become self-reinforcing.

The degree of price volatility frequently observed in housing markets cannot usually be found in other durable goods markets. Car and domestic appliance producers face similar 'stock-adjustment' demand characteristics, yet economies of scale in their production tend to generate oligopolistic industrial structures. This enables firms to hold prices relatively steady during downturns in demand. They prefer to accept the resultant possibly greater fluctuations in volumes in order to sustain the margins necessary to finance their large amounts of fixed capital. Such firm strategies are not realistic in housebuilding, because of the ease of entry and exit from the industry and the competition they face in the housing market from existing housing owners. This means that, in downturns, there are always large numbers of suppliers prepared to cut prices for a quick sale when financial pressures dictate.

This pricing characteristic of housebuilding is ignored by those who, over the decades, have argued that housing production should become far more capital intensive, like a 'real' consumer goods industry. The volatility of their returns, however, implies that housebuilding firms with highly capital intensive production methods face a high chance of going bust during the next major market downturn. Nevertheless, huge experiments in capital-intensive 'industrialised' housebuilding were undertaken in a number of European countries from the 1950s to the 1980s via subsidised social house-building programmes (Donnison 1967; Barlow & Duncan 1994; Harloe 1995). Large, specialist housebuilders emerged and governments tried to create the market conditions that would enable them to reap cost savings through scale economies and innovation. Unfortunately, few of the scale economies in production materialised and most of the large housebuilders that grew up disappeared as soon as public funding ceased, as did their proprietary new building systems (Ball 1988; Glendinning & Muthesius 1994; Gann 1996).

Short- and long-term demand effects

Some causes of changes in housing demand are short-term, business cycle related factors, such as rising incomes and interest rates. So, unsurprisingly, housebuilding tends to fluctuate in line with the business cycle; with the degree of output and price variation being greater than that for the rest of the economy on average, because of the stock adjustment characteristics of new housing demand, discussed above. There are, however, several key demand features that have longer impacts. They include variations in house-hold numbers generated by population and social changes; migration into prosperous regions; technologies of living (the tram/streetcar, the bus and the motor car being the most historically notable ones); shortages caused by catastrophic events like war; and public policy towards such matters as subsidies and tax breaks for particular types of housing. These, when combined, tend to create 'long' housebuilding cycles that are superimposed on the business cycle. Many of these longer-term factors are extended lag responses to specific technological or policy 'shock' events, which makes it difficult to generalise about housebuilding long-cycles, though many have tried (e.g. Hickman 1973).

Differences in long-term housing investment shares

Housebuilding varies in importance between countries over long periods of time. This characteristic is summarised in the data provided in Table 9.1, where countries are ranked by the long-term significance of housebuild-ing as a share of GDP. The country with the most housebuilding over the

Table 9.1 Housing investment as a share of national income, 1956–2000: cross country comparisons.

	Mean (%)	Maximum (%)	Minimum (%)	Std dev.	Std/mean
Germany	6.4	8.1	4.8	0.9	0.15
France	5.7	7.8	4.1	1.2	0.20
Japan	5.6	8.8	3.6	1.3	0.23
Netherlands	5.3	6.4	3.9	0.6	0.12
Canada	5.3	7.4	3.8	1.0	0.19
USA	4.4	5.7	3.2	0.6	0.14
UK	3.5	4.7	2.6	0.5	0.14

Source: OECD.

last half a century has been Germany, followed quite closely by France, Japan, the Netherlands and Canada. The USA trails almost 2% behind Germany and the lowest, the UK, by almost 3%. These differences can be explained by several factors. Germany is at the highest rank, because of the housing boom during the period after reunification in the 1990s and is now converging towards the investment shares of other countries after a long process of downward adjustment (Ball 2005b). The USA provides little subsidised low-income housing, unlike the European countries listed, which probably accounts for most of the difference over the longer term, although the housebuilding boom in the 2000s has boosted its housing output significantly in recent years. The UK is exceptional, probably because of its restricted land supply in growth regions and a correspondingly high propensity to repair and upgrade existing dwellings (Barker 2004).

Once these differences are taken into account, a crude estimate of the typical long-term share of housing investment in the annual national income of an advanced economy with moderately expanding household numbers would seem to be around 4 to 5%, with the extra percentage point depending on the social attitude to subsidising the housing conditions of lower-income groups. It has been argued that housing investment declines as a share of national income as national income rises above a certain per capita level (Malpezzi & Wachter 2005), but the long-cycle characteristics of these data make it hard to isolate any such effect across this range of higher income countries.

Table 9.1 also suggests that there are maximum amounts of housing investment with which a well-functioning economy can cope. It shows that housing investment shares have never risen above 7 to 8% of GDP for the countries listed, even when there are chronic shortages. This is unsurprising as such percentage figures imply a huge allocation of a country's existing resources into housebuilding. Not only does this deny those resources to other activities, frequently generating inflationary pressures at the same time, but it also necessitates substantial knock-on investments in building materials industries, the training of skilled labour and urban infrastructure. Furthermore, when the housing boom is over, all those resources have to be redirected elsewhere again, which can generate substantial and long-lasting readjustment costs – as Germany experienced for a decade after its mid-1990s housebuilding boom. These factors highlight the difficulties of expanding housing supply rapidly to meet sharp increases in demand.

Long-term housing investment volatility

The degree of volatility in housing investment GDP shares can be measured by looking at the standard deviations of annual residential investment shares in national income, as shown in Table 9.1. Typically, housing investment fluctuates annually by around 0.5 to 1% of GDP, with the countries with the largest shares of housing investment in national income, not surprisingly, experiencing the largest absolute fluctuations in those shares. When weighted by their respective means, however, the standard deviations across countries are quite similar. Overall, housebuilding volume fluctuations are not atypically large when compared with other capital goods industries (Ball *et al.* 1996).

House prices, as well as output levels, exhibit marked cyclical patterns, but their volatility is less consistent across countries, as was shown for recent years in Chapter 5. None the less, it is hard to identify countries with persistently more stable new housing markets in terms of both prices and quantities. This conclusion is unsurprising as there is no reason to expect differences between countries in housing demand shocks over the long run. Yet it is an important one when investigating cross-country differences in housebuilding industries, for it suggests that institutional differences on the supply side, rather than features of demand, are where answers are to be found.

A lack of globalisation

Housebuilding institutions do not seem to travel well. In some industries, such as the automobile industry, the benefits of high volumes and international differences in macroeconomic cycles have encouraged firms to globalise. So, in that industry and many others, firm practices are now international in character. In contrast, cross-country diversification has not occurred widely in housebuilding, even though cycles of housing investment in each country tend not to coincide (Ball 1999).

Perhaps, low scale economies and the importance of local information on construction, land and housing markets militate against internationalisation. There are some examples. Two of the UK's largest housebuilders have become significant producers in the USA in recent years, while a US major owned a UK subsidiary for a number of years before recently selling to a UK housebuilder. Such moves are presumably influenced by the persistent differences in the timing of the housing market cycles in those two countries.

In the sections below, it will be argued that housebuilding practices arise from the broader institutional context in which firms operate and these tend to be country specific. Therefore, it may be hard for firms to transmit innovatory practices by setting up subsidiaries in other countries.

The market framework of housebuilding

What do general market data imply for housebuilders? First, they highlight that housing supply is a risky business. Production and land purchase decisions have to be made on the basis of forecasts of highly uncertain prospects. Second, it is also extremely difficult to forecast how long a market upswing will last and the extent to which markets are dampened or exacerbated by business cycle effects. Third, extensive econometric research shows that price behaviour in the housing market may be irrational in the sense that forecasts of future market performance are based on recent experience – i.e. adaptive expectations (DiPasquale & Wheaton 1994; Muellbauer & Murphy 1997; Meen 2001). This may help to explain why the ending of the upswing phases of market cycles tends to come as a shock event, which radically alters subsequent behaviour and housebuilder performance.

The consequences for homebuilders of this type of market structure are significant. Most importantly, substantial market risk has to be taken account of in the organisation of production. Furthermore, housing market cycles can be the opportunity for spectacular profit making but, also, equally spectacular loss making. This gives the industry some of the rhythms that Schumpter (1942) suggested occur in industries over the course of the business cycle: organic expansion and optimism during upswings and substantial industrial restructuring during downswings (Maddison 1992).

Functional organisation of the housebuilding process

There are three prime functional aspects of housing development:

1. *Residential land development* Land has to be acquired, the appropriate regulatory permissions sought, and the site prepared with infrastructure so that homes can be built on individual serviced plots. With redevelopment sites, this may require the demolition of an existing structure or wholesale land reclamation.
2. *Housing production* The actual building of dwellings – from substructure to completed and fitted-out superstructure.
3. *House marketing and sales* Completed housing is transferred to ultimate users, either through sales to individual homeowners or via some type of landlord. This process involves sales in various types of owner-occupied market (e.g. speculative for purchasers of completed dwellings, pre-sales or one-off contracts with owner 'builders') or rental market (e.g. sales to private landlords of single or multi-family units or contracts with social housing agencies).

Figure 9.1 illustrates these three functions and their interrelationships. Next to each function in the diagram is a box highlighting the relations to other agencies and markets. A Venn diagram is used in Figure 9.1, rather than a sequential series of boxes, to highlight the fact that the three housing development functions are interrelated and may be institutionally combined in different ways.

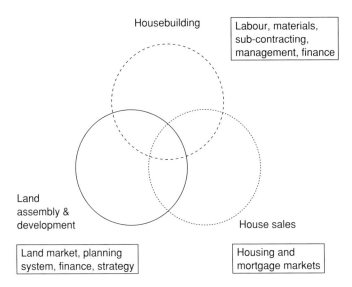

Figure 9.1 Overlapping functions in housing development.

Speculative housebuilding of single-family dwellings for homeowners clearly demarks the process sequentially from land assembly through to sales. Even there, though, homebuilders are keen on pre-sales before starting to build. In social housebuilding, land assembly, project conception and finance have traditionally been initiated by social housing agencies themselves. In which case, land assembly and house 'sales' take place at the time of project approval and actual building subsequently takes place when contracts are let to private building contractors. Large-scale private landlords might adopt a similar procurement strategy to social landlords. In both the large social and private landlord cases, development companies could also approach landlords with projects they wish to build on land they have already assembled, or offer off-the-peg standardised building designs completed at a fixed price for construction on sites already prepared by the landlord.

There are also differences between the organisation of the overall housing development process in relation to single-family and multi-family housing. Multi-family structures are generally more complex and capital intensive than single-family ones, because of the greater need for load-bearing walls plus common access and other facilities. This tends to mean that the developers of multi-family dwellings have to be larger to gain access to capital. They also have to be more focused on design and construction matters than in the single-family case, where repeat designs and simple construction formats are more common.

Such descriptions are inevitably generalisations, because the possible combinations of the three functions and their relationships to other interlinked markets are manifold, and there is little point in describing them all in detail here. Several features, nonetheless, are common in descriptions of them:

- A network of interrelationships is described.
- The physical characteristics of the overall housing development process are significant influences on housebuilding organisational relationships.
- Economic and financial factors play an important role in determining organisational structures.
- Public policy with regard to housing tenures, land markets and building processes have considerable effects on institutional housebuilding arrangements.

The overriding point is that different ways of organising the housing development process are often associated with distinct housing outcomes.

One way of exploring these varying ways of housebuilding is to categorise each of them as distinct structures of housing provision. In this way, the functions of agencies in the production process can be mapped out for each type of housing development. This has the benefit of recognising that any agency or firm in housing development is involved in a network of interrelationships and enables a mapping out of the constraints and influences on individual agency behaviour. Specific theories are still needed, none the less, to understand what institutional arrangements are important and why they exist.

Housing production influences on structures of housing provision

A useful starting-point when examining housebuilding institutional structures is the functional distinction between land development and actual housebuilding, because both require particular types of management and finance structures.

Labour relations

One of the most important factors relating to production is the employment relationship. Housebuilding involves a construction process and so requires a specific range of construction-related labour competences. Most on-site tasks in housebuilding are amenable to be broken down into priced jobs and let out to subcontractors and other specialists, which is common in many countries.

Subcontracting has a number of important advantages for housebuilders. Amongst the benefits are that it lowers general overhead costs; enables activity specialisation, because specialists can be more fully employed working for several clients; facilitates responses to fluctuations in workloads; simplifies administration and some regulatory factors, such as taxation and employment legislation (and may facilitate tax advantages for subcontractors); encourages high work speeds; and lowers supervision costs as managers only have to check that work has been done properly and on time and, then, pay out the agreed sum, rather than have to monitor work effort continuously (Eccles 1981a; Ball 1996; Costantino *et al.* 2001). The relative importance of each aspect is a matter for some speculation in the literature but measurement difficulties mean that an accurate ranking of them is never likely to be achieved.

House builders can impose financial penalties on non-performing subcontractors and build up long-term relationships with core ones to ensure that they are generally available, have access to the appropriate pools of skilled labour (which may including a training element), can cope with any innovations that may occur, and can self-police their own quality and prices. Often subcontractors are single individuals, providing tools and labour and Eccles has termed such organisational arrangements as 'quasi-firms' to indicate the relationships involved (Eccles 1981b).

The average ratio of subcontracting to directly employed labour in the UK was 70% in a 2004 study of volume housebuilders that collectively produced a third of national output. With the exception of some tidying up and snagging, typically all manual work was subcontracted: to individuals, gangs of trades people or to sub-assembly specialists. However, a small fraction of firms had strategies of employing significant proportions of trades directly, and health and safety legislation required direct responsibility for some activities, such as the driving of on-site vehicles like forklift trucks. Some professional tasks were also outsourced, particularly those associated with design, law and land-use planning. Firms retained overall control by employing permanent career staff for site supervision, managerial, marketing, sales, finance, input procurement, some legal and some design tasks. Relationships with subcontractors were often long-term ones and close. For example, a number of the largest housebuilding firms funded the salaries of subcontractors' trainees and expected some of the more talented of them eventually to enter managerial positions within their own enterprises. The firms would purchase most general materials used by subcontractors to ensure their quality, delivery and fitness for purpose and to gain purchasing economies (Ball 2005a).

In the USA, Bureau of Census returns suggest that around 65% of house builders' costs were subcontracting payments in 1997 and that this had hardly changed in 20 years (quoted in Costantino *et al.* 2001). Many subcontractors are very small enterprises (Eccles 1981b).

These sorts of subcontracting relationships, and their benefits, have become famous since the discovery of 'Japanese' manufacturing methods in North America and Europe in the 1980s (Ricketts 1994; Kay 1996). Yet, similar ones have existed since, at least, the nineteenth century in many countries' housebuilding industries (Price 1980) and have been common for a very long time in Japanese building itself (Reeves 2002).

Above the smallest sizes, subcontractors themselves often hire part of their workforces on time, price and task-specific bases – whilst, at the same time, employing a core of competent skilled workers and supervisors. So, a hierarchical tree of work patterns – embodying market and non-market relationships – can frequently be observed in housing production.

Another common employment option for housebuilders is to hire workers on a temporary hourly or daily basis. In this situation, the problem of directly monitoring work effort arises. This encourages the use of standardisation and simple techniques of production with easily observed results, so that relatively unskilled workers can be hired – and fired if they do not keep up with normal work rates.

Subcontracting and day-working considerably aid the flexibility of the housebuilding industry in coping with uncertain demand. When house builders' output falls, they do not have to lay off workers, but instead merely issue fewer contracts or hire fewer workers; a similar situation exists with plant when it is hired.

Such self and temporary hiring employment techniques have implications for the types of production methods used, as the latter have to be effective in the context of those employment practices. Generally, this means that techniques are relatively simple, do not use much sophisticated capital equipment and change slowly. When equipment is complex or expensive, it is hired complete with skilled operatives to avoid any potential skill difficulties. The same occurs with more technically complex materials or fittings.

The capital tied up in housing production, therefore, is generally small for employment practice reasons, as well as to ensure flexibility in the face of varying demand. Surveys show that production capital is often financed out of retained profits and short-term credit loans, though land stocks are usually too expensive to be funded in this way (Hillebrandt 1971).

Such an organisation of production maximises the possibility of resources being fully employed elsewhere when one particular housebuilder has insufficient work. In well-developed subcontract markets, workers and plant exist in an institutional framework of information networks about job opportunities. These are often informal in nature but facilitate mobility.

Overall, consequently, housebuilding inputs, including labour, should be more fully and effectively employed in countries that have construction industries with 'flexible' labour practices. In contrast, countries requiring direct employment in 'main contractor' or 'functional subcontractor' firms, and which impose high costs hiring-and-firing, are likely to impose significant periods of idle time on building workers. This idle time may occur through more extensive periods of unemployment or it may lower firm efficiency, with firms holding on to underemployed staff because it is too expensive to lay them off. As a result, firms may be reluctant to employ extra workers because of future workload uncertainties or because of the cost associated with hiring when subsequent firing is expensive to undertake. Theory and the fact that building firms adopt the flexible employment model whenever they can both suggest that the enforced direct employment and high labour market transaction costs options are more expensive and less efficient modes of operation.

Another influence on employment practices relates to features of the local physical geography. In countries and regions where the climate makes it impossible to build in the deepest winter months, for example, the large-scale switching of resources between housebuilding and other activities is obviously imperative at different seasons of the year. Traditional migrations are made between, say, summer housebuilding and winter forestry or between educational establishments and summer vacation building sites. Similarly, in countries with large agricultural sectors that have heavy demands for labour only at peak times, such as harvests, another pattern of seasonal job shifts in and out of housebuilding tends to occur.

Some have argued that labour subcontracting is bad for building quality and productivity, because it leads, first, to rushed work and, second, to a slow decline in the skill level of the construction workforce (Clarke & Wall 1996). The first claim is suspect because of the information asymmetry problem, mentioned earlier. The second argument is a 'tragedy of the commons' externality-type argument in which no one is prepared to train skilled workers because they will always be poached by others. It is difficult to see how the nature of the employment relation changes that argument much, however, because the incentives for a trained worker to move to a better paid job would not alter as long as firms free-ride on other's training expenses. Compulsory industry-wide training levies and grants to firms offering training are policies aim at internalising these externalities, as, for example, with the Construction Industry Training Board in the UK (http://www.citb.org.uk).

The subcontracting of tasks has important implications for the firm structure of housebuilders. It means that at low levels of output, housebuilders can be very small entities indeed. A one-proprietor entity, for example, can hire outside help for most construction tasks. Even larger firms, when measured by their output, need only have a limited direct production workforce, consisting primarily of those managing subcontractors or ensuring a steady flow of materials or skilled operatives to fix incomplete or poorly done tasks.

Subcontracting may also arise as a means of avoiding taxes in contexts where the effective tax rate on the self-employed is lower than on directly employed workers. Such tax effects, for instance, contributed to the rise of labour-only self-employment in the UK from the 1970s onwards. Conversely, a recent tightening of UK tax rules and legislation creating a more flexible labour market have led to a growth again in the share of direct employment.

Subcontracting, it can be concluded, has significant impacts on firm organisational structures. The practice considerably enhances the ease of entry and exit from housebuilding and, hence, the degree of competition within the industry. Yet, some countries, especially in Europe, ban extensive subcontracting and their employment laws require workers to be hired on a permanent basis. This is the case in France, for example, although some subcontracting has been permissible there since 2001. The arguments above would suggest that such a ban leads to higher construction costs. Of particular interest in the context of the arguments being made here is that the legislation would also be predicted to create a different array of types of housebuilding firms from those prevalent in countries with extensive subcontracting or day labour.

In the French situation, it is to be expected that most firms obey the spirit of the law and employ large, direct workforces. On the basis of the arguments outlined above, therefore, they would be predicted to be bigger in terms of employment size than in the subcontracting institutional framework and face higher labour- and plant-related costs. Such cost pressures, furthermore, encourage firms to diversify in order to steady workloads and cover overhead costs. They pass the resultant extra costs on to clients in higher building prices.

This argument, consequently, predicts that the scale and scope of housebuilding firms will be greater in countries with strict employment legislation, and housebuilding costs in such countries will be relatively high. Some French evidence seems to confirm this prediction, particularly the fact that large construction firms have increasingly moved into housebuilding (Campagnac 1992; Campagnac & Winch 1995) as part of a diversified portfolio of construction activities.

Some housebuilders in strong labour legislation countries chose to ignore restrictive laws and subcontract illegally. This leads to 'formal' and 'informal' construction sectors. Informality is prevalent in housebuilding because of the frequently small scale of activity, which makes it difficult for governments to police. This dualism can be seen, for example, in Germany, particularly between those building workers permanently living in the country and the large influx of extra building workers from lower-wage European countries. In France, the problem of monitoring informal building labour has helped to generate further legislation. Since 1990, for example, the signing, and registering, of a 'construction contract' is compulsory before a house is built. The claimed objective is to provide better protection for clients, but it also 'formalises' building work, so that it has to conform to employment law. The system, in practice, has unsurprisingly proved difficult to administer. The professional body representing house builders (Fédération française des constructeurs des maisons individuelles) has produced a statement on the need to ensure full enforcement of the law, because understandably they regard the employing of cheaper, illegal, casual labour as unfair competition. It claims that over half of single-family dwellings are constructed illegally (Bâtirama 2002). Thus, labour legislation, ostensibly aimed at improving the efficiency of the construction industry, actually mitigates against competition based on relative efficiency and, instead, it encourages enterprises to compete by making a strategic decision about whether or not to conform to labour and tax laws.

Traditional small builders and small proprietor-run firms tend not to be affected by restrictive labour legislation. It consequently protects them to a degree from competition from larger, more 'modern' developers and builders. This may help explain why a traditional type of housebuilding, owner development, is so prevalent in countries such as France and Germany. In it, individual homeowners buy plots of land and then hire some organisation to build their home for them. It may be a builder, who provides an off-the-peg design or an architect and a group of independent 'jobbing' builders specialising in particular housebuilding trades. Owner development represents around half of all the new dwellings produced each year in France. In respect of single-family housing, the data suggest that most in France are owner developed (Table 9.2). In Germany, many owner-occupied houses are built in a similar way, and it is common in Europe's other Mediterranean shoreline countries. This owner self-build market is ideal terrain for small builders, but they share it with larger firms that sell and build standardised designs, sometimes in a partially prefabricated form.

Even in countries with a much higher preponderance of mass-market house builders, there are some individuals who buy land and hire agents to design and build their homes (Barlow *et al.* 2001). In those countries, however, it is probable that such methods tend to occur at the upper end of the market; yet, as can be seen, it is the owner occupied mass market in France. One cause of the difference (it is being hypothesised here) is labour regulations

Table 9.2   Types of new developments and dwellings in France.

Type of development	% share in 1999	Type of dwelling	Starts in 2001 (thousands)	% share in 2001
Owner developer*	52	Single houses	172	48
Construction firms	27	Grouped houses	43	12
Social and semi-public developers	12	Flats	128	36
Other	9	Other	14	4
Total	100		357	100

* Owner occupiers that commission a dwelling to be built on a plot of land they already own.

Sources: *Dwellings*, INSEE; Developments, Ministère de l'équipement, des transports et du logement, Paris – DAEI-SES: Sitadel.

in construction and their implications for the competitive position of particular types of housebuilding firm. Unfortunately, there is insufficient information to explore the argument in any more detail.

Firm specialisation

Many firms find that they can keep management costs and risks down by specialising in only one form of housebuilding (e.g. single-family owner occupation or large multi-family structures). Different housing types often require distinct construction processes and, hence, skills to manage them. When structures are more complex, design, materials procurement and logistics matters become more complicated and some firms may outsource professional tasks, such as design and engineering work, on similar principles to those with regard to the subcontracting of manual trades.

Despite the advantages of market specialisation, some firms still undertake different types of building. This is particularly common in continental European countries, such as the Netherlands, France and Spain. When they do so, construction firms frequently use the M-form type of management structure (Williamson 1981), using quasi-independent subsidiaries to limit management diseconomies. Firms' strategic choices over the market segments in which to be active, therefore, have implications for their internal organisational structures and management needs. Yet, if scale economies in production are low, the benefits of extra size may be limited, or even be negative as management diseconomies set in. When firms diversify, consequently, possible increased unit costs in production may have to be compensated for by other benefits, such as risk reduction caused by weak correlation in demand variations between construction sectors or spatial markets.

Diversification and financial influences

A noticeable difference exists between countries with regard to whether major housebuilding firms are independent firms or operate as divisions of larger enterprises with diverse activities across construction and other industries. Typically, in English-speaking countries such as Australia, the UK and the USA, the large housebuilders are stand-alone firms or have only a limited range of other activities. In contrast, in continental Europe and Japan, housebuilders tend to be parts of conglomerates.

Likely reasons for this differentiation relate to sources of corporate finance and taxation variations, as discussed in the general finance literature (Rajan & Zingales 1995; La Porta *et al.* 2000). Though no detailed empirical research has been undertaken on this issue for housebuilding, such explanations seem applicable to it. In countries where stock markets play a key role, as in the English-speaking countries, potential agency problems between owners, managers and creditors tend to lead to the need for transparent public information. This encourages housebuilders to specialise in that business only and to be publicly quoted. Where more emphasis is placed on debt finance through banking institutions, credit monitoring may be less public and, so, conglomerate corporate structures are more common.

The land market and residential development

Land assembly and development together form the second major functional element of housebuilding. There are two main issues to consider in the context of the organisational structure of housebuilding. The first concerns the land market and residential development and the second is between land development and housing production. Once again, there are a large variety of potential organisational outcomes, so only some key characteristics are examined.

The land market and residential development

Residential development involves the conception of housing projects; the acquisition of land sites on which to build them; the negotiation of the prices to pay for land; and decisions on holdings of land stocks (or 'banks'). The land market is like any other in that prices are determined by the interaction of demand and supply. In the aggregate, the land market can consequently be represented in the normal competitive way. What is important for examining the organisational relationship between the land market and housing development, however, is the way in which actual land plots are bought and sold.

A distinctive feature of the land market is that each building plot has unique locational characteristics. Land sites, consequently, are imperfect substitutes for each other. Moreover, and partially because of this locational characteristic, what is built on any particular site is not a standard product but a unique array of built structures. A land purchase decision, therefore, is simultaneously one about a decision to undertake a specific type of housing project. A developer consequently has to plan a project in its form and time flow and also calculate likely costs, uncertainties and returns. The decision to invest in the project is then based on the firm's overall strategic objectives.

Land development is highly risky. Risks are affected by seven key factors:

1. Construction issues related to the costs and time of completion of the built structures.
2. Individual project success, the prices at which the new dwellings can be sold and the likely time profile of sales.
3. General housing market conditions.
4. Interest rates and other finance matters, because land purchase, holding and the early groundwork and infrastructure stages of development all require funding and, probably, external finance.
5. Regulatory hurdles, particularly with regard to building regulations and land-use planning controls.
6. The price paid for land sites.
7. The scale of any impact fees or planning obligations required by local government before permitting development.

Together, these factors underlie developers' estimates of probable cost, revenue and profit outcomes. Such calculations determine what a developer is prepared to bid for an individual plot of land at any point in time. Risk premiums need to be factored into any potential land bid and require skill and judgement to price correctly. These risk premiums are an important determinant of land prices and assessing development risk is a key element in negotiations between developers, landowners and planning and other regulatory officials. Different developers vary in their project proposals for particular sites, their risk assessments of them and on their general degree of risk adversity. This means that there is likely to be a range of bid prices for land, depending on the scheme envisaged and developers' expectations about future housing market conditions.

The land development process, furthermore, is often more capital intensive than housebuilding, which intensifies the risks. Land has to be purchased, time must be spent passing through regulatory procedures, and the site has to undergo any necessary and expensive works required to enable individual building plots to be prepared.

The construction and project risk characteristics of individual sites can be pooled by firms by developing more than one site at a time. Greater firm size may also lower borrowing costs as lenders can more easily monitor loans. The land development process, consequently, suggests that greater firm size is a benefit. The size of the risk pooling benefits depends on the spatial level at which risk-pooling ceases to outweigh any counteracting management diseconomies of scale.

Landowners and developers negotiate over the price and timing of land purchase. Land acquisition can either take the form of outright purchase or an option, which is a futures contract to acquire land at a later date subject to specified conditions. The nature of the land purchase negotiation has implications for firm organisation. In those negotiations, the transparency of a site's development value will be a key issue. If there have been many similar recent land transactions in a locality, a land's value as a residential site is easy to identify for both parties, so the negotiations should be straightforward. In many situations, however, there is greater uncertainty over a site's development value. In such situations, negotiation is more significant and strategic.

Figure 9.2 illustrates some factors that influence landowner and developer negotiation strategies. Landowners' positions are influenced by the state of the local land market and their alternative best options. In order to strike a good bargain, developers are likely to emphasise the potential riskiness of their proposed development. They may emphasise their superior knowledge of the local housing market and the planning and other regulatory systems, which enable them to maximise both their and landowners' returns if landowners co-operate. Impact fees and planning obligations payable to the local municipality further complicate land negotiations. With these, developers again generally have superior knowledge compared with landowners and they can assist landowners over such matters, if the price is right.

Land banks may also offer developers negotiating advantages by smoothing their throughput of land. Land banking helps consequently to facilitate a strategic view by developers of the land market. These put developers in a good negotiating position with landowners, because the latter will know that the former can take their housebuilding activity elsewhere.

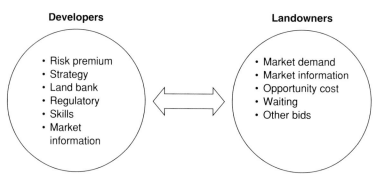

Figure 9.2   Negotiating over development profit and land price.

Spatial land strategies also form part of inter-developer competition – a large development in a locality by one developer, for instance, may block a similar move by another one for fear of creating local oversupply.

There are scale advantages in residential land purchase and development: larger enterprises have employee skill bases, capital bases and land banks that enable them to spread risks, lower financing costs, improve negotiating positions with landowners and facilitate strategic actions. This does not mean that smaller developers are necessarily fully competed out of the land market, rather that their operations are likely to be more risky and credit constrained.

Land development and housing production

An obvious producer firm distinction in housing is between those enterprises that purely undertake land development, those that solely build housing by acquiring pre-serviced building plots, and those enterprises that combine both the land development and building functions. In some country cases, the actual division between these types of firm, and the relative market shares they have, is strongly influenced by government policies. Yet, in most situations, market forces seem to be the prime cause of the separation or combination of land development and housebuilding. This section provides some suggestions as to what those forces might be.

Government policy has the greatest influence in Europe. This is not surprising as, in many European countries, land-use planning and housing policies are strongly interventionist. The introduction of large-scale social housing programmes in the middle decades of the twentieth century, for example, was, in part, based on criticism of pre-existing housing development and its design, as well as constituting a sustained attempt to provide better housing for low income groups (Swenarton 1981). As a result, social housing landlords became major land developers from the 1920s onwards, as well as large-scale landlords. They undertook the development function in new housing, for many years priding themselves on their revolutionary estate designs and built forms; whilst they overwhelmingly hired private building contractors to build the actual structures. There was some attempt to municipalise housebuilding completely, by bringing it under the control of state housing agencies or local authorities. Such moves tend to have only limited impact in new building, though they were far more influential in social housing repair and maintenance (Briscoe 1990).

In the twentieth century, furthermore, policies were introduced in Europe that made public or semi-public authorities key land development agencies for all types of property development, for example, in the Netherlands, France, Germany and Sweden (Barlow & King 1992; Golland & Boelhouwer 2002). These bodies, generally under municipal control, took over the function of traditional private sector land developers, relying for funding on central or regional government grants and public sector banks for loans. In most of these countries, however, such land development practices generally did not become universal, so that purely private land developers continued to exist in large numbers.

Residential land development in France

France illustrates the multiple types of development framework that can arise when a series of land policy measures are enacted over the years. In it, land may be developed by the public sector directly, or by semi-public companies (Sociétés d'économie mixtes, SEMs) set up under the control of the local municipality. Most French municipalities create and control a large number of SEMs, not only for property development, but also for a wide range of other purposes, such as transport, waste collection and sports facilities. Property SEMs benefit from the municipality's right of compulsory purchase when they are set up to undertake development and assemble sites. As a result of this eminent domain attribute, they are particularly common when 'brownfield' land is redeveloped. When SEM-organised sites have been cleared in cities or assembled in suburbs, and made ready for development, they are then sold mainly to private property developers, with imposed constraints and guidelines about the type of housing to be built (in terms of architectural design, standard, proportion of affordable housing, etc.).

Another common French process of land development is the ZAC (*Zone d'aménagement concerté*) system. In those schemes, the municipality designates a number of localities where the public and the private sector agree to develop various types of property. The planning process is simplified and speeded up, and the public sector takes on the land development function and private developers (who may be individual home-owners) agree to follow certain guidelines and specifications on design, uses, and environmental and social standards, for instance. ZACs are often used for urban expansion and new suburb development.

The use of specific policy-ordained mechanisms for land development varies considerably from one area of France to another; with local market conditions, policy objectives and political agendas having a considerable influence on the actual forms of land development that take place. In some cities, the management of land release and development is very liberal, in others it is under tight control by the municipality, such as in Rennes (Le Galès 2001).

This type of land policy undoubtedly has had a considerable influence on the types of housebuilders that exist in France and their relative market shares. A strong role for local government as land developer and the often loose planning controls in non-urban areas, for example, both make it possible for many small developers and owner builders to find sites and put up a house or two. So, it is hard for private sector developers to build up large, sustainable market shares as speculative house builders.

French land and planning policies, consequently, contribute to an understanding of why owner self-build has such a large share of its housing market. The significance of the policy process, furthermore, suggests that the most successful strategy for private residential builders is to become heavily involved in local politics, which is what seems to happen.

Private land developers and builders: separation and combination

Purely private sector land developers are, of course, the most common type of developer in market economies, apart from in a handful of European countries. Yet, it is still possible to observe significant differences in the institutional structure of the development process. Most notably, there is often an organisational separation between land development and housing construction; at the same time, the two aspects are also often undertaken by one enterprise in a combined way. These two forms, independent developers and builders and combined developer–builders may even exist in the same housing market. The separate arrangement is common, for example, in Australia and the USA,[1] and it was prevalent in Britain's primarily private rental housing system prior to 1914 (Ball 2001). In contrast, in modern Britain, development and building are now generally combined under the control of one housebuilding firm that buys sites, erects homes and sells them. Why should such distinctions occur and why are they important?

One likely reason for developer–builders relates to the improved branding and quality control feasible as a result. In addition, the relative riskiness of the two aspects of development and building and the competitiveness of land markets in different countries may play a part. It was noted earlier that land development was a more risky activity than that of building, so its returns should be larger in order to compensate for the extra risk. When relatively small house builders can buy serviced sites from land developers, they can enter and exit the industry easily without the encumbrance of land development procedures and associated capital costs. They can choose their sites if they wish from more than one developer, spreading project-specific risk and encouraging competition between land developers.

In competitive land and housing markets, project-specific risk is heightened by competition. Builders' and developers' decisions to build and put land plots on to the market might also lead to excess supply, so that market-based risk is similarly high. Being able to sell plots to builders who then build houses and sell them, spreads these risks between developers and builders. Each has to commit less capital for their respective stages of the housebuilding process and, equally importantly, the time that capital has to be committed before a profit can be taken is far less than for firms that both develop and build.

The suggested hypothesis here, in summary, is that in competitive markets differences in risk and returns between the development and building aspects of housebuilding create a tendency for the land development and construction sides of housebuilding to be separated. Combined developer–builders may well still exist in competition with such firms, but the predominant tendency would be towards separation. In such market contexts, furthermore, there should a large turnover of housebuilding and real estate development firms, because of the ease of entry and exit and the scale of risk. Such a firm structure has been reported by several studies of housebuilding in the USA and Canada (Clawson 1971; Grebler 1973; Buzzelli 2001). A recent study, furthermore, suggests that there are systematic spatial variations in the average size of homebuilders in such markets. These depend on, for example, whether the urban area is growing, when firms tend to be larger, or whether the locality contains small-scale development restrictive local governments, where firms tend to be smaller (Somerville 1999).

When land supply is restricted, in contrast, as it is in most of urban Britain, the attractiveness of combining housing development and building is greater. In this market context, holders of residential land sites develop a degree of strategic advantage through the land they own. With restricted land supply, the riskiness of development is diminished as individual project risk is less than in the competitive market case, and there is less chance of spatial competition between builders generating overbuilding. So, in the contexts of limited land supply, combining development and housebuilding heightens firms' influences on local housing and land markets. If, for instance, developers sold plots on to separate house builders whenever they were offered the current market price for land, then the latter would determine when and how much new housing was supplied.

Private multi-family housing

With private sector multi-family housing, the distribution of project risk between land development and housing production is skewed much more towards housing production than it is in the single-family case. Multi-family housing requires much more building work in terms of load-bearing foundations and walls, access facilities and communal services. Individual dwellings, moreover, have to be created all at the same time as they are contained within the same structure; whereas single-family housing can be produced on a piecemeal basis and a development built through over time. It, hence, is more costly, capital demanding and risky in terms of market timing to build multi-family than single-family housing.

Project risk may also be greater in terms of the likely success of a specific multi-family built structure in comparison with standardised single-family housing built in a successful, expanding suburb. Where multi-family housing is built on a single site by a private investor, the benefit of combining land development and housing production consequently is often overwhelming. The actual building work is likely to be contracted out, but the developer retains control of that building process and the sale or letting of the finished units.

The risks, costs and capital requirements of multi-family structures tend to mean that many private multi-family dwellings are 'one-off' developments by small-scale developers, who either hold on to a handful of completed buildings as investments, or sell them on to investors or homeowners. Such factors also encourage the formation of apartment owner co-operatives, where legislation and tax laws are attractive; these exist in countries as different as Sweden and Turkey. The co-operative then becomes the land developer and builder and co-operative members own rights to use specific dwellings and have the ability to sell those rights.

Another common practice is that groups of individuals are persuaded to set up co-operatives by professional developers that undertake their land development business by using such ownership devices. The members of the co-operatives then, in effect, provide the development financing for the entrepreneurs who, in a competitive market, will have to accept a lower return than that for a speculative multi-family residential development, because of the reduced risk. Moral hazard becomes a problem in such contexts, as co-operative members have to trust the developer to carry out the works as agreed.

The capital requirements of multi-family residences encourage the existence of larger firms, particularly in regions or countries where land supply is tight, apartment living the norm and urban densities are high. Spain and Hong Kong are contrasting examples of the practice. In Hong Kong, a few major developers are said to dominate the new housing market, using the subcontracting production model (Chiang & Tang 2002).

With the international trend towards some higher-income groups moving back into inner-city localities, new types of combined developer–builder firms have been evolving in recent years. They find sites, assemble them from fragmented owners when necessary, raise funds, undertake the path through the regulatory process, set up sales offices, and control the image and building qualities of their projects to appeal to marketing-generated purchaser profiles. In many of the world's major cities, such developers have evolved. Once again, sector specialisation seems to bring benefits to such enterprises, because many do not stray far from their targeted markets.

The structure of the Japanese housebuilding industry is somewhat different from that elsewhere for two reasons: there are extreme urban land shortages and the existence of a number of large firms amongst a sea of small producers. There is a high share of infill building where existing dwellings are demolished on a piecemeal basis and their sites used for single-family or multi-dwelling units ('scrap and build'). Around 40% of new dwellings were created in this way annually between 1993 and 2003. In addition, there are a number of large producers using industrial prefabricated techniques (Oizumi 2006).

The dynamics of industrial change

The ease of entry and exit from housebuilding and the riskiness of land development means that housebuilding is an industry with substantial enterprise turnover, as noted above. Firm change is driven by the property market cycle and regulatory changes, rather than by the technological factors, scale and scope economies and international trade pressures that are common in many manufacturing industries (Chandler 1977; Porter 1990). During upswings in the housing market, particularly if they are long-lasting, new entrants flood into housebuilding and existing firms expand. The subsequent downturn, however, leads to a shrinkage in both the number of active firms and the size of those remaining, with the unluckiest or most over-committed ones failing.

Take-overs add to the process of firm change. During housing market upswings, firms may find it cheaper and quicker to acquire land by taking over another builder than through direct purchase in the land market. Similarly, surviving firms may acquire the land and other assets of the failing firms cheaply during housing market slumps (Ball 1988).

Occasionally, changing demands for housing create new market segments in which specialist firms can grow. The inner-city 'loft' and 'luxury apartment' markets have already been mentioned. Retirement housing is another case where specialists have emerged with rising retiree wealth and the growing need for specialist care facilities with ageing populations. Both these markets, moreover, have benefited from regulatory change, particularly in planning and infrastructure provision.

Regulation in the broadest sense, furthermore, is not simply a government domain, but can arise, for example, from changing financial market practices. From the 1950s to the 1990s, many large UK housebuilders were parts of far larger construction conglomerates. This is rarely the case now, a development aided by the demand for greater financial transparency required by modern capital market lenders, mentioned above.

Conclusions

This chapter has examined reasons for differences in the organisational structure of housebuilding in different countries. It focused analysis on potential economies of scale, market factors, information asymmetries, regulation and risk. The great variety of ways in which housing is built can broadly be explained in terms of a limited range of concepts commonly used in industrial economics. Market instability is an important factor, but is insufficient to provide a full explanation because it is a common feature of durable goods industries, most of which are not organised in the same ways as housebuilding. Locational specificity is important, especially with regard to the land market. The type of housing being built and the markets in which they are sold are further influences. Information is particularly important in explaining the economic characteristics of house-building, because of the nature of both the development and production processes. Strategic behaviour enters the equation, particularly through behaviour with regard to the land market and residential development strategies. Regulation in labour markets also has considerable consequences for firm structures. Land availability and the impact of planning regimes on it both affect the range of functions undertaken by individual enterprises and the size of firms.

Note

1   An interesting history of such a developer, Newland Communities, can be found at http://www.newlandcommunities.com.

10

The influence of size economies and planning regulations on the housebuilding industry

Introduction

Much has been written on the impact of land-use planning, zoning and other regulations on housing supply and recent housing market booms have heightened interest in the issue.[1] The topic has a long pedigree in the UK, with urban containment written into the post-1947 planning system, and the Barker Review has again brought the issue to political prominence (Barker 2004). 'Smart growth' and other land development restrictions have led to a recent surge of interest in the USA, with several commentators highlighting the impact of such regulation on housing supply in a growing number of US cities (Glaeser & Gyourko 2005).

In contrast to this renaissance of interest in housing supply, there are few studies of the impact of planning on the industry that it actually regulates: real estate development. The implicit assumption of planning and land supply studies consequently is that the transmission mechanism from planning policy to housing output is certain and direct in terms of the quantitative and supply timing impacts of land availability. This assumption is obviously open to question. Studies in the UK, for example, suggest that less than half of the land allocated to housing is actually built upon within five years (Bramley & Leishman 2005). The reasons for this leakage are likely to be varied but suggest a need to investigate supply side processes in more detail before coming to conclusions about how to improve supply price elasticities, though it is widely recognised that far less is known about the supply than the demand side of the housing market (Rosenthal 1999).

Moreover, the structure of the housing supply-side may be influenced by the nature of the regulation of it, that is, by the type of land-use controls in existence. The specific question addressed here is: 'Do land-use planning systems encourage the existence of particular housebuilding industry structures through their impacts on firm size?'

Concentration in the housebuilding industry

The housebuilding industry has traditionally been treated as consisting of a multitude of small firms with high levels of entry and exit: a close approximation to a perfectly competitive industry. Some authors continue to argue that empirically this still remains the case (Buzzelli 2001). Yet, although the data are patchy, there is evidence that there are quite high levels of concentration in many countries' housebuilding industries.

It has long been recognised that large-scale housebuilders may arise in specific contexts. For example, large firms grew up rapidly in the 1920s and 1930s housebuilding boom in the UK (Ball 1983; Jackson 1991) and, also, during the 1950s and 1960s in the USA (Grebler 1973). Yet few of these firms had a sustained life span and they tended to disappear or shrink significantly in size when their respective housing markets entered periods of turbulence and supply-side decline.

Many of the world's housing markets have been experiencing unprecedented boom conditions over the last decade or so. In such sellers' markets, it is to be expected that some building firms will grow rapidly. This has raised concentration ratios in several countries as a result. Yet, the question remains, however, as to whether such increasing concentration is predominantly cyclical in character, as in earlier periods, or is highlighting more fundamental shifts in industrial structure.

Fundamental changes, for example, may arise from the growth of scale or scope economies, which could occur in production, finance, the procurement of inputs, in marketing and sales or in the benefits of strategic behaviour in relation to other competitors. Changes in the regulatory land-use planning environment may have had an impact as well. These characteristics can broadly be separated into those that arise from benefits of larger firm size in a free market context and the influences of regulation on firm structure.

This chapter will examine them by investigating the benefits of greater firm size in more detail and undertaking a comparative investigation of firm size hierarchies in the UK and the USA. As Chapter 9 noted, there are considerable variations in the structure of housebuilding industries across the world but the UK and US industries have a number of similarities that make them more comparable than most. Although in the USA, planning regulations have tightened up land supply in many parts of the country in recent years, it is still the case that, in aggregate, planning induced constraints on land supply are far less than in the UK.

The significance of volume housebuilders in Britain

Conventions in the available UK statistics make it useful to define a volume housebuilder as a firm producing over 500 dwellings a year though, as will be argued below, this output level may be a cut-off point for important scale effects as well. That output is equivalent to an annual turnover of slightly over £100m (around $180m or €150m) at 2004 new house price levels.

As Table 10.1 shows, there were 36 UK volume housebuilders in 2004 and they constructed 61% of new private housing output.[2] The remaining 40% was built by a far larger number of other smaller developers and 'self-builders' – future homeowners who organise the housebuilding process themselves. (Many small firms do not build in any one year and many self-builders do not bother with the expense of the NHBC warranty, but the data are comprehensive for the firm sector of the industry as sales depend on having such a warranty.)

The size distribution of housebuilders in the UK is right-skewed, in common with housebuilding industries in many countries, with a relatively small number of larger firms and a long tail of small producers. Entry and exit at the small firm end of the distribution is high and many such firms also do not build every year. At the other end of the firm size distribution range, changes in larger firms are commonly driven by takeovers and mergers and to a lesser extent by differences in internal output growth, rather than through bankruptcy. Social rental housebuilding, undertaken on a contract basis, accounts for about a tenth of total UK output. Some

Table 10.1   Size of UK private housebuilders 2004.

No. of starts per firm	None	<500	500–2000	2000+
Share of private output	0	39	13	48
No. of firms registered with NHBC	10 600	5800	22	14

Source: Calculations based on NHBC data.

firms specialise in the social sector and the size distribution is similar to that in private housing, though at a much smaller scale.

At 61% in 2004, the share of volume housebuilders in total output is sharply up from earlier decades. In 1978, for example, their share was only 33%, around half of the current level (Ball 1983). Furthermore, it seems that the increase in the volume builders' share of housing output has been a fairly continuous process because, by 1988, the top 40 firms (roughly equivalent to the extant volume builders) produced 48% of private housing output, rising to 54% in 1993 (Ball 1996). These data consequently suggest that housebuilder concentration in the UK is a trend rather than a cyclical phenomenon.

The number of volume producers, in addition, has been relatively constant over time – 29 in 1978 and 36 in 2003. However, their annual total output when measured in dwelling units almost doubled between those two years: building approximately 50 000 dwellings in 1978 and 95 000 in 2003, and these firms experienced an even greater increase in their turnovers, given the marked rises in real house prices between those two dates.

Within the 36 volume builders, there is a marked L-shaped distribution in the firm-size hierarchy with a long tail of firms that produce only slightly more than the 500 mark. This is shown in Figure 10.1, where the top 23 firms are ranked by size. The number of truly high volume producers is small: only 11 build more than 2000 homes a year and only three more than 10 000 units.[3] The degree of concentration of output amongst the top five firms is particularly high. Their annual outputs are equivalent to a third of UK private sector housebuilding and at firm sizes below them, the cumulative share of output decreases rapidly, with the top ten firms altogether building 46% and the top 25 around 55% of annual national housebuilding.

Data are also available for planning applications to built dwellings[4] and they are good indicators of firms' future outputs. The data in Figure 10.2 suggest a close correspondence between the annual planning applications each firm makes and their current output levels. In 2004, the top 40 housebuilders applied to build 117 000 dwellings on 1350 sites in Britain, which was equivalent to almost three-quarters of the private housing starts that occurred in that year. It is also interesting to note that the number of sites is relatively small, indicating that in specific towns and suburbs land site conversions to new housing are actually few in number each year.

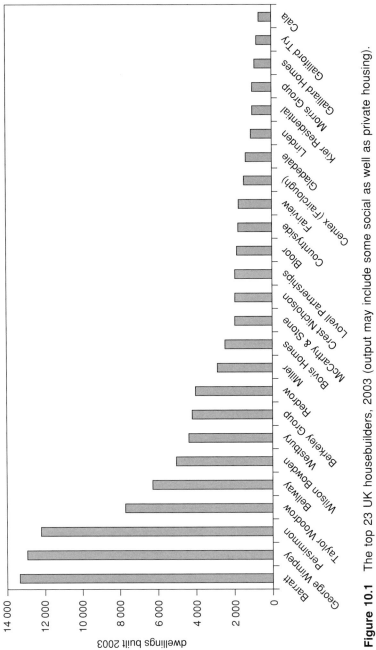

Figure 10.1   The top 23 UK housebuilders, 2003 (output may include some social as well as private housing).

Source: Home Builders Federation, from company accounts.

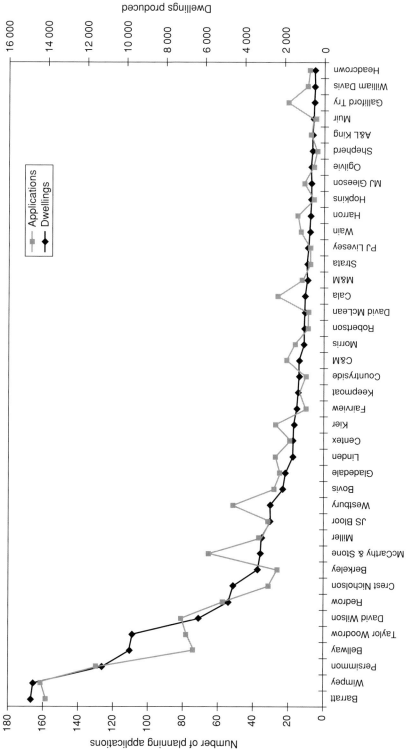

Figure 10.2 Number of planning applications made and dwellings built by size of firm, 2003–4.

Source: ODPM and company accounts.

Table 10.2   English regional housebuilding concentration ratios, 2003–4.
English regional planning decisions, applications by large housebuilders and
private housing starts.

	No. of applications by the top ten* housebuilders	Dwellings in top 10 firm's applications as % of annual private starts*	Share of top two in top ten's applications*
North East	45	89	35
South East	146	46	25
West Mids.	73	43	46
Yorks and Humber	82	42	48
London	64	39	50
East Mids.	47	38	36
North West	73	35	36
South West	62	33	43
East England	39	16	42

* Measured by highest overall number of dwellings in detail planning applications in region, 2003–04.

Source: Estimates from information from ODPM and EMAP Glenigan.

Planning-based data, consequently, confirm the high national new housing
market shares of the larger housebuilders and highlight their significance
in relatively thin local land development processes. These planning data
are also available at the regional level and, when the activities of the top
ten housebuilders in each English region are considered, the results re-
emphasise the degree of concentration (Table 10.2). In the English regions
on average in 2002/3, the number of planning applications by the top ten
housebuilders active in a region was equivalent to 42% of all the private
sector dwellings started in that year.

Seven of the nine English regions have broadly similar concentration ratios,
with the North East having a much higher ratio and the East a much smaller
one. In addition, the distribution of planning applications amongst the top
ten is heavily concentrated towards the largest firms, with the top two firms
in each region responsible for 40% of the top ten's applications on average.
Furthermore, the same firm names tend to reappear as applying for the
largest numbers of dwellings in each region year-on-year, as is indicated
for Southern England in Table 10.3. Below the 10 000-a-year output level
of the top three to four firms, housebuilders tend to specialise in a select
number of regions, the location of which depends on individual firm
histories.

Overall, the data suggest that in any English region the currently active,
and soon to be built on, housebuilding sites are relatively small in number
and the majority are owned by a limited number of volume housebuilders.

Table 10.3 Top ten housebuilders in regions of southern England, ranked according to dwelling numbers in planning applications.

London

2004–03	2003–02	2002–01
Berkeley	Berkeley	Berkeley
Barratt	Wimpey	Barratt
Wimpey	Crest Nicholson	Wimpey
Bellway	Bellway	Crest Nicholson
David Wilson	Barratt	Bellway
Weston	Gladedale	Fairview
Higgins	Higgins	Higgins
Taylor Woodrow	Durkan	Rialto
Telford	Fairview	Gladedale
Goldcrest	Rialto	Durkan

South East

2004–03	2003–02	2002–01
Wimpey	Wimpey	Barratt
Barratt	Wilcon	Wimpey
Crest Nicolson	Barratt	Taylor Woodrow
Bellway	Redrow	McCarthy & Stone
Persimmon	Berkeley	David Wilson
Berkley	Bovis	Berkeley
Taylor Woodrow	David Wilson	Persimmon
McCarthy & Stone	Taylor Woodrow	Wilcon
David Wilson	Persimmon	Bovis
Redrow	McCarthy & Stone	Redrow

South West

2004–03	2003–02	2002–01
Persimmon	Persimmon	Barratt
Barratt	Barratt	Persimmon
Crest Nicholson	Crest Nicholson	Bellway
Westbury	Wilcon	Westbury
Bovis	McCarthy & Stone	McCarthy & Stone
Wimpey	Kingsley	Wilcon
Redrow	Westbury	Wimpey
Newland	Bovis	Kingsley
Taylor Woodrow	Bellway	Bovis
Bellway	Wimpey	Crest Nicholson

East

2004–03	2003–02	2002–01
Crest Nicolson	Persimmon	Persimmon
Persimmon	Wimpey	Bovis
Wimpey	Wilson Connolly	Wilson Connolly
Taylor Woodrow	Bovis	Wimpey
JS Bloor	Swan Hill	Construct Reason
Kier	Barratt	Barratt
Hopkins	Westbury	Swan Hill
PJ Livesey	Construct Reason	Westbury
Redrow	Malcolm Bullock	Malcolm Bullock
Kenford	Galliford Try	Galliford Try

Source: Based on data compiled by EMAP Glenigan.

Most new housebuilding in any particular locality exists at only a few sites and spatially there is a concentration of housebuilding into a few sub-urban growth and urban regeneration areas.

International comparisons

International data are patchy, yet the available information suggests that Britain probably has one of the most concentrated housebuilding indus-tries amongst the world's advanced economies. The level of concentration is certainly far higher than in the USA, where the top 25 housebuilders account for 30% of private housing output in contrast to 55% in the UK. Furthermore, large US builders tend to produce in the high household and income growth regions, so that their total outputs are a product of high housebuilding rates in those localities, whereas housebuilding con-centration ratios are substantial throughout the UK.

In functional terms, the major housebuilders in both countries have broadly similar characteristics of product specialisation, a wide geographic spread of operations, a public ownership structure, localised operating divisions, and the actual work of erecting and fitting out homes is generally sub-contracted. One key distinction between the USA and UK is that pure land development companies are common in the former, selling individual plots on to small builders or to households that contract builders to erect their own specific designs; whereas such procedures are rarer in the UK. Instead, the standardised house types of the major firms are the most common form of new single-family housing (Hooper 2000).

Size-wise, the largest firms in the USA are much bigger than in the UK, with the top two in the USA producing over three times as many homes as the equivalent British ones. Typically, the current largest homebuilders originated from small family firms, producing in one US city or region. They subsequently became major producers by growing rapidly through organic expansion and acquisitions in localities with high housing demand spread widely across the USA.[5] They build in most market segments from first-time buyer to luxury and retiree, though most focus on the prime owner occupied market of single-family homes.

Spatial diversification is a common cause of increased size. It helps firms to survive housing market downturns and even to benefit from them, because at times of depressed housing markets less successful firms or their land banks can be purchased for attractive prices. For example, the largest firm in terms of units produced (44 000 homes in 2004) is D. R. Horton. It began in 1978 in Dallas/Fort Worth and only started expanding into other markets a decade later in 1987, with a spatial diversification strategy based on involvement in the most active homebuilding markets across the USA. It now has 51 divisions in 21 states.

The local-builder-made-good history is common amongst the largest house-builders in the UK as well. In contrast to common US practice, however, UK firms do not have mortgage finance divisions because of the different characteristics of the two countries' mortgage markets. In addition, more of the larger UK housebuilding firms have originated from initially being part of larger construction enterprises operating across all fields of construction. During the first half of the 1990s, this multi-sectoral construction firm model virtually disappeared in the UK (Hillebrandt & Lansley 1995), although such multi-division construction/development company ownership patterns are still typical of the larger housebuilding enterprises in many other European countries, such as France, Spain and the Netherlands, as noted in Chapter 9.

In both the UK and USA, the volume producers consequently are now generally publicly-quoted firms and with activities primarily based on private housebuilding. Focusing on one activity improves transparency. The high cost and risks of land banks make borrowing essential and lenders tend to prefer stock listed enterprises as their performance is then easier to monitor. As a result, public quotation and specialisation in house-building tend to go hand-in-hand for volume builders. Nevertheless, stock markets traditionally put a significant risk-premium on residential real estate development. High leverage ratios tend to damage stock prices and lead to higher bank lending and mortgage borrowing costs as well. This encourages housebuilders to rely heavily on reinvested profits for their investment funds (Barker 2004).

Therefore, in many respects, the American and British housebuilding industries are similar. Where they differ markedly is in their concentration ratios. To recap, the 25 largest producers in the USA have around a 30% market share, whereas the UK ones have a 55% one. When only the shares of the top five firms in total private housing output are compared, the difference is even greater, with the UK top five having a 33% market share and the US top five having just 10%. This difference may be attributable to the sheer geographic scale of the USA compared with Britain, which could be argued to make it hard for firms to cover large parts of the country. However, such an explanation fits poorly with the wide geographic spread of the largest US housebuilding firms and geography, of itself, does not seem an insuperable constraint given the multi-divisional nature of house-building enterprises in the two countries. More generally, the common

M-form divisional structure of the modern corporation and the global reach of many of them, as described and analysed by Williamson (1985), and the existence of many international corporations suggests that geography is not a fundamental barrier to firm size.

Australia also has a far less concentrated housebuilding industry than the UK, one that is significantly less than in the USA as well, with the top ten firms having only 15% of the market in the late 1990s (DIST 1999).

Scale economies and the organisation of housing production

An obvious explanation for the existence of large firms is that scale economies exist throughout the current range of firm outputs. Several scale economy benefits, for example, can be suggested for volume producers. In contrast to smaller producers, volume firms:

- are wholly profit-driven and focused on housebuilding;
- have the volumes to facilitate task specialisation and the incentives to employ the best available workforce in all aspects of their businesses;
- have the scale, management skill and products to treat housebuilding as a continuous flow process and derive economies by doing so;
- have the capabilities to understand and manage project information flows, uncertainties and risks;
- are more likely to minimise 'non-productive time' (e.g. when people are on site but waiting for an earlier task to be finished, when they are measuring or working out what a job entails, when they are waiting for materials, etc.). Such deadweight time can be substantial and, so, is a key determinant of overall construction productivity and costs;
- work continuously in localities and build up long-term relationships with subcontractors and suppliers;
- have the greatest market power and purchasing muscle to try to ensure that subcontractors and suppliers deliver and undertake work according to predetermined schedules.

The multi-divisional organisation of regional subsidiaries

Individual firms are actually made up of a series of relatively small regional subsidiaries. Typically, divisions are set up as corporately independent subsidiaries of the parent firm. Overall headquarters staff of the parent are generally limited to a small range of people necessary to undertake the corporate functions that cannot be efficiently carried out at divisional level.

The 51 divisions of the largest US housebuilder have already been noted. One of the UK's largest housebuilders operates with a headquarters staff of only around 30 and has 18 functional subsidiaries, each specialising in a particular area of the country. Some large firms also have an intermediate level of management between headquarters and operating divisions but, again, it will have a small number of personnel.

A typical regional division builds around 500–1000 dwellings a year. Given the larger size of individual building sites in the USA, the operating divisions of firms there tend to produce higher unit volumes in comparison with the UK, where land supply constraints typically lead to smaller plot sizes and harder to build on urban regeneration sites. Nevertheless, there seems to be an optimal divisional size determined by production costs. It is not possible to obtain detailed cost data on such optimal sizes but discussions with firm managers highlight the significance of production costs in determining divisional structures. UK firms when interviewed argue that below a certain size unit overhead costs rise, so that small divisional sizes are only tolerated when they are growing or subject to a temporary demand shock. At the other extreme if too many units are built by one division, management diseconomies begin to bite deeply and, therefore, firms generally find it useful to spin off another new division. The optimal size in the UK anecdotally seems to be around 500 to 600 units a year. Some firms may have super-divisions that can rise to 1000 units a year, but they usually depend on exceptional conditions rather than distinctive organisational strategies.

The principal determinants of optimal divisional size are the number of sites a housebuilder is working on at any point in time and the cost curves associated with building on a multiplicity of sites. For any given level of market demand, sales potential is saturated more quickly if the firm builds on only a limited number of sites because of the imperfect substitutability of housing across space for individual consumers. In other words, builders' experience has shown them that specific sites will only generate a certain range of sales in a given time period. More sites must be brought on stream if a higher turnover is desired and production rates on individual sites are geared to the level of sales on them. Sites, in turn, cannot be too closely spaced otherwise they drain sales off each other. Firms can try to avoid such problems by building in different market segments but, again, to do so often means building on separate sites at some distance from each other.

The size of a housebuilding division, therefore, depends on the number and geographic spread of sites and the practical possibilities of divisional staff being able to visit them on a regular basis. For example, the largest UK firms build on over two hundred sites spread across the country and will have a commensurately large number of divisions to manage and serve them. The functions within those divisions will be broadly common, leading to a fairly fixed matrix of staff numbers and occupational requirements.

This site driven nature of housebuilders' operations has important implications for any individual firms' share of a local new housing market. Firms generally are not successful when they try to concentrate too much of their activity in one local market area. This characteristic dilutes – though does not negate – the potential impact of any firm's local market power.

Production economies of greater size

The question arises of whether there are further production economies of scale above the divisional level. Unfortunately, severe data limitations make investigation of this issue difficult. There are some available data in the UK relating to labour utilisation and operating profit to turnover ratios for the top 25 firms.[6]

In terms of labour utilisation, the evidence of scale economies for the larger firms with outputs above those of a typical housebuilding division is weak. It is unlikely that the larger firms will gain any scale economies in site utilisation of labour. Virtually all manual work on housebuilding sites is sub-contracted, so that the housebuilders active in any locality share a common pool of subcontractors. Non-manual labour, in contrast, is generally employed directly by housebuilders to undertake such tasks as management, input procurement, cost measurement and valuation, marketing and finance. Much of this labour input (typically, around 30% of total labour utilisation in the UK industry) is a fixed overhead cost of a firm's operations and, so, there might be possibilities for the largest firms to economise on such overhead costs. However, regression analysis of the relationship between the directly employed workforces of the top 24 UK firms and their number of completions shows a linear relationship only (Figure 10.3).[7]

This result is indicative of constant returns to scale above around the 500 dwellings level. The estimate suggests that every additional 2.7 dwellings produced is typically associated with approximately another person employed throughout the range of larger private housebuilder firm sizes.[8]

The multi-divisional nature of firms' production and the narrow size range of those divisions helps to explain why scale economies in production do not exist above the 500–1000 units a year output level. Larger firms are

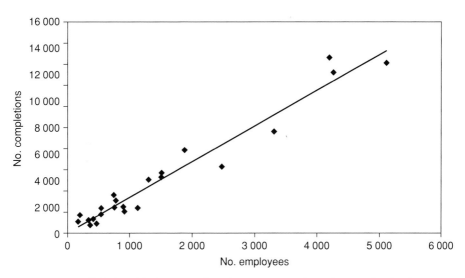

Figure 10.3 Relationship between housing output and employees for the largest UK housebuilders.

Note: Estimates based on 2003 data from company accounts.

aggregates of production units of around that size, so greater size is simply correlated with wider geographic spread, rather than differences in either units' costs or methods of production.

Other potential sources of scale economies

Three other potential sources of scale economies for the largest enterprises relate to finance, marketing, input procurement and innovation.

With regard to finance, it could be argued that the largest firms are more able to raise funds from investors and banks. While some studies have found that small housebuilders do suffer from difficulties in raising external finance, this is less likely to be so for volume producers. In the UK, all of them have annual turnovers of £100m or more and are publicly quoted. Therefore, any finance-related gains are likely to be small or non-existent. There is a general complaint that housebuilders' shares trade at earnings discounts compared with other industries. However, this affects all firms, no matter their size, because of uncertainties over house price forecasts in a volatile housing market and difficulties in putting accurate valuations on firms' major assets, their land banks.

Marketing benefits for the largest producers also seem limited. Because housing markets are essentially local, the extra benefits of a national profile are not that great. Instead, sales effort is put at the level of local divisions. While national branding may have some consumer impact in terms of familiarity, there may be some offsetting negative effects of a national profile associated with bad publicity. For example, reputations for poor build quality can have adverse impacts across all the divisions of larger firms.[9]

Input procurement is also unlikely to provide additional benefits of scale. Construction labour markets are local in nature and there are possibilities for workers of employment in more construction sub-sectors than housing. This means that the largest firms are unlikely to have any procurement advantages over more regionally specialist builders. Some firms, when interviewed, suggest that subsidising the training of sub-contractors' skilled work forces brings benefits in terms of quality and sub-contractor loyalty.[10] However, again, the smaller regionally-concentrated volume builders have as much possibility of undertaking this practice as the larger firms.

The same local principle applies to land acquisition, so that the largest firms are unlikely to have any land procurement advantages with respect to landowners in specific localities. Moreover, volume builders of all sizes are not usually constrained by the potentially large size of some land parcels. Where large land sites are acquired, even by relatively small firms, it is possible for them to sell on tracts (or options) to other housebuilders and land investors. This practice is often desirable in order to spread site-specific risk (Ball 1996).

With regard to materials procurement, there may be purchasing economies of scale, because of the greater volumes of specific materials required at an annual output of 14 000 dwellings compared with, say, 500, and the negotiating muscle such volumes bestow on the largest housebuilders. But the costs of materials are considerably less per dwelling than either those for land or labour, so that the overall impact on total unit costs is unlikely to be that great.

Innovation also does not seem to give the largest firms much of a competitive edge either. For example, traditional brick-and-block techniques prevail in England and Wales. In Scotland, factory produced timber-frame are more common but they are used by firms across the whole range of sizes and usually produced by independent firms prepared to sell to all comers.[11] In housing, the largest cannot easily derive an edge in housebuilding by investing in R&D and using patented technology (Ball 1999). However, some of the largest UK housebuilders are now experimenting with such strategies, though whether, in practice, this will lead to firm specific benefits is a matter of conjecture at present.

Housebuilder returns and competition

If greater size does enable larger firms to earn higher margins, either through scale economies or market power, this should be reflected in the relative profitability of firms of different sizes. Conversely, unit returns should be constant with respect to size if such benefits do not exist. It is difficult to procure meaningful information on the returns on capital in house-building, either at one point in time or over time. However, evidence from available cross-section data[12] on operating profits and firm size does not suggest that larger firms are actually making higher unit returns than smaller ones.

Figure 10.4 compares annual operating profits with the output in 2003 of the 23 largest UK housebuilders. The plotted regression line is linear, which suggests that operating profits, when weighted by a firm's average house selling price, rise linearly with output.[13] This cross-sectional profits analysis suggests that, even if some firms do have significant market shares, they are currently unable to make significant higher returns relative to

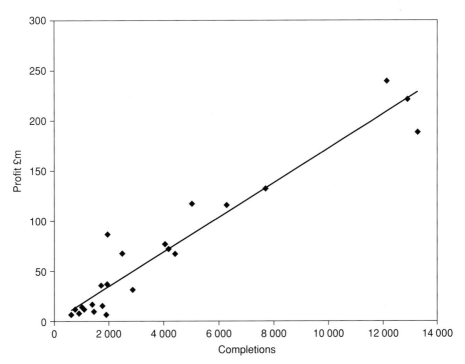

Figure 10.4   Gross operating profits and number of dwellings built 2003 (operating profit weighted by average selling price).

Note: Estimates based on 2003 data from company accounts.

other firms. One probable reason for this is that most potential sources of scale economy are exhausted before the output levels of the largest firms. Their frequent dominant market positions in new housing markets consequently do not seem to enable larger firms to add a higher than average mark-up above cost to their dwellings compared with those sold by other volume housebuilders.

Theoretically, it is easy to understand why local housing markets may still remain competitive despite large single firm market shares for new dwellings. Typical arguments highlighting potential competitive forces would refer to the competition from owners of existing dwellings or contestability in the form of the ability of other builders to enter local markets if existing developer returns become too high (Barker 2004).

Diversification benefits of size

The empirical analysis above was cross-sectional for one year only. This excludes the impact of one potentially important benefit of size, spatial diversification, because those benefits are derived over full housing market cycles and data are not available for such a long period of time.

Larger firm size probably does provide the significant benefit of making it possible to operate across several regions. In this way, firms may be able to diversify away some of the downside risk of local housing market fluctuations, especially of prices. For example, although Meen found that housing output levels across the nine English regions had similar cycles – suggesting that regional diversification has little impact on fluctuations in output volumes – there are significant differences in the amplitude and timing of regional house price cycles, with consequent knock-on effects on residential development profitability (Meen 1996; 2001). Such market diversification gains may, therefore, be considerable and help to explain why larger firms have grown in importance over time.

Regional diversification gains from size, therefore, may help to explain why larger, spatially diversified, firms increase their market shares at the expense of smaller firms. They are more likely to survive sharp housing market downturns than smaller volume builders, because the latter are inevitably more regionally and housing market segment specialised and, so, face a higher risk of failure in a housing market downturn. The largest firms are also at less risk of takeover. It should be noted, however, that the size benefits of diversification gains are isolated to the firms themselves, in terms of their probability of survival, because such diversification benefits do not produce any direct efficiency gains.

The regional diversification benefit of size may be even greater in the USA than the UK, because there are weaker correlations at the inter-regional and metropolitan area levels for housing output and price cycles (Pollakowski & Ray 1997). However, historically, USA house prices have not fluctuated to the same degree as those in the UK (see Chapter 3).[14]

Barriers to entry and the UK planning system

Ease of market entry is a key test of whether a market is competitive or not, because it is impossible for existing firms to collude with all potential entrants and, in a free market, new entrants would be attracted whenever margins rose above the norm. The question arises consequently of how easy it is to enter a regional housing market in the UK.

Ease of entry is generally regarded as a characteristic of housebuilding because of its low fixed capital requirements and mobile workforces. In principle, entrants simply have to buy a few plots of land, hire subcontract labour and buy some materials in order to set up in business: hence, the small firm characterisation of the industry.

Yet entry cannot be that easy in the UK as small builders' market shares have been steadily declining, as noted earlier. Similarly, to set up from scratch as a volume builder is also arduous. There are two potential constraints, both of them related to the land market. The first is a pipeline effect: how long does it take to set up production at somewhere near the optimal output size? The second is a potential land-use plan entry-barrier effect as a market 'outsider' when land supply is constrained below free market clearing levels.

With regard to the pipeline effect, to produce around 500 units annually in a regionally-based operation requires a number of years' investment in setting up an operation and assembling residential development land. A three-year land bank is roughly needed to ensure continuous production and to avoid a lack of sites holding up production. The arithmetic of typical sales from any one site and the three years' time horizon means that an entrant to a regional market has to purchase between 15 and 45 sites to enter it. Not only does that require a considerable amount of capital but it also creates a significant procurement exercise. Land sites have to be identified, purchased and the proposed developments on them put up for planning approval. This whole process takes considerable time. New entrants consequently face high risks that demand in a housing market may have weakened significantly by the time their products are ready for sale. The institutional framework of land assembly consequently imposes on new entrants high sunk costs and significant uncertainties, which together act as a significant deterrent to entry. Those costs and uncertainties are increased the longer the planning process takes and the more uncertain is its outcome. The UK system of requiring detailed planning permission for every new development, therefore, may act as a significant barrier to entry.

Concerning the land-use plan entry-barrier effect, any system of restricting land supply through a forward looking plan is likely to lower housebuilder competition for a number of reasons. With less land to go around, higher land costs will act as a barrier to entry for undercapitalised (typically small) builders. In addition, such a land-use plan reduces the uncertainty of where to purchase land by indicating the location of permitted urban growth during the period of the plan. This simultaneously provides important information on where and how much land needs to be bought to block its acquisition by others. Early movers into such a planned land market, therefore, may easily end up making it hard for others to compete with them.

The nature of the UK planning system confers additional information benefits on 'insiders', including existing residential developers, at both stages of the planning process: plan formulation and the granting of planning permission.

First, a local development framework identifies a ten-year horizon of new housing land, with a pipeline of five years of currently developable land (Rydin 2003).[15] In formulating land availability plans as part of this process, local planning authorities consult with existing residential developers and landowners. There is anecdotal evidence from local plan inquiries over the last decade or so that individual developers are active in lobbying to bring their own sites into the category of being allocated for development in the next period, while overtly or covertly lobbying to have their competitors' sites not allocated. Potential future new entrants to a housing market obviously have no say in this process at all.

Second, planning permission applications are assessed on a wide range of criteria, some of which are locally specific and not widely publicised. There is an imperfect correspondence between granting planning permission and the allocation of sites in a local development framework. In principle, allocated sites may be refused and non-allocated sites granted permission for a development as part of an often-praised flexibility in the UK system (Cullingworth & Nadin 2001). If refused permission, developers may appeal to central government adjudicators, who may override the local decision. The result is that high success ratios in this procedure require extensive negotiating ability; detailed knowledge of local planning criteria and comparable policies elsewhere; knowledge of the appeals systems and precedents; and an ability to hire expensive consultants and planning lawyers. Moreover, a firm's housing products need to have design and production characteristics that can easily be adapted to varying local planning requirements. These criteria favour larger firms and those with extensive prior experience of local planning policies (i.e. insiders).

So, in both its tight restrictions on land supply in many localities with high housing demand and in its institutions, the UK planning system may well favour larger, incumbent firms over others.

What are the implications of such restrictions on competition? Two possibilities need to be considered. The first is the potential for market power, either as monopolies or oligopolies. The empirical finding relating to the constant profit margin per unit of output discussed earlier does not indicate that the largest firms are able to command higher returns, so the monopoly argument looks weak. However, relatively constant profit margins cannot of themselves rule out the possibility of explicit or tacit collusion between firms in local new housing markets – in fact, they could be an outcome of such strategic market behaviour. There is simply no hard evidence on whether such market practices exist or not. Yet, given the volatility of the UK housing market, it seems unlikely that explicit collusion could be maintained between housebuilders across the whole of a market cycle, especially at times when margins are falling sharply. If firms have an expectation that any agreement to restrict competition will unravel at some unknown stage in the further, they are less likely to commit to a collusive agreement.

Excess returns, consequently, do not seem to be a major issue. Nonetheless, there may be subtler and potentially more damaging economic effects of the altered competitive environment under strong planning constraint. These relate to such matters as supply responses to rising prices and rates of innovation.

Arguments about investment under uncertainty suggest that firms have a 'real option' benefit from waiting because more information will then be available to them. This option value of waiting has to be overcome if investment is to take place (Dixit & Pindyck 1994). One possible counter to the information benefits of delay is the fear that a competitor will make earlier moves and, hence, take the market from the hesitant investor. Evidence of this real option type of effect in residential housing has been found by Mayer & Sommerville (2002). They found that builders of multi-storey apartments in Vancouver respond to market uncertainty by delaying building, but that this effect was negated when there were many other competitors in a locality.

By limiting the possibility of competition and providing information on the pattern of future development, the UK planning system may undermine counteracting influences to real option induced investment delay. House-builders having residential development land with planning permission can be cautious with respect to rising house prices. In other words, they can raise their outputs slowly in response to increasing demand, safe in the knowledge that potential competitors cannot enter the market and satisfy pent-up demand because of planning-induced land shortages. If this hypothesis is correct, the initial restriction of land supply by the planning system induces a further weakening of supply responses by altering competition amongst housebuilders.

A similar argument can be made with respect to innovations. Firms can adopt wait-and-see attitudes to product and process innovation, knowing that others cannot enter using innovations to capture their market, because such entrants could never obtain sufficient land to do so. This may help to explain why, for example, modern timber frame techniques are more prevalent in Scotland than in England. Their more rapid introduction in Scotland and their slow penetration into the English market may consequently have something to do with the markedly greater restrictiveness of the planning system in England, as well as the relatively minor differences in climate between the two countries and the highly thermal values of timber-frame over traditional brick-and-block techniques.

Conclusion

This chapter has examined concentration in the UK housebuilding industry and compared it with that in the USA. The degree of concentration in the UK is particularly high and it has been growing for many decades. A series of potential scale and scope economies were examined to see whether they might explain growing concentration. Scale economies in production, procurement, marketing and finance seem to be important at smaller firm sizes but appear to be exhausted at output levels well below those of the largest firms. However, diversification size benefits were identified in terms of permitting a wider spatial spread of housing markets in which firms are active when demand fluctuations between those markets are imperfectly correlated. However, none of these characteristics were unique to the UK and, so, cannot provide a full explanation for the exceptional importance of large firms there.

What does distinguish the UK situation is its planning system. Long-term restrictions on residential land supply exist in areas of high housing demand. Moreover, the planning process is complex and contains significant discretion. It was argued here that these characteristics of the land market probably explain much of the high level of concentration.

There is no evidence of widespread monopoly abuse of their market power by the largest housebuilders. In fact, on a cross-sectional basis, their profits per dwelling seem to be no more than those of smaller firms. However, such high degrees of concentration and the way in which the planning system regulates the land market with no concern for the competitive implications of its actions do suggest that competition might be blunted. One possible effect is that by reducing uncertainty over competitors' actions, the planning system allows firms to focus primarily on uncertainties surrounding the state of the housing market and invest accordingly. In setting up their business strategies, firms do not have to fear a flood of competing dwellings in a particular housing market. They can advantageously smooth out production rates and be relaxed about innovations, costs and the non-price elements of competition.

This, of course, does not mean that the planning system is an implicit conspiracy to sustain the market positions of a few major housebuilders. It obviously is not and planners and developers are often at loggerheads over insufficient land release, delay and conflicting objectives. This suggested outcome of institutional framework of British housing supply, if it is correct, seems rather to be a classic case of the law of unintended consequences.

Notes

1   See surveys in Cheshire & Sheppard (2002, 2004); Evans (2004); Pogodzinski & Sass (1991).
2   In the UK, most private housing has warranty insurance and inspection for potential defects from an industry body called the National House-Building Council. This has proved to be a useful source of firm data.
3   The data are for 2003. 2004 figures show marked growth for some firms. For example, Taylor Woodrow grew by 18% and produced over 9000 homes and, so, has effectively joined the top four volume homes group.
4   Source: Office of the Deputy Prime Minister.
5   Brief company histories are available on companies' Websites.
6   The data are derived from company accounts and are produced in the trade magazine, *Housebuilder*.
7   The linear regression estimate is: $y = 2.7x - 12.1$ ($R^2 = 0.95$), where y = number of completions and x = number of direct employees.

8   Interestingly, Cho in her study of Korean housebuilding firms found that scale economies were exhausted above the 500-unit level as well (Cho 2003).

9   In recent years, an annual British housebuilding consumer satisfaction survey has been posted on the Web and there is not a close ranking of build quality with firm size (www.constructingexcellence.org.uk).

10 This practice is undertaken by around half of the top ten housebuilders.

11 The Scottish divisions of the larger firms, moreover, may use timber-frame techniques, while the English ones stick to more traditional methods.

12 The raw data are derived from companies and published in the *Housebuilder*.

13 The profits regression equation is:

Profit (£m) = 0.96 + 0.0171 × Dwellings (R^2 = 0.92), which implies that every additional dwelling increased operating profits by around £17 000 in 2004.

14 Chapter 12 considers some wider scale and scope economies in construction.

15 The UK Government currently proposes to extend this to fifteen years with more stringent criteria on ensuring that the five-year pipeline is a realistic one (ODPM 2005).

11

Construction and real estate professions and practices

Introduction

Both the construction and real estate industries extensively use professional workers and independent, professionally based, specialist consultancies and practices. This chapter explores some of the economic reasons for their existence and frequent organisational independence. In fact, examining these issues raises many questions about how enterprises in real estate and construction in general relate to each other. The argument downplays the explanations frequently found in historical investigations that emphasise status and power.[1] This is not to say that professions have little influence on the nature of the production processes of which they are a part – in fact, it will be argued here that they have a significant effect – but rather that the roles of professions have economic foundations that stem beyond the restriction of trade.

To an extent, some of the ground has already been covered in the chapters on real estate brokers, because they are one type of real estate profession (with many sub-categories). However, the issues focused on there related to particular aspects of the professional–client relationship, namely, the incentives associated with a small percentage fee and also the effects of the nature of a firm's business activities – specifically residential versus commercial brokerage. Here, a somewhat different perspective is taken because of the broader range of professions being considered, although this should be viewed more as an adjustment of the focus than a reformulation of the approach. More emphasis is placed on the significance of characteristics such as the signalling of competence and innovatory practices. As with real estate brokerage, there is an examination of firm structures and some discussion of the impact of globalisation on professional practices.

What is a profession?

There is no general precise definition of a profession. In the modern world, to a great extent, a professional worker is self-defined and the term profession is generally applied widely to journalists, economists, financial analysts and many others. Profession, in this sense, becomes virtually synonymous with 'middle-class job'. The term is also used to denote a mode of behaviour. To be 'professional' in common parlance is to undertake a task conscientiously and with skill. This common-sense notion highlights an important characteristic of a profession – the ability to signal to others that someone has competence and integrity. Another key aspect is that the tasks that professions undertake require specific 'skills', extensive knowledge acquired through lengthy education and experience. Professional people, therefore, have specialist knowledge. To maximise their earnings from using this knowledge, they have to signal this skill to potential clients and employers and simultaneously indicate that they will use their talents to the best of their ability in the interests of those who employ them.

The 'professional ideal' when translated into economic terms is a statement that an 'agent' is both highly competent at agreed tasks and has self-interests that are at one with the aims of the 'principal' that hires her or him. This is important because the information that is available to the principal and to the agent is different (i.e. is asymmetrical), with the agent having knowledge that he or she may wish to hide from the principal. That private, hidden information relates to the quality of work done. This may be poor either because the agent has insufficient skill or because they did not do the job properly. The 'professional ideal' is a statement that asymmetrical knowledge is not a problem for the client, because professionals do not take advantage of hidden knowledge. This ideal is often unachievable and situations where the principal–agent relationship fails to live up to it have spawned a huge literature in economics.

The information problem for the principal occurs at two stages: when appointing someone to undertake specific tasks and during the actual execution of those tasks. To win the job, professionals may lie about their skills, what work is required and how much it will cost the client and then fail to do the job properly. Professional people, by their nature, are likely to be adept at exercising 'opportunism' – that is, the ability to operate in their own self interest rather than those of an employer or client. If they are so minded, in order to win work, they can be highly accomplished at disguising the actual limits of their abilities and the true cost of a job. When undertaking the tasks, they can be similarly skilled at hiding shirking, any unnecessary effort done to maximise revenue, and plain incompetence. Finally, after the job has been completed, they may attempt to avoid liability for any mistakes made during it. Clients, consequently, have to place much trust in the professionals they hire. A client, for example, has to accept a lawyer's judgement of success in a legal matter or expensively consult others to check on that judgement. They then have to rely on the advocate pursuing their case in the best possible way with the utmost vigour.

The fundamental problem for the client, consequently, is being able to discriminate between good and bad professionals. When private information is widespread, it might cause a market to fail, because if clients cannot distinguish between the good and bad, they will be unwilling to pay much for the service. This will make it uneconomic for professionals to spend time in training to gain the competence that clients want. The bad will have driven out the good, because adverse selection has ensured that the low price, bad quality option is the only feasible one.

Once a professional is employed, the problem of cheating (moral hazard) arises and the client will bear the cost of it. The client needs mechanisms for checking on the behaviour of professionals as they work, or of drawing up incentives that ensure that the interests of the principal and agent are closely combined. Clients, of course, typically in many parts of real estate and construction, are not final consumers but other businesses.

Such information asymmetries may create significant problems in real estate and help to explain the potentially conflicting nature of construction and the reasons for its organisational structure (Ball 1988; Winch 2001; 2002). What is needed are means in the public domain to enable competent, honest professionals convincingly to distinguish themselves from the incompetent and dishonest. Clients simultaneously need ways of finding out about professionals. Professional bodies and professional practices/firms are the institutional means by which this information trade is made possible at low transaction cost.

The most common means for professionals to indicate their abilities and integrity is for them to acquire formal educational qualifications and join a professional body. In this way, professionals overcome the adverse selection problem by indicating publicly that they are competent and that clients are actually buying high quality advice from them. The formal creation of a profession, with rules of conduct and non-trivial requirements for entry, may actually make a market for professional advice feasible, because without such an institution there is no means of identifying the competent from those who are not.

Membership of a professional body generally requires evidence of educational attainment and, often, further demonstration of practical experience. In addition, members of professional bodies are bound by rules of behaviour. Joining a professional association, thus, is costly in terms of acquiring the competence as well as paying the annual fees. The investment, however, has a pay-off in terms of improving a person's credibility as a professional.

One way of looking at the function of educational qualifications and professional association membership is that they help to turn individuals' competences into reputations that are public goods. Being able to refer to a person's educational qualifications or membership of a professional body greatly reduces the search costs of finding out about their abilities, because people will have general knowledge about a degree-giving body or a professional body at relatively low cost. The less well known, or the lower the reputation, of the university or professional association, the more limited is the benefit of acquiring accreditation from them. A rational professional, therefore, would invest in accreditation until the extra cost of acquiring better quality qualifications equalled the additional expected earnings.

Universities, through their educational activities and standards, not only transfer knowledge to an individual but also confer on him or her a reputation for competence by virtue of the reputation of the university and its specific courses. Universities and professional bodies, furthermore, can mutually gain by co-operating. Professional bodies can advise on courses and screen the ones that they find acceptable, raising the desirability of those courses to students. Universities simultaneously enhance the reputation of those professional institutes by allowing them to undertake such roles.

In some instances, the state further reinforces such reputational effects by requiring membership of a professional institution before being able to practise. Architects in the UK, for example, have to be registered with the Architects Registration Board and can only do so by demonstrating evidence of qualifications and competence. Governments tend to enforce membership when public safety is at risk – as with health related activities and the safety of built structures – or when the law itself is involved, such as over who can represent people in court. Governments, in addition, offer charters to professional bodies that give them *de facto* monopoly rights over professional activities in particular spheres. By doing this, governments implicitly transfer all or part of the role of regulation to the professional body in question. This might be done for efficiency reasons, for example, because it is seen as more effective or, for distributional reasons, say, to reduce public costs by imposing them on the profession itself.

Lobbying by self-interested professionals may be effective in turning policy to their advantage. In particular, professionals are likely to prefer low external control in order to limit monitoring and reporting costs; to constrain potential adverse publicity that public accountability might bring; to be in a position to facilitate greater control over the education and the role of the profession; and, perhaps, to be granted official sanction for restrictive trade practices. The rent-seeking and public good aspects of the relationship between governments and professional bodies are likely to be intertwined and complex. Even so, professional bodies can claim to be some of the oldest examples of that modern vogue, the public–private partnership.

Professions in real estate and construction

There are a large number of distinct professions associated with the provision of built structures. They fall into three general functional types:

1. *Market professionals* They offer advice on market conditions; act as agents for parties in transactions and management; assist in market search in a variety of ways – site or office user identification, building planning and land-use planning advice, etc.; and, finally, undertake valuations.
2. *Production professionals* They provide skills in the design and management of building projects. Architects, and structural and consulting engineers provide the main design input, aided by other specialists, such as heating and ventilation and lift (elevator) engineers. Valuation engineers interrelate with the design professions to try to maximise value for money in meeting design objectives, through advice on layout, building materials, the building process, etc. Construction management may involve a mix of professions, generally under the guise of a project manager or some similar sort of management structure.
3. *Information and monitoring professionals* On the information side, they evaluate market conditions by providing data and analysis on construction costs, and assist in the formulation of specific projects by providing cost estimates for designs and planned construction programmes. Monitoring roles compare work outcomes with initial plans and construction costs with initial estimates. Any variations in initial specifications will also be costed and monitored, and additional claims for payment formulated and submitted to the client. These tasks are generally undertaken in Britain by quantity surveyors.

Construction and real estate are areas of economic activity with large numbers of professions. Activities are labour intensive with a marked division of labour, highlighting the productive benefits of extensive specialisation. A significant number of the specialisms are 'white collar', knowledge-based ones where competence needs to be signalled to prospective employers and clients. These areas consequently are ideally suited to the professional approach to the formation of labour markets and the associated service markets in which professional labour is the key input. Professional bodies, once they are established, play important roles in influencing the markets in which their designated professions operate. Professionalism in Britain is particularly extensive and fragmented. This is probably because the professions had an early start there, with rapid industrialisation and urbanisation starting in the eighteenth century – many decades before elsewhere. Historically, individual professions have often been able to win state recognition and royal charters but are less successful at excluding others from doing so. In Britain, for instance, there is not an over-arching profession with pre-eminence across many aspects of professional advice and management in the development process, although this has been more the case with architecture in a number of other European countries. Finally, British professional bodies have been particularly successful at reinforcing their permanence by forming extensive partnerships with education providers. In this way, they have helped to establish their callings as worthy careers.

On the one hand, professional fragmentation has been argued to be a cause of conflict and inefficiency in the British construction industry for many years. It was a theme of Bowley's influential book (Bowley 1966) and has been commented on at regular intervals ever since. On the other hand, the large number of professions may have the beneficial effect of intensifying competition and keeping monopolistic practices amongst the professions in check.

The competences of specific construction and real estate professions overlap considerably. For example, many would claim to be able to manage a real estate project, especially smaller scale ones. The roles of architects and engineers in design are another case in point. This overlap increases substitutability, so if individual professions raise their fees they may find other professions underbidding them. Competitive rivalry between professions encourages them to expand their respective numbers. Profession size is important in terms of being able to influence education, the significance of representation on industry bodies and in relation to government. These inducements to expand memberships increase labour supply, thereby

Table 11.1 Some professions associated with real estate and construction in the UK.

Professional body	Membership, 2001
British Institute of Architectural Technologists	7 500
Chartered Institute of Building	40 000
Chartered Institution of Building Services Engineers (CIBSE)	15 000
Institution of Civil Engineers	75 000
Institution of Structural Engineers	22 000
Royal Institute of British Architects	32 000
Royal Institution of Chartered Surveyors	86 000

Source: Relevant Webpages.

limiting the possibility of a monopolistic restricting of labour supply through tight controls on profession numbers.

Table 11.1 lists some of the relevant professional organisations in the UK. A brief survey of their Web page material shows a strong similarity in the professional aims of such organisations and those in other countries would profess similar themes. RIBA's mission statement exemplifies the ideal of a professional body: 'The advancement of architecture and the promotion of the acquirement of the knowledge of the arts and sciences connected therewith'.[2] The language may be grand and arcane but professional promotion and education are identified as the core themes.

There is considerable inertia in the number and scope of professional institutions. Setting up a professional body is costly, so new ones tend only to evolve if they can do more for specific groups than an already existing professional body. Pre-existing bodies also have the advantage of prior links with government and the educational sector. Size matters in achieving institutional aims, so starting from small beginnings is often hard, because a professional body needs to have significant weight in order to be successful in promoting an identifiable, widely recognised profession.

There are scale and scope economies in operating nationally and, increasingly, internationally. Overhead costs are high, so a professional institution must have a large membership to keep fees within reasonable limits. One means of achieving this is for an institution to draw related activities under its umbrella. The traditional practice divisions of the Royal Institution of Chartered Surveyors (RICS) illustrate the diversity of specialisms that may be contained within one professional body – general surveying practice, quantity surveying, land agency and agricultural services, building surveying, planning and development, land surveying, mineral surveying and auctioneers of fine art. Size breeds success – as indicated by the several previously independent surveying professions over the years that have opted to join RICS: the independent quantity surveyors body joined in the early 1980s and, more recently, the much smaller technical surveyors group in 2000.

Not all professionals are likely to be members of their field's professional institution, unless it is a legal requirement of being able to practise. Even those who choose not to join their professional body still benefit from that institution's attempts to improve or sustain the status of the profession and lobby in its interests. One of the implicit aims of a professional body, therefore, is to keep the number of such free-riders low. If free-riding is high, the professional body loses prestige and is less able to control the rules of entry to the profession. This, in turn, may weaken the profession itself.

Co-ordination and co-operation

So far, the relationship between a single professional and a client wanting a new building has been examined in terms of the (hidden) real competence and behaviour of the professional. In practice, a variety of different types of professional come together. To achieve client objectives, each type of specialist has not only to be competent but also to perform as the client believes they have agreed. This requires them to achieve a specific set of predetermined aims and co-operate with others in doing so. The moral hazard of behaving in a different way from that agreed in the initial contract/agreement becomes significantly more complex in those intertwined relationships than in a straightforward direct one with clients.

Trust between professionals is vital, because not every task can be laid out in minute detail, nor can all events be forecast. Each specialist will also have information on a project that others do not, because of their particular skill base and their specific involvement in the project. Co-operation and trust are not costless. Undertaking work in a way that someone else can follow on from easily may take more time, for example, than doing it in a slapdash fashion. Furthermore, if something goes wrong or not according to plan, accepting responsibility for the problem may lead to considerable personal costs; whereas trying to pass the blame on to others creates the chance to avoid responsibility, but at a potentially high cost in terms of the confusion, misinformation and delay generated.

A simple prisoners' dilemma game illustrates the reasons why professionals may persistently fail to co-operate. Assume there is a complex building project that involves input from two enterprises: one is a firm of project managers that instruct all the construction workers on a site, and the other, an architectural practice that makes the design and provides drawings to the project manager. If problems arise in the execution of those drawings, the architect may have to accept liability for the cost and will have to provide amendments in a timely fashion. Yet the project manager, to increase earnings, could unreasonably claim that the initial drawings were hard to understand and contained hidden and unexpected tasks. When construction problems arise, moreover, the project manager could try to blame the architect's drawings. In a similar vein, the architect might be uncooperative by producing poorly specified drawings and by trying to pass blame on to the project manager when things go wrong because of their inadequacy. When both the project manager and architect adopt opportunistic strategies, the worst situation is created, with much time lost in arguments, poor resolution of problems and the possibility of lengthy litigation. If the project manager and architect co-operate, project costs are kept down but when one or other fails to co-operate costs rise, and the highest costs occur when both refuse to co-operate.

These possibilities are illustrated in the pay-off matrix shown in Table 11.2. This matrix identifies four possibilities in a project: (1) both parties co-operate with each other; (2) the architect fails to co-operate but the project manager is prepared to; (3) the reverse of (2); and (4) neither co-operates. In each cell, the left-hand number is the net profit to the project manager in each of the specified situations and the central one is the architect's net profit. The right hand number in brackets is the project's overall cost. (The numbers are in £m and, for simplicity, both the project manager and the architect are assumed to have the prospect of similar returns.) If both co-operate, the project comes out at the lowest cost (£30m); if only one party is awkward, the project's cost rises to £40m; and, if both fail to co-operate, costs are greatest at £70m. In situations where one party is trying to be co-operative and the other is not, the pay-off to the non co-operative partner is assumed to be the greatest, while the other loses out because the difficult one exploits helpfulness.

Table 11.2   Co-operation in building.

		ARCHITECT	
		Co-operate	Don't co-operate
PROJECT MANAGER	Co-operate	7, 7 (30)	1, 5 (40)
	Don't co-operate	5, 1 (40)	3, 3 (70)

It is obviously preferable if the architect and project manager co-operate with each other, but are they likely to? If one does not trust the other, it would be irrational for them to co-operate, because each would then fear that they would end up being in the loser's position of finding that the other is trying to profit from their helpfulness. So, unless both can trust each other, the most rational strategy for them is to be unco-operative and the costs of the project will be at their greatest and the client loses the most.

This extreme case of no co-operation indicates that institutional rules and arrangements are likely to arise to minimise the adverse consequences of non-co-operation. It is also assumed for simplicity that the outcomes were certain; whereas in practice large building projects contain many uncertainties, which need to be managed and dealt with in a co-operative way. Furthermore, the illustration was of a simple two-agent relationship, whereas in real estate and construction multiple suppliers often exist, as on large construction sites, which make relationships far more complex, the possibilities of opportunism greater and detection of it more difficult.

Encouraging co-operation

Detailed contracts

The obvious way to try to ensure parties do as required is to specify what is needed in good initial contracts. These can lay out a whole set of rules, incentives and procedures in relation to uncertain events. Typical construction-related ones include decision-making hierarchies, compensation for unseen events (atypical weather, client changes of mind, etc.), penalties and performance bonuses, payment triggers and rates for additional work, conflict resolution processes, standardised event procedures (including adjudication), effort monitoring and quality controls (Murdoch & Hughes 2000).

It is obviously costly to write such contracts and many run to hundreds of pages. As potential issues are likely to emerge time and again within building work, standard forms of contract emerge and remain in existence for long periods of time. This reduces the expense of contract writing, because all eventualities do not have to be thought of from scratch but are encapsulated in this type of public good. The 1995 Engineering and Construction Contract, for example, is commonly used in the UK. Sometimes parties fail to agree on standard forms of contract because one participant feels they are unreasonable. Early in the twentieth century, for instance, there was stand off between architects and building contractors in the UK, which was only resolved through state pressure, as the public sector was in danger of being a significant loser from the dispute (Ball 1988).

Contracts can also vary in terms of their basic incentive structures. Typical ones in construction are fee-based, fixed price and incentive formulations. Each of them is designed to assign risk and rewards in distinct ways and are consequently best in specific situations (Winch 2002).

Not only are contracts expensive to write, they are also inevitably incomplete. People have to think about all potential eventualities in the future, successfully negotiate over them, and write them down in a way that can be understood by the outside authorities assigned to enforce contracts (Hart 1995). Such issues are identified as 'bounded rationality' in the transaction costs literature (Williamson 1985). They imply that alternatives to contracts are also necessary.

Requiring credible commitments

Commitments are demonstrations of good faith arising through the imposition of severe cost penalties on agents if relationships break down. A typical method in construction is for an agent to post a bond, which is forfeited in specified circumstances. Other options would be the imposition of high fee charges for dispute resolution or large, upfront and unrecoverable, project specific investments.

Repeated interaction

The game above implicitly assumed that the architect and project manager were only going to work together on one project, so that it did not matter whether they failed to reciprocate any offer of trust, because they would never work together again. If, alternatively, they are likely to work together repeatedly, they are more likely to come to an understanding and to co-operate in order to avoid recriminations in future. Put another way, there is now a cost to defecting which alters long-term pay-offs, so that the co-operate-fully option is more likely to occur.

Such repeat situations are observed in the real world of real estate and building but, even so, pairing together repeatedly is generally infrequent because clients choose their teams for reasons other than the fact that each has an implicit hold over the others through their repeated coming together on projects.

Reputations

Clients do not necessarily have to observe how agents behave or interact. They can ask others and rely on reputations. It is common for clients to take professional advice on the specialist professional teams to hire. Alternatively, they can delegate this task to an experienced individual or firm as project manager and rely on their information about agents' reputations.

Minimise the pay-offs to opportunistic behaviour

One way of thinking of the consequence of repeat interaction is that it narrows the pay-offs between co-operating and not co-operating. There are other ways of doing this, all of which aim to minimise the degree of asymmetrical information and the situations in which it might have a significant effect on cost outcomes. Common devices involve commitments, mentioned above, or designing management structures with the aim of limiting opportunistic behaviour possibilities for any professional in a team. Partnering between construction-related enterprises and clients is another modern option (Mohr & Spekman 1994; Bresnen & Marshall 2000). In this formulation, providers of construction and real estate services commit themselves to close relationships with their clients. This is undertaken via formalising mutual objectives, agreeing on managerial rather than contractual/external problem resolution procedures and continually searching for measurable improvements – though the vagueness of the term 'partnering' still makes the exercise an uncertain one.[3]

Purchase from specialist intermediaries

Another option for clients is to rent or buy a completed structure from a specialist developer, rather than initiate a development themselves. Developers are repeat users of agencies in construction and are likely to have superior skills and information regarding them and the technicalities of construction process. They should consequently procure buildings more cheaply than novices.

Undertake extensive monitoring

When information is one-sided, clients have incentives to improve the knowledge they have through continuous monitoring and quality control. Clients, for example, may set up parallel professional teams to those actually undertaking specific tasks as monitors of the former and sources of advice as the project proceeds. The cost of this route makes it more likely on complex, large-scale projects. It is also an option better suited to some circumstances than others. Where, for instance, considerable creative or innovative input is required, and participants need to be highly personally motivated, the extra surveillance may be stifling in its effects.

The limits of professionalism

There are obviously limits to what professionalism as a practice can achieve. The discussion of incentives, co-ordination and co-operation in the previous section, for instance, hardly made reference to the ideals of professionalism.

Promotion rather than control

Overall, professionalism has greatest success with adverse selection problems. Professional bodies can help to maintain educational standards and signal their members' competences. They are far weaker when confronted with cheating (moral hazard). When faced with breaches of their rules, professional bodies have limited information on which to judge the existence of misbehaviour, constrained processes and only weak sanctions to impose on transgressors. There is also a natural reluctance of fellow professionals to discipline colleagues.

Once there is sufficient evidence for professional bodies to discipline a member, there also is often enough evidence to secure a ruling in a court of law but, if there is no such evidence, the member may be able to take legal redress against any disciplinary body for defamation of character. The threat of legal action itself helps to turn professional investigations into slow, quasi-legal processes for fear of the liabilities that could be imposed if faster and broader, but less legally scrupulous, procedures were followed. Disciplining those few found to be at fault is unlikely to alter the behaviour of others, because the chance of being found out and punished is remote. Consequently, the pay-offs to a group of skilled personnel of having a professional body that was strict towards its members are small.

Unsurprisingly, therefore, professional bodies concentrate on 'promoting the profession' and education, rather than on disciplining members for failing to behave in conformity with broadly defined professional ethics. This emphasis, in fact, is true of all professional bodies rather than simply of real estate and construction-related ones. Some, like doctors' organisations, may have strict disciplinary rules but they tend to exist only for fear that the state may instigate compulsory disciplinary measures if such voluntary schemes are not put in place and are shown to have some effect.

Anecdotal evidence for the limited disciplinary role of real estate and construction related professional bodies is the extremely low profile that this aspect of their activities has on their Websites. It is also extremely difficult in general to pursue cases against such professionals because of complexity and the extent of hidden information. As a result, the costs of complaint often outweigh the benefits. Take, for example, the experience of the Architects Registration Board set up in Britain in 1997 as a statutory regulatory, rather than a professional, body. It does publish the annual number of consumer complaints against registered architects. In 2003, when around 30 000 architects were registered, it dealt with less than 900 enquiries from consumers about architects' services.[4] These data either suggest a high degree of honesty on the part of architects or that aggrieved parties see little benefit in pursuing this particular grievance route.

Inter-professional conflict

The structuring and rivalry of professions do not aid the generation of inter-professional trust and co-operation. Real estate and construction professions are renowned for their mutual animosity and lack of respect for each other's skills. This is partly because of the experience of trying to co-operate but, also, because of competition between them over their relative status and areas of competence. In some cases, there are fundamental differences in their roles: such as those between land-use planners, who often wish to control land use in non-market ways, and property advisers, who are trying to maximise client returns. Moreover, as each profession tries to raise its own profile or to spread into a wider range of activities, it inevitably comes into conflict with other professions. For example, who should have overall control of the management of a building project? This has historically been a major battleground between architects, construction firms and others.

Mere difference itself is important. Professional bodies promote a profession, via shared identities and experiences and peer group emulation, and over many years they have been highly successful at doing this. Yet, this process intensifies distrust and disdain for other related professions, with professional colleagues more likely to swap anecdotes about bad instances of inter-professional co-operation than good ones. This negativity would correspond to the results of studies in experimental economics, which show that people tend to trust those similar to them but not those who are different and that experiences of failed trust are cumulative, with poor experiences in the past affecting subsequent behaviour and reputation (Glaeser *et al.* 2000; Clark and Sefton 2001). Even if two individuals from different professions wish to co-operate, they may still have conflicting viewpoints and ways of working because of differences in the interests and outlooks of their professions.

As there are far more professions in real estate and construction than in most industries, the problems of professional co-operation are particularly acute. They are exacerbated by conditions of change, which relate to technology, product mix and the state of the real estate and construction cycles. All this makes attempts at team building and co-operation especially important but simultaneously difficult.

Self-interest over public interest

There are several other areas, apart from the limits of co-operation, where professionalism promotes the self-interest of specific groups more than general interests. Monopoly and other restrictions of trade are obvious examples. Entry requirements, for example, might be made excessively tough or approved courses restricted with the aim of limiting potential recruits in order to raise the future earnings of existing members.

Other self-interested actions may be significant as well. The educational requirements laid down by professional bodies might emphasise factors that differentiate a profession at the expense of more generally useful skills commonly needed in building (e.g. by playing down quantitative, financial, managerial or team-working skills). Professional bodies might also be resistant to technical changes that require new competences or erode existing roles. Screening devices might be set to ensure greater group homogeneity rather than being based on more objective technical criteria.

Professional bodies, as was argued earlier, do generate public goods but, once entrenched, their actions are difficult to monitor or contest, except in blatant cases, such as when in direct contradiction of competition law. By becoming quasi-regulatory bodies, albeit remaining in the private sphere, they consequently fall foul of the general observation that it can be difficult to regulate the regulators.

Reputation, firm size and the size of professional bodies

The limits of professionalism in dealing with moral hazard problems influence the characteristics of professional practices and firms. For, if a professional institution cannot induce client confidence, individuals and firms may have more success.

The traditional characteristic of many professions is one of many small-scale private practices, consisting of an individual owner or a few qualified professionals as partners, plus a handful of ancillary staff and juniors. Such organisations tend to serve only a local market, because locality gives them a means to gain a reputation. Even when a local client does not have repeated contact with a professional, each mixes in the same neighbourhood business milieu and, so, can gather knowledge about each other relatively costlessly. Clients also have a relatively costless means of retribution for bad work, because they can easily spread damaging allegations about misconduct within such a narrow spatial market. This sanction regarding reputation limits the threat of opportunistic behaviour by the professional.

More generally, probity is one of the important assets of most professional firms for gaining clients. The precise importance of probity, of course, varies with the type of service being provided. With architects, 'creativity' is central (Blau 1984; Winch & Schneider 1993) and for others, perhaps, innovation or interpersonal skills. No matter the most important characteristic, each involves creating and maintaining a reputation.

Many professions' tasks involve actions that have only limited economies of scale. Hence, as long as there is sufficient work around to enable specialisation to occur in the first place, production-oriented scale economies may often be limited thereafter. This is not surprising as such skilled tasks are labour-intensive. The range of specialisms in a local market depends on the scale of that market, with greater professional specialisation as market size thresholds are achieved. Small, localised professional practices may, therefore, take on a variety of tasks to keep up turnover.

When firms operate at a wider spatial scale than the local, firm size often matters for their reputations because the information-rich context of the local market no longer holds. Instead, size becomes an important symbol of a firm's abilities. A large, well-known and long established firm implies expertise and competence even to those with no direct knowledge of them. If all clients are locally based, this extra signal is unnecessary. Market-makers might also emerge in some contexts, with knowledge of the abilities and behaviour of small firms that can be transmitted to clients, either directly as their employees (as in the case of national housebuilders and local subcontractors) or as their professional agents (as with planning consultants and expert witnesses).

Even so, what is often necessary for nationally and internationally based professional practices to flourish extensively is the existence of client firms that also operate at such spatial levels. Being able to use the same professional agency across a wide variety of markets, moreover, may reduce the transaction costs of hiring professional services.

The scale of international activities in real estate has grown significantly in recent decades; not only in real estate but also in construction, where around 10% of services now involve a supplier based in another country (Campagnac *et al.* 2000). This has led to new tiers of large international professional firms emerging in many real estate and construction professional activities. They may form temporary teams (or more permanent link-ups in formal and semi-formal partnerships) as well as being in direct competition with each other, depending on the nature of particular markets, individual projects and specific complementarities.

The importance of client spatial reach was seen earlier in the analysis of the spatial spread of real estate service providers in Chapter 6, and this characteristic has been emphasised in the general literature on professional enterprises (Aharoni 1993; 1997; Brock *et al.* 1999). However, as noted earlier, there are likely to be scale and scope advantages to size as well. Those advantages may mean that, once established, large nationals might easily encroach on local markets and purely local providers disappear or remain only in specialist niches.

Scale and scope advantages generally extend into spheres beyond the remit of the direct skill competence of the professional and, so, do not contradict the observation of limited scale economies there. Instead, they refer to such factors as the benefits of market diversification, the economical provision of complementary services, knowledge transfer from one market to another, an ability to retain key staff by offering them career paths that take them through a range of activities and levels of seniority by moving from one office or activity to another, an ability to draw together ideas and disparate groups with the organisation to generate innovations, and a capacity to transmit innovations to new markets.

Of course, there are downsides to size. The effects of mistakes can be as easily transmitted as more positive corporate information. The case of the demise of Arthur Anderson worldwide in the wake of the Enron scandal is a frequently-cited instance. Yet Anderson was a rare exception rather than suggesting that benefits and costs of a global spread in accountancy services are finely balanced.

The routes to becoming an international professional practice are varied. They may be client driven, when, say, a multinational company takes its usual professional teams with it to new regions or countries, or when designers win national or international competitions. The preferred professional agency then can gain a foothold in broader markets. Alternatively, financial backers of real estate and other building investments may push for international rather than local professionals, because they are more aware of their competences and wish to be assured about project risks. Firms may also set up their own subsidiaries in new markets. This, however, is often a slow way to gain a reputation and contacts. A faster route, and one that has been particularly common internationally in recent years, is for professional firms to form partnerships with those already active in new localities or to take them over.

Firm sizes and internal organisation

There are now similar arrays of firm types in many real estate and construction professions, with a mega-tier of a handful of well-known international firms and a much larger number of nationally-focused or local ones. The smaller enterprises may still be traditional practices and partnerships. In contrast, many of the larger ones have converted to a corporate status, possibly with a public listing of their shares.

In common with professional practices in other industries, many in real estate and construction have relatively autonomous offices in each country or sub-division with a relatively light touch of central management. This reflects the typically collegial nature of governance at partner/ director level and the need to incentivise senior staff. Relatively permissive central management structures also echo the significance of local information in a context of differing business practices between countries (Maister 1982; Greenwood *et al.* 1990). As much professional work in real estate and construction is a co-operative effort, both within one organisation and between them, a series of practices and behaviours evolve to facilitate co-ordination. Research into them to date has been greatest with regard to architecture (Winch & Schneider 1993; Schmidt 2003; Lui & Ngo 2004; Winch 2005).

Large professional firms generally have internal management structures more common to major firms in general than to those in small professional practices. These include complex managerial hierarchies, profit or cost centres, corporate strategies, formal recruitment and promotion procedures, and other staff incentive structures. In part, larger professional firms adopt these managerial characteristics because of their size and the need to manage geographically spread businesses. Yet, with their staff, they face similar principal–agent problems and information asymmetries to those described above between client and professional. Detailed employee monitoring and other management practices help to avoid the threat of non-conforming behaviour by employees.

Employment practices in real estate and construction are the commonplace ones noted in studies of accountancy and law firms. Junior staff – often recent recruits from universities – do much of the work, associates supervise and train them, and partners or directors spend much of their time winning work. This hierarchy is often humorously termed 'grinders, minders and finders'. The more senior categories add value to the lower experience levels of the juniors. In addition, there is widespread implicit encouragement of those not marked for promotion to leave, so that they can be replaced by cheaper recent graduates (Maister 1982). This crude but effective incentive system not only encourages prodigious work rates for relatively low pay, it additionally induces significant job mobility between firms/practices and encourages the ambitious or more rebellious individuals to set up new enterprises. Such employment practices consequently act as an important conduit for knowledge transfer, innovation and competition.

Large professional practices and firms are generally strong supporters of the relevant professional institutions. That gives them influence over the general strategy of those institutions and also sustains the quality and educational attainment of their own recruits. Professional bodies, therefore, can generally easily encompass the needs of both large and small practices, because both gain considerably from the roles they perform.

Conclusions

It has been argued here that information problems are at the heart of the rationale for professionalism and professional institutions, both in terms of identifying skills (adverse selection) and minimising the effects of professionals failing to conform to the agreed aims of the client (moral hazard). It has been suggested that professionalism is better at coping with adverse selection rather than moral hazard problems, whereas the reputation of practices and larger firms was more likely to minimise moral hazard effects. The large number of professions related to real estate and construction was suggested to be a result of the complexities of the physical and market-oriented aspects of property development and the benefits of specialisation that arise as a result. Professional organisations also have their own scale economies and market structures, with cumulative processes that tend to favour the larger bodies over the smaller ones.

When evaluating the balance between the market efficiency inducing aspects of professionalism and the ones that constrain efficiency for the benefit of a profession's members, the overall conditions of market competition are significant. Competition in real estate and construction is generally high. There are a large number of professions with overlapping functions, limited incentives for individual professional bodies to restrict labour supply and growing international competition. As this is the case, it is likely that the beneficial effects of professionalism in terms of overcoming some of the problems of hidden knowledge outweigh the monopolistic tendencies inherent in creating a professional body.

This conclusion, however, can only be a matter of judgement of particular contexts, because of the extensive existence of private information. It is consequently hard to measure precise effects. A case for widespread public intervention, nevertheless, seems weak. The general policy that seems to underlie most governments' attitudes to the professions is one of setting broadly permissive legislative framework, informal monitoring and threats of intervention to limited monopolistic abuse. There is one caveat to this generally optimistic conclusion in the area of education. Because education is such an important part of the professional remit, and so much of it is publicly funded, there may be a case for better overviews of the educational requirements of professional bodies to ensure they do not encourage the negative aspects of professionalism. The problem then arises of defining what is a good education for the professions involved in real estate and construction, who should decide it, and who should monitor and control it. Unsurprisingly, most governments have avoided this contentious issue.

Notes

1 See, for example, the classic studies by Perkin (1989) and Lockwood (1989).
2 http://www.architecture.com
3 The UK's Construction Industry Board provides a good summary of partnering at http://www.ciboard.org.uk/Procrmnt/Partner.htm. For a more academic treatment, see Mohr and Spekman (1994).
4 *2004 Annual Report of Architects Registration Board* (http://www.arb.org.uk).

12

The distinctiveness of large construction firms

Introduction

Several aspects of the construction industry have already been covered in the previous chapters on analytical approaches, housebuilders and the professions. This chapter focuses on the non-housebuilding firms, which are generally known as contractors, because they undertake building work for known clients having won contracts from them. Although in the modern construction world, contractual relations can be extremely complex, contractors are usually the principal managers and executors of the construction process. They are the production lynchpins, turning initial concepts of building and infrastructure – and the designs made – into reality through the mobilisation of the necessary resources in something generally approximating to the most efficacious way. They are normally termed 'construction firms', though other terms like 'speculative housebuilders', 'specialist contractors' and other sundry enterprises simultaneously exist. For the sake of argument, the common labelling convention of construction firms will be adhered to here.

The scale of activity in contracting can go from the very small – such as minor repairs and small jobbing work – to the large and the truly gigantic, such as major office and retail complexes, industrial plants, significant public buildings, tunnels, bridges, airports and other transportation facilities. The technology used can similarly stretch physically from the mundane use of paintbrush and screwdriver to the previously untried edges of human knowledge, with a similar range evident in management and process techniques.

Somewhere along this continuum of products and technologies are economic pressures that lead to the growth of giant firms. In virtually every
country, the construction industry may be characterised by a mass of
small enterprises. Yet, above them is a size pyramid around whose apex
are industrial giants and most of their business is in contracting. For
example, in 2004 the largest UK construction firm had an annual turnover approaching £5 billion and they were only 21st in the global league,
according to one well-known league table (see later). Furthermore, the largest
firms have become significantly bigger in terms of their real turnovers
over the last decade or so.

How do such giants arise in an industry with precious little proprietary
technology and limited fixed assets? The existing literature is surprisingly silent on this matter. The discussion aims to provide some useful
pointers.

The pervasiveness of large construction firms

Market shares

There are no standardised international statistics on concentration ratios
in the construction industry but a few examples illustrate that, though
by no means the most concentrated of industries, larger firms in construction do tend to have significant market shares. Substantial amounts
of work are then subcontracted on by them but, obviously, they still play
the central co-ordinating role.

In the USA, for example, in 1997 firms with turnovers of $10 million
or more (the highest identified category in the data) had around a 45%
share of total non-residential construction, about 40% of which was
then subcontracted, according to the Census Bureau. In Australia in the
late 1990s, the five largest companies had a 16% share of non-residential
building and the top four civil engineers had a 25% share (DIST 1999).
In the UK, the top ten firms probably had roughly 25–30% of the non-
residential market in 2004 (author's own estimates based on two disparate
sources). A study of the Hong Kong market found high levels of concentration in residential property development with 60% of that market
shared between the top five developers in the first half of the 1990s. These
were predominantly local firms, while overseas contractors with relatively
high levels of concentration predominated in the other construction market sectors of public building and civil engineering. In contrast, general
building contracting was characterised by low levels of concentration and

local firms only (Chiang *et al.* 2001). China has until recently been run entirely on non-market economy principles and during that era there was a deliberate creation of giant enterprises within construction via decrees and state procurement practices. Those firms still play important roles (Xu *et al.* 2005).

International reach

Large firms are significant in many countries. Figure 12.1 lists the world's fifty largest construction firms by country of origin in two ways. The first column ranks them by total turnover and the second by turnover not in their country of origin to indicate the degree of international trade. Two Asian countries, Japan and China, lead the firm numbers amongst the world's fifty leading construction companies, followed by the USA. China apart, no developing countries feature and only a few Asian ones.[1] A surprisingly large proportion of the giant construction firms come from Europe, nineteen out of the fifty in fact, with some quite small-sized countries from there managing to feature in the world's top fifty. This Europe bias is heightened when it is recognised that the two largest firms are both French, while Germany, Spain and Sweden all feature in the top six, followed by a raft of Japanese producers. The USA only has one firm in the top ten at number five. The pecking order of giant construction firms consequently cannot simply be explained by the relative economic size of national economies, though advanced economies seem to be their principal location, with the exception of China.

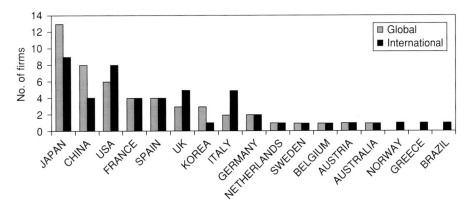

Figure 12.1   Number of firms in top fifty contractors ranked globally and by international activity by country of origin.

Note: 'Global' is the ranking by total construction contracting turnover; 'International' is the ranking by turnover outside the country of origin.

Source: Calibrated from data in *Engineering News-Record*.

The international trade in construction rankings also highlight some interesting regional differences (Figure 12.1). All three featured Asian countries in the giant firm rankings have noticeably fewer firms in the international top fifty than in the global ranking, which includes their domestic markets. Instead, Italy, the UK and the USA have a notably higher representation in international trade and three additional countries make an appearance, two of them small European ones.

The overall evidence from these data is that, while it may the case that large construction firms are common in many countries, they seem to play particularly important roles in parts of Asia and Europe.

Scale economies and the transferability of construction technologies

Scale and scope economies would be obvious explanations of the existence of giant firms, if they were present. Unfortunately, there are few studies available to provide the evidence. At a minimum, the presence of so many large firms indicates that significant diseconomies of scale are unlikely to exist but such an observation hardly constitutes a robust test of the benefits of size. The likely gains from specialisation suggest at least some scale economies above small firm sizes yet many such obvious scale economies would seem to be exhausted way before the size of the construction majors. A study of an intermediate size range of publicly quoted UK firms, for instance, found no evidence of a positive relationship between firm turnover and profitability. However, further suggestions on potential scale benefits are made in later sections.

One other characteristic of giant construction firms is their multi-divisional nature. Divisions act as semi-autonomous entities in their specialist sphere, typically with separate profit and loss accounts. They are hierarchically linked to the rest of the enterprise through a hierarchical bureaucratic structure, in which resources are allocated between competing divisions. As Williamson argues, such multi-divisional organisation design limits information overload at the centre and minimises threats of opportunistic behaviour in subordinates (Williamson 1985).

One possible constraint on scale benefits is that it is difficult for any individual construction firm to gain significant long-term advantages through technical competence. Fixed capital is generally low and where it is more important, as in some areas of civil engineering, it can be acquired from suppliers by all firms with few barriers imposed by patents and exclusive

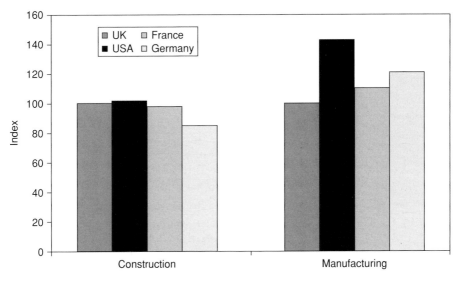

Figure 12.2 Comparative international productivity in construction and manufacturing. Indexes of total factor productivity, 1999.
Source: O'Mahony & de Boer (2002).

arrangements. New ways of doing things can equally be learnt by others, so that catch-up tends to be relatively quick. The only exception to this observation may exist in developing and very small countries, which may not have the indigenous resources, including skilled labour, to achieve rapid catch-up and, so, have to import construction technologies by hiring overseas contractors. This 'skills deficit' effect has been a long-term generator of international construction business (Linder 1994).

If technologies are highly mobile and easily acquirable, it is to be expected that construction productivity is relatively similar across countries and would be predicted to be more so than in many other industries. Studies of productivity based solely on labour inputs suggest this is not the case. They show quite significant variations but they are influenced by the choice of technique and the mix of types of construction work. Total factor productivity measures, which take account of other inputs as well as labour, are less affected by those factors. Instead, they show quite similar levels of productivity across several major economies (Figure 12.2, where the atypically lower score for Germany could be due to post-reunification factors). This similarity in construction productivity contrasts which the much greater variation existing between manufacturing sectors, where firm and industry specific influences seem to matter far more (O'Mahony & de Boer 2002; Ive *et al.* 2003).

General and construction-specific influences on firm size

A prime reason for large firms is that scale and scope economies exist, which give them competitive advantages over smaller producers. As the textbooks explain, scale and scope economies derive from a number of sources: technical, managerial, financial, marketing, purchasing and research and development. In addition, firms may benefit from external economies, including networks of suppliers and pools of skilled labour. Particular industries and the firms within them can then be examined for the significance of each of those factors. Construction is like any other industry in this respect. However, its distinctive characteristics are likely to mean that some sources of scale and scope economies are likely to be more important than others. The absence, for example, of product dedicated, high fixed-capital production processes has already been highlighted. What the literature suggests is that investigations of market–firm boundaries and country-specific factors are likely to be of particular importance.

The boundaries of the firm debate

The most popular way of examining construction markets, organisations and the boundaries between them is the transaction cost approach (Chapter 2). Greatest application of it is associated with explaining subcontracting (Winch 1989; 2002; Bridge & Tisdell 2004; Rodney Turner 2004). The general reasons for subcontracting were discussed earlier, in Chapter 9, and relate primarily to optimal resource employment issues and incentives. However, in its aims transaction cost economising goes beyond mere identification of a set of potential influences by endeavouring to quantify which activities are subcontracted. Moreover, the dynamics of the theory suggest that those tasks that are subcontracted should be the same for all firms operating in common institutional environments, rather than be influenced by features such as firm size. (For instance, it assumes that asset specificity occurs at any scale.) Large firms consequently should do no more tasks than smaller ones, so the sole difference is that they are involved in more transactions, which in construction generally means more markets. In other words, the prediction is that they are bigger only because they are in more places, not because they do things differently.

To an extent, this prediction is borne out in the earlier analysis of UK housebuilders (Chapter 10), where firms across a wide size range (beyond a minimum output efficiency point) were argued to undertake similar types of activity. However, the predictions of transaction cost economics are not fully corroborated by the housebuilding case study. First, some firms clearly do things differently in terms of the degree of subcontracting they undertake and their choice of technique (Ball 2005a). Second, scale was argued in Chapter 10 to give larger firms some advantages in both their input and output markets. There is consequently evidence of the importance of strategic behaviour, both in terms of within-firm competences and in relation to markets, which conforms more closely to what are often termed the resource-based and Porter-based views than to transaction cost economics (Chapter 2). This is surely likely to be the case in general construction as well as in housebuilding. It is hard to think that some of the world's giant construction firms are just the same as much smaller companies, apart from being multiplied manyfold in turnover.

Concern over the lack of firm specificity in transaction cost economics has led several construction industry specialists to promote the resource-based view of firms as a means of explaining firm competences. De Haan and his colleagues have undertaken a series of case studies of construction firms, which they suggest supports the resource-based view (De Haan *et al.* 2002). One recent study has an ingenious matrix of firm types, technologies and associated plausible market conditions, drawing from both transaction cost economics and the resource based view literatures (Bridge & Tisdell 2004). However, these approaches still do not convincingly enable the question to be asked of why giant construction firms exist. The problem is that identifying differences in the competences or market circumstances of more or less successful firms does not of itself explain why those differences occur or what effects they have. Only potentially refutable causal statements stand a chance of doing that. As Chapter 2 argued, the task of assembling such a theory comprehensively is hard, to say the least, when dealing with such entities as markets, institutions and organisations. They are open to so many causal influences and many factors are difficult to distinguish or to measure.

Fortunately, a number of causal statements can be made about existing large construction firms. Essentially, the argument is to look for the drivers of corporate change, because a dynamic process is more likely to enable evaluation of an underlying theory than a static one. The argument is that large construction firms arise because they benefit from a mix of institutional, technological and market factors and that these elements tend to interrelate and have effects on each other over time. As such, in terms of organisation theory it is an eclectic economic viewpoint.

An illustration of the argument directly relates to subcontracting. Rather than seeing subcontracting as a potential prospect for a given set of technically necessary processes, another hypothesis is to treat it as making possible new activities (i.e. technologies) within firms, which open new opportunities. If a construction firm employs all the resources necessary to undertake a range of tasks in a (usually weakly) hierarchical system, much of that firm's effort is going to be involved with monitoring and controlling what takes place before contracts are won, during their execution, and in their aftermath until all outstanding matters are resolved. This is not simply a series of internal events but also necessitates dealing with many third parties over these issues. The focus will be on progressing jobs to ensure a profit and limiting adverse consequences as they arise.

Subcontracting widens firm options as well as transfers particular tasks within a project to others. Firms are able to do different things as a result and to act strategically, including winning and managing particular arrays and types of project, developing new competences and innovating, all of which may lead to increased productivity. In this way, production and transaction technologies change (i.e. firm competences are transformed, rather than just tasks being transferred from one party to another). Subcontracting permits economies of scale by enabling firms to specialise and simultaneously to manage a much larger array of projects. The proposition holds equally for subcontracting enterprises. They can focus on their specialisms and above a certain size gain managerial and other within-firm benefits.

So, in an industry like construction – which is associated with a mixture of physical technologies (i.e. built structures and the means by which they are created) and managerial and personnel technologies (i.e. organisation and personal capabilities) – subcontracting changes and improves the overall technology mix, particularly in a dynamic context. A useful working hypothesis is to suggest that the greater the number of projects undertaken by enterprises, the higher is their productive efficiency. Firm size consequently matters.

Gains arise for a variety of reasons, including learning-by-doing plus certain features of firm architecture examined below. The scale at which these effects run out is an empirical matter. The objective here is not to postulate on the causes of all potential scope and scale economies but, rather, to identify certain factors that make giant firms a viable form of business organisation. So, the question arises even in a speculative exercise, such as the one here, are economies likely to be exhausted well below the giant firm category? The possibility that they do run out does not preclude the existence of very large firms, either if constant returns to scale still exist or because large firms have better survival rates. The largest firms then are simply no more efficient producers than their smaller brethren. Even so, it is worthwhile exploring more positive scale factors.

Information and communications technology is likely to have increased optimal sizes, by improving communication, information handling and analysis. Consequently, the threat of information overload has been reduced and means of constraining opportunism through enhanced analysis and monitoring options enabled.

One significant development in recent years has been the growing complexity of relationships within projects as more and more independent specialists are drawn in on a contractual-relational basis (Pryke 2004). Conceptually 'subcontracting' as a result has increasingly become a generic term for the relationships between independent agencies on projects, rather than a precise legal description. Such an increasingly complex and ingenious array of networks suggests that the principle of organisational specialisation has now extended far beyond the traditional manual trades– contractor–professional divisions. These developments further enhance the potential for greater firm scale.

The housebuilding industry provides a practical illustration of these principles. By decentralising and subcontracting, small groups of senior managers and support staff can successfully direct operations of firms with annual turnovers running into billions. Furthermore, lean management systems generally exist throughout firm-subsidiary hierarchies (Chapter 10). The absence of a requirement to undertake proprietary fixed investment (excluding land), a common cause of scale in many manufacturing industries, in this way becomes paradoxically a means to larger firm scale rather than an impediment to it.

Country-specific market influences

Institutional characteristics vary across countries and some are more conducive to the growth of giant construction enterprises than others. Parts relate to broad business practices and the 'social embeddedness' of norms (Porter 1990; Williamson 2000). Some of these will favour large firms, whereas elsewhere the environment is less propitious for giant enterprises. Other factors relate to more construction specific issues (Winch 2000). For example, Reeves argues that the nature of subcontracting relationships in the Japanese construction industry, whereby subcontractors link themselves to one contractor in relationships of trust, has enabled the largest contractors to grow substantially in size (Reeves 2002). Contractor relationships in Hong Kong similarly have a degree of specificity as well as familiar construction attributes (Chiang *et al.* 2001).

Of particular relevance is the procurement environment. Many countries' construction markets are weakly exposed to international competition, either through the direct favouring of domestic producers in such areas as public procurement or via a myriad of institutional barriers. Construction markets tend to be more open in areas where it is less feasible to use local providers, such as in areas of design and specialist engineering, than in general construction.

Constrained construction markets are particularly commonplace in some regions of the world, including much of continental Europe and Asia. Behind formal and informal trade barriers, large firms can grow, especially if favoured in public policies. Size in such cases does not relate to efficiency but rather to market power.

Even without explicit or implicit trade barriers, domestic firms tend to have a competitive edge through their knowledge and embeddedness in the local environment. Large firms may grow up behind such 'natural' protective barriers, although these are probably weakening over time.

The amount of construction work affects the potential for large firms by influencing potential turnover in domestic markets. Countries with higher levels of construction output relative to national income tend to have larger firms. The types of work matter as well. Larger, more complex projects favour the growth of larger firms.

Financial factors

Finance encourages large firms to emerge in a variety of ways. They relate, first, to the characteristics of projects, second, to the gains arising from the pooling of projects and, third, from variations in the characteristics of lenders to construction firms.

The most obvious finance characteristic relates to the size of projects. The ability to raise finance at lowest cost is important in any project above the smallest, because firms have to have the ability to be able to finance working capital, to post performance bonds where required, and to bear project risks and fund losses if problems arise. If contractors face borrowing difficulties or suddenly collapse and cannot complete projects (either as project managers or as main contractors) substantial costs are imposed on clients. So, other things being equal, clients are likely to prefer larger firms because of their financial strength. Lenders providing project funding to either the client or the contractor are also likely to lend to and offer preferential terms to larger firms for the same reason. Such issues clearly correlate with firm size and constitute an obvious scale economy.

These project-based features are reproduced and enhanced in concession contracting programmes that encourage private consortia to provide the initial capital finance for public works, as well as the design and construction expertise to create them, and subsequently to run them for a fee (Winch 2002). Such approaches have grown in popularity in recent decades and have helped to give larger firms a competitive edge.

Because of the inherent risk involved in construction work, the financial soundness of suppliers is a significant consideration. Larger projects generally heighten the costs of failure for a given level of risk and, so, clients with large schemes are likely to be particularly risk-averse when appointing project teams. Greater firm size lowers supplier default risk of the client. There are numerous cases of even substantial firms with high reputations and previous records of success getting into financial difficulties as a result of particular large schemes. Therefore, the risk aspect of the financial benefits of size is likely to be significant up to very large firm sizes.

Another aspect of the financial benefits of size relates to the insurance principle, whereby the average outcome will approach the expected outcome, the greater the number of events. On this principle, one way of reducing the possibility of firm-specific failure caused by a number of its projects making substantial losses simultaneously is for the firm to have a large portfolio of contracts. Clients can observe the operation of the insurance principle within large firms and recognise the implied lower supplier default risk for them. The firm scale required to ensure engagement of the insurance principle is obviously greater the larger the projects undertaken. Clients of big schemes are thereby encouraged to employ large-scale suppliers. The operation of the insurance principle in an environment of large projects consequently encourages the emergence of very large firms.

There is another effect of the pooling of projects: in this case it relates to the overall profitability of firms. This can be seen by conceiving of individual projects as being an asset to a construction firm once their contracts have been won. Projects can conceptually be classified on the basis of their expected return and the risk associated with it. (Typically, in practice, this exercise will not be done in terms of sophisticated return modelling but as a product of the experience of personnel within a firm.) However the risk and return calculation is made, any construction contract has in its financial aspects characteristics similar to those of a financial asset: an expected return and a risk associated with that return. The principles of modern portfolio theory (Reilly & Brown 1999) can consequently be applied to construction firms' portfolios of projects and firms can move to the efficient frontier through an appropriate strategy of diversification in their project mix.

This financial optimisation process is more complicated in construction because of the much higher transaction costs in building than involved in the acquisition of a portfolio of financial assets and the greater lumpiness of construction projects. Both the transaction and lumpiness aspects of construction suggest that larger firms are more likely to have a project mix with the appropriate diversification characteristics than smaller ones. On this reasoning, very large firms should have higher rates of return than smaller ones because they are more likely to achieve a composition of activities that brings them closer to the efficiency frontier.

Little empirical research has been undertaken in the area of diversification, risk and returns in construction. However, one piece of research has identified a benefit of lower volatility in aggregate turnover when firms diversify across construction activities (Ball 2003a).

The third finance effect is a country-specific institutional one: the type of financial system and its influence on firm behaviour. This issue was raised earlier, in the chapter on international housebuilding (Chapter 9). Some countries' financial systems are more market-based. In them, share issues and stock markets are important sources of finance, indicators of firm capabilities to other lenders, and generate threats of hostile takeovers. Some other countries' finance systems are more financial institution–producer firm relationship based. In these, financial relationships are more hands-on and personal, through long-term bank lending and supervision, interconnected share holdings, a lower emphasis of stock market processes and little threat of hostile takeover.

There is now an extensive literature identifying important effects on firm structure and behaviour arising from such institutional differences (Rajan & Zingales 1995; Levine 1997; Allen & Gale 1999; Rajan & Zingales 2001). One consequence relates to the scope of firms. Market-based finance systems demand accounting transparency, so that impersonal investors can make decisions on firm worth. This gives strong disincentives to the formation and continued viability of broad-based companies, because such companies' accounts are unlikely to reveal hidden problems in particular areas of activity. The situation is different in bank-based finance systems. They permit continuous confidential financial monitoring and, so, diversified and conglomerate enterprises are sustainable. There is a clear cross-country correlation in construction between the existence of giant firms and relationship-based financial systems. Nine of the top ten global construction enterprises come from countries with such financial systems. Furthermore, construction enterprises in such countries are more likely to be spread across a wider range of construction activities and, possibly, to be subsidiaries of companies that straddle a number of industries.

Motivation, reputation and firm competences

There is a growing literature on the importance of non-pecuniary sources of motivation, which can better be created within organisations than in market relations. Such theories argue that workers are willing to put in high rather than low efforts for little variation in wages if they identify with the goals of the organisation for which they work. A flexibility is assumed in individuals' preference functions, so that organisations can inculcate a sense of greater personal self-esteem in workers if they achieve the goals set down by the organisation and peer groups within it. A clear example of such behaviour is suggested in the way in which training programmes mould recruits into soldiers in that very large organisation, the US Army (Akerlof & Kranton 2005). The mutual benefits of identity to worker and organisation supplement the motivational benefits of monetary incentives, which can be costly and ineffective as a sole motivator (Prendergast 1999).

Large firms on this identity type of argument can provide employees with greater motivation and a career path, which in the cultural environment of construction can be particularly important to productivity and goal achievement. For example, in a recent survey by the author of recruitment into the UK housebuilding industry, a number of respondents complained of the difficulty of hiring the best staff, because they preferred the glamour of working for well-known major companies on the largest, most prestigious construction projects (Ball 2005a).

Although this identity argument is applied to direct employee motivation, it could equally be relevant to boundary of the firm. Work tasks may, therefore, remain within companies because of the motivational gains derived from within-firm rather than subcontractor activity. Such motivational gains then join up with other within-firm benefits that differentiate its competences, such as keeping important information confidential and out of the reach of competitors, knowledge transfer from one market to another, specialisation in particular areas of construction, building up a reputation and brand, training and so on.

Large construction firms' turnovers are not the same as their within-firm activities because of the extent of subcontracting. Earlier, it was argued that extensive subcontracting aided the growth of very large construction firms by permitting lean management structures within them. The motivational argument clearly pulls in the opposite direction of keeping work within firms. This tension helps to determine what the outcomes are in terms of firms' competences. When taken together, they can help to explain why successful very large construction firms exist that seem to be able to overcome the potential diseconomies arising from very large bureaucratic structures. At its most simple, this argument suggests that motivated managers of a construction major can simultaneously and effectively organise complex hierarchies of relationships across the large number of projects undertaken by it.

Such capacities are aided by reputations for competence and reliability (Lui & Ngo 2004; Wong *et al.* 2005). Large construction firms achieve such reputations through such efforts as branding and sustaining work quality and client satisfaction. However, the insurance principle highlighted earlier works in the sphere of reputation as well as profitability. Reputations can be damaged by features such as unforeseen events, opportunistic behaviour, mistakes or employee incompetence. When these affect large projects, reputations of even quite large firms can suffer as a result. The overall impact of such one-off events on the largest firms, however, is likely to be less because they have a bigger pool of ongoing projects, so that the impact of one unfortunate scheme on overall corporate reputation is likely to be lessened.

Conclusions

Large firms are a feature of construction around the world. Yet their existence seems paradoxical in a context of an industry renowned for high resource mobility, low amounts of fixed capital and few patented technologies. Neither production process nor product characteristics arguments can be used to explain why the industry's giants exist. In principle, a small independent team of competent project managers could effectively run virtually all construction projects and groups of relatively small-scale independent specialists could co-operate in producing them.

The existence of giant firms also poses problems for theory, because the organisational theories commonly used in construction economics cannot adequately explain the size range of firms. Transaction cost economics focuses on whether assets are jointly or separately owned, the boundaries of firms, rather than their relative sizes. Resource-based views describe competences but again do not distinguish between competences at the various potential firm turnover levels. This raises doubts about the ability of such theories to comprehend fully the nature of organisational arrangements in the industry and the array of firms there. Though, to be fair, industrial economics in general does not have adequate explanations for the observed distribution of firm sizes in industries (Sutton 1997).

The characteristics examined here specifically tried to focus on issues that distinguished the very large firms from others. The issues considered were a variety of county-specific characteristics, the role of subcontracting in limiting potential diseconomies of size, issues associated with finance, and factors associated with worker motivation and firm reputations. Though there is little or no empirical evidence to go on, there is no reason in principle why such factors cannot continue to provide significant benefits up to very large firms sizes, counteracting potential diseconomies of scale. Another explanation would be that only constant returns to scale exist through wide ranges of firm size. Large firms then exist because probabilistic events lead to such outcomes.

If the scale benefits arguments are right, this does not necessarily mean that larger firms are the most efficient producers. A number of the country-specific factors, for example, concern barriers to trade, which are likely to hamper efficiency rather than improve it. Similarly, other benefits are linked to firm growth and survival, rather than lowering the overall cost of construction work.

Note

1   The precise rankings may be affected by the methodology by which *Engineering News-Record* data are collected (Strassman & Wells 1988).

13

Multi-agent governance in property-led urban regeneration

Introduction

New forms of governance involving participation by people from a wide variety of social backgrounds are a topical issue in public policy. One arena where such partnerships have been around for over a decade in the UK is urban regeneration, where local government and other public sector agencies enter into partnership with others from the private, voluntary and community sectors. The research reported here examines the efficiency and effectiveness of such governance structures in urban regeneration projects that involve a large property element. An institutional perspective is used to highlight the potential benefits and costs of such a governance model. The results of an empirical survey of the views of participants in such partnerships are then reported. Respondents highlighted the weaknesses, rather than benefits, of this hybrid multi-agency approach, emphasising problems of time and cost overruns and a lack of trusting, co-operative interrelationships. The theoretical analysis, however, does point to ways in which more positive outcomes could be achieved.

Urban regeneration partnerships

Urban regeneration partnerships (URPs) were first introduced under the Conservative governments of the early 1990s, then taken over and strengthened by New Labour (Tiesdell & Allmendinger 2001). They exist under a number of 'flagship' urban programmes, including the Single Regeneration Budget, the New Deal for Communities and the Neighbourhood Renewal Strategy (DETR 2001).

In URPs, local government and other public sector agencies enter into partnership with others from the private, voluntary and community sectors. The prime aim of such partnerships is to maximise the social and economic benefits of physical regeneration (SEU 2001). Since the early 1990s, there have been well over a thousand of them throughout Britain. They have spent public funds and stimulated other investments running into billions of pounds (Ball & Maginn 2005). In aggregate, consequently, they have been significant policy vehicles aimed at tackling multiple deprivation. They have had notable impacts on the spatial structures of modern British cities through their property development aspects. They have also been central to the growing market for mixed-use developments, because access to public funding depends on providing such mixed uses.

Partnership working is now common both within the private sector and in public sector procurement from the private sector but there is still a clear hierarchy in these formulations. The URP formulation extends the bounds of partnership by requiring extensive co-operation between agencies with widely different objectives, modes of working and principal–agent relationships. There is also no clear hierarchy but a principle of equal partners. Nor is there an initial detailed menu of desired outcomes or penalties for their non-achievement; instead the aim is for a partnership to produce mutually agreed outputs in relation to regeneration (Carley *et al.* 2000).

Three issues in particular are argued here to influence the chances of URP success:

1. The extent to which agencies' objectives and the constraints they face correspond.
2. The nature of principal–agent relationships.
3. The influence of institutional cultures on agents' behaviours within the partnership framework.

The relative significance of these factors will depend on the type of regeneration activity in question and the frequency of co-operation. Each issue will now be considered in turn.

Agency objectives and constraints

The theoretical and practical literature on negotiation highlights that successful co-operation depends on having clear, well-defined objectives on which all parties agree and towards which they are prepared to work (Raiffa 1982;

HBR 2000). The aims of individual negotiators, furthermore, influence their behaviour during negotiation. With broad prior agreement on objectives, individuals are likely to be accommodating; whereas with a widespread variety of initial views, intransigence and lengthy, fruitless discussions are more likely. The objectives of each agency in URPs are often substantially different, which may hinder the easy discovery of common ground.

Public sector agencies focus on aims outlined in national or local government policies or in the programmes of local public service providers. Such objectives also mean that public sector agencies, especially local authorities, are generally the initiators of URP schemes.

As initiators, they face the problem of attracting other partners to join them. Their best tactic may be to be as vague as possible about project objectives in order to attract the interest of other partners in the hope that once committed to negotiations, partners will then resolve any difficulties over conflicting agendas. Such a tactic of putting on a positive gloss, however, may impose high costs on already potentially difficult negotiations and a lack of clear objectives is a widely voiced complaint about URPs.

Private sector agencies, as profit-making entities, want returns on their investments in URPs, so that for them revenues generally have to exceed costs. Nevertheless, profit-maximisation may be tempered by 'social responsibility' aims, which could induce them to become involved in regeneration projects even when they are loss-making for them.

Voluntary bodies' objectives vary considerably depending on their charters. 'Voluntary' in the UK refers only to the non-profit, social interest nature of organisational objectives. Staff below board level may be salaried and often have training as professionals, rather than conform to the classic, unpaid, mutual-aid image of volunteer work championed in the social capital literature (Etzioni 1995; Putnam 2000). The scale and scope of individual voluntary organisations range from the small and local to the national and large; involving highly specialised activities or more general ones; and encompassing faith, single issue and quasi-political organisations. Many such bodies receive public sector funding and receiving it may depend on participation in URPs (Ball & Maginn 2005).

Some of the most active voluntary sector organisations in URPs are registered social landlords (RSLs), which provide new or refurbished housing for lower-income groups, and these are often important 'property developers' within regeneration schemes. Local authorities themselves may also take on a property developer role when the regeneration project involves the rehabilitation or partial demolition of existing rundown local authority housing estates; this has been a common theme of UK urban regeneration schemes.

Common involvement in physical redevelopment may form the basis for good co-operation between the local, voluntary and private sectors, because they all have experience of the problems of brownfield redevelopment and building refurbishment. It may also lead to conflict if each sector's development activities preclude those of the others or impose costs on them.

The *community sector* refers to residents and small businesses in regeneration localities. Clear initial aims rarely exist for such a diverse group of people, rather views emerge in response to specific regeneration proposals. In common with low propensities to vote in relation to local government as a whole, community responses are often marked by apathy rather than substantial local engagement (Purdue 2001; Shaw & Davidson 2002).

To summarise, in principle there are a wide variety of aims across each of the four types of agency and substantial potential divergences between their aims. This may lead to lengthy negotiations to try to reach agreement or to the need for compromises that constrain potential organisational efficiency and effectiveness and lead to sub-optimal outcomes. Alternatively, the partnership may have to be wound up before it embarks upon its regeneration activities through a total failure to agree.

There have been a number of well-publicised cases where regeneration partnerships have collapsed, or been delayed for many years, despite lengthy negotiations. In London, Project Vauxhall, a multi-million pound residential regeneration project on the Ethelred Estate in Lambeth involving the local authority and two developers, was abandoned in 2001 after the community rejected proposals. Similarly, a proposed £1.6 billion commercial and residential regeneration of the Elephant and Castle area collapsed in 2002, when the council terminated its four-year relationship with a private developer consortium – at a cost of £5m to the latter – over a dispute about profit sharing (Wehner 2002). The failure to redevelop the huge acreage of railway lands in the King's Cross area for almost forty years resulted from irresolvable conflicts between community groups, local government and private developers.

It is not simply the degree to which initial interests diverge. Each type of agency also faces distinct constraints, which may make it hard for them to align their positions closely with others'. For example, developers are likely to be highly cost conscious, whereas the community may be less so, as it bears few direct costs. Such potentially conflicting constraints may limit the possibility of the agency transformation that is often hoped for via partnership (Mackintosh 1992).

Principal–agent issues

Individuals represent organisations within partnership structures. As a result, principal–agent issues arise, where the organisation is the principal and the individual representative, the agent (Molho 1997). The principal–agent problem is encapsulated in the question: 'Do individuals maximise the benefits of partnerships to the bodies they represent or does self-interest (opportunism) motivate their actions as well?'

It is clearly possible for opportunism to prevail across all organisational types. Opportunism, moreover, does not mean that agents wilfully or corruptly go against the interest of their organisations. Instead, and more commonly, it means that representatives are risk or effort averse. For example, they may rely on procedure to ensure that blame for any failure does not fall on them rather than doing what seems most likely to achieve partnership success.

Potential principal–agent problems can be greatest in situations where principals have the least ability to impose costs on their agents. Most public, private or voluntary bodies have the sanction of dismissal or denial of promotion if employees acting as their agents go against their wishes. Potential sanctions are far more limited in situations where the agents have weaker links with their nominal principals. Business and residential community representatives often fall within the latter category. When elected, turnout is often low and the election is usually a one-off event with few effective mechanisms for recall or accountability. Furthermore, many of such representatives in URPs are appointed by the bodies initiating partnerships, possibly after informal soundings, because that is the only way to find representatives (Foley & Martin 2000; Edwards *et al.* 2003).

The local community itself may have jaundiced opinions of 'career activists', those who may take paid 'community representative' employment and/or be prepared to pay high time costs in attending meetings, and of local 'godfathers and mothers' acting as self-declared community leaders (Lowndes & Skelcher 1998; Miller 2000). Such representatives, furthermore, will have a long experience of relationships with other bodies, especially local authorities and those 'histories' will have an important influence on current interrelationships. Those experiences may bring wisdom, yet they may also colour current actions in an irrational way with events taking place years earlier affecting current perceptions in a changed context (Stewart & Taylor 1995; Atkinson & Cope 1997).

Differences in organisational cultures

It is now widely recognised in the organisational literature that enterprise culture has an important impact on how an organisation functions and its members behave (Kreps 1990b). With URPs, organisations from widely different backgrounds and cultures are brought together to form a new organisation and, so, such cultural differences can exacerbate the problems of effective co-operation.

Organisational cultural differences exist across all four sectors – public, private, voluntary and community. Bodies committed to partnership working have incentives to minimise such cultural differences. In the context of British URPs, the Government, the private sector and parts of the voluntary sector (such as large RSLs and long-established community regeneration organisations) are likely to employ as partnership representatives similar types of personnel – typically professionals, often with degrees – and they become the facilitators of partnership co-operation (Diamond 2002). It is common to find professionals who have worked in two, or sometimes all three, of these partnership sectors over the course of their careers. This is unsurprising as property-related regeneration is now such a large and established UK business, so that organisations within it will wish to employ staff that understand how the partnership process works and the languages and organisational procedures that are associated with it.

An important element in building up co-operative relationships is the need to establish trust amongst the various types of partners (Southern 2002). Studies have shown that trusting relationships are more likely to arise between similar groups of people and types of organisation than when there is a great deal of dissimilarity (Powell 1996; Sydlow 1997). Personnel from those agencies, consequently, would be predicted to find it easier to build up trust between themselves than with community representatives. This is especially likely in deprived areas, where community representatives may well come from distinct social backgrounds, with different educational and work experiences and, possibly, a jaundiced view of such professionals. From these deductions, a prediction can be made that a greater lack of trust is likely to be found, on average, between the community and other agencies in partnerships.

Trust is not about having the same views. Differences of opinion are likely to exist between partnership representatives because of the different aims of the organisations that they represent. Several commentators have even highlighted such differences as positive aspects of partnership working as they cause people to rethink their perceptions and ideas in positive ways (Hastings 1996). Instead, the question of trust concerns such issues as the ability of one partner to stick to agreements once made.

The pros and cons of urban regeneration partnerships

There are several potential *benefits* of undertaking partnership working. The four most important are generally regarded as associated with knowledge, resources, synergy and redistribution.

1. *Superior pooled knowledge* This is perhaps the most commonly cited benefit. Local authority officers can gain insights from working with property developers or other businesses or property developers can more readily understand the constraints faced by local government, for example. With regard to community representatives, the actual experience of social deprivation and living or working in a locality may provide superior local knowledge that is essential for successful regeneration. This knowledge is assumed to be hidden from the outside world and, so, unavailable from statistics or the knowledge base of local authority officials or external experts. Such community knowledge may take two forms: better *information* about local preferences and conditions or a superior *understanding* of potential solutions.
2. *Extra resources* By combining the public and private sector, additional resources can be brought into regeneration. Co-operation between the public and private sectors means that projects can be formulated and public funds spent in ways that enhance the potential for property development or other private sector business activity. Under some URP programmes, such leveraging has been a direct aim. In the Single Regeneration Budget, for example, proposed schemes had to identify the extra investments leveraged by public sector funding.

   In part, 'extra resources' is an externality argument. If a partnership outcome can reverse some of the external costs of a locality that are associated with neighbourhood decline, this is likely to induce more private sector investment. However, such externality benefits often have distributional implications – say, benefiting new entrants to the locality more than existing ones, or benefiting businesses more than residents. Such distributional factors may heighten the conflict between community and private sector interests over what should happen to a locality.

3. *Synergy* Synergy is the mantra of all partnership working and, therefore, it is unsurprisingly applied to URPs as well. Co-operating organisations may lead to outputs that are greater and more usefully varied than would occur otherwise because they merge distinct resources and talents when working together. This has a dynamic component as well, with greater experience of partnership working leading to the further rewards of learning to work together and transformations of organisations and behaviours that make individual agencies more receptive and productive within the partnership framework.

4. *Redistribution* Redistribution may be predetermined as, for example, when central government allocates national resources to a specific locality. Alternatively, it may be the outcome of a regeneration project and the negotiations contained within it. Public funding may lead to betterment gain for developers or to more subsidised housing for low-income groups. Community power is also argued to lead to a greater redistribution of resources to the deprived in society. Such outcomes may be in the form of direct subsidy or in terms of enhanced social skills and 'social capital'. Within deprived communities, it is argued individuals lack a sense of self worth and skill bases – deficits that can be overcome through the work, negotiation and co-operation resulting from active involvement within a regeneration partnership. Successful co-operation within the community, furthermore, strengthens and even creates community institutions that permanently add to the social capital of a community (Taylor 1995). Not all redistribution, of course, is socially desirable, so that the redistributional gains of URPs refer specially to socially-preferred distributional outcomes.

The *costs* of partnership working are associated with 'effectiveness' – which is the ability to achieve project aims, the aspirations of individual partners and to mobilise the actions leading to the benefits listed above – and 'efficiency' – which is the transactions and wider project costs of achieving such outcomes. Both of these issues are comparative in nature, because they implicitly or explicitly relate partnership working to some other organisational form.

With regard to effectiveness, negotiation theory suggests that co-operation is most likely when: (1) potential partners work towards well-defined ends that are limited in scope (with preferably a singular aim) and (2) in situations where partners can build up trust. The process of co-operation, furthermore, is aided by the possibility of bilateral, private negotiations (rather than stand-offs in public fora) and where there is a competent facilitator/'strong' leader. These criteria indicate why business-led 'urban regimes' in the USA are likely to have had some success. In fact, US 'urban regime theory' has been an influential strand in city-level governance theory (Stone 1993). Yet, several studies argue that urban politics in the UK and elsewhere in Europe emanate from a wide milieu of social forces and is subject to more limiting constraints on potential activity than is recognised in urban regime theory (Stoker & Mossberger 1994; Harding 1997). Public accountability requirements in the UK, for example, more often constrain one-to-one negotiations that exclude other partners than is the case in the USA.

Other efficiency and effectiveness factors are associated with the time taken in negotiations and the desirability of the compromises that may have to be reached. The larger the number of partners, the greater the costs such factors impose. The costs of delay impact differentially on distinct partners as well, which means that some partners can adopt delaying tactics knowing that they are imposing costs that are hard for others to retaliate against. Some agencies may also be put off by procedures that are likely to seem bureaucratic and inflexible in order to be seen to be fair to all participants. The pressures to achieve agreement, moreover, may predominate over cost-effective outcomes. One-off rather than repeat situations of co-operation are likely to lead to lower rates of success, as the pay-offs to each participant of co-operation are likely to be less in such contexts.

Empirical investigation of URP governance structures

While it is possible to make deductive statements about potential benefits and costs of partnership working, it is an empirical matter whether the positive or negative aspects of partnering outweigh the other. The heterogeneity of URP projects and the difficulty of aggregating costs and benefits make it difficult to build up case study empirical material and derive generalisations from it (Ball 2003b). Nonetheless, it is possible to ask agents that have been in partnerships about their views on the efficiency and effectiveness of partnerships and whether co-operation overall is achievable. This was undertaken in the empirical research report, described below, to explore the extent to which the experience of participants corresponded to the theoretical deductions about partnership working discussed in previous sections.

London was chosen as the case study area. The London property market has some distinctive characteristics from those of other areas in the UK. It is by far the UK's largest market for offices, has the highest house prices, contains marked property cycles, and has many uses competing for scarce space. This, consequently, means that there are often likely to be substantial land-use conflicts between different agents and interest groups, and a variety of arenas in which those conflicts are worked out. London has also received a large share of the aggregate allocation of regeneration funding, particularly with respect to property-led regeneration. Despite its geographic and social distinctiveness, therefore, London is in many ways an ideal location to undertake an analysis of co-operation.

Nevertheless, it may be the case that the distinctiveness of London and the frequent intensity of its urban politics do impact on the partnership process in urban regeneration. The empirical regeneration literature in the UK to date, however, has not felt it necessary to distinguish the London context from the rest of the UK. A wider geographic range of empirical material would obviously be preferable, but outside the scope of this study.

The sample of people drawn up to interview was developed in two ways. The first approach was a functionally-based one, the second was a project-based one. The functionally based strategy aimed to get a good spread of agencies involved in regeneration. It involved identifying local authorities with significant regeneration activity and RSLs active in regeneration in London. One person per organisation was interviewed. A similar functionally-based approach was adopted with property consultants and non-social housing developers. The project-based one identified particular regeneration schemes and interviews were conducted with as many partners as possible working on those projects. A variety of types of project were chosen, ranging from relatively small to large schemes and from social housing to mixed or primarily commercial developments.

In-depth semi-structured interviews were conducted. The interview schedule comprised a total of 26 questions focusing on a range of issues associated with URPs that included: (1) agents' roles within them; (2) advantages and disadvantages; (3) the efficiency and effectiveness of URP decision-making bodies; and (4) the nature of relationships between the partners. Almost 120 agencies were contacted; around half of those contacted were happy to be interviewed; the low number of community respondents was a disappointment and, so, they are left out of the main result reporting.

To avoid putting too much researcher interpretation on the responses, which is evident in much of the empirical research undertaken in this field, answers were grouped and coded. This enabled quantification of the number of times particular issues were raised and calculation of the percentage of respondents voicing any particular topic. Respondents could then be separated by agency type to see whether specific types of agency had particular concerns about URP governance.

Most of the questions asked were open-ended, allowing respondents to identify themselves what they thought were the most pressing issues and which other agencies they found it hardest or easiest to co-operate with. This approach was adopted to avoid leading respondents into giving positive or negative comments when they might otherwise not have done so. It, however, is a weak form of questioning because inter-viewees may not raise issues even when they have an opinion on them. Silence, in other words, does not mean agreement with URP principles. Yet, the view was taken, after a piloting exercise, that the questions were sufficiently well structured to elicit concerns if they were felt strongly by respondents.

Results

The views of the participants

The overall reaction found was that participants had considerable reservations about the efficiency and effectiveness of the URP model. The property developer[1] respondents and, particularly, the property consultants were the most critical, but even local authorities had reservations. The overall critical stance can be seen by comparing the four most frequently cited positive and negative responses, shown in Figure 13.1, where it can be seen that far more respondents voiced concerns over URP processes than supported the principle. Furthermore, the types of complaint correspond to outcomes expected in theoretical analysis above when the interests and behaviour of the various agencies are too divergent to make efficient and effective co-operation possible. The process as a result is regarded quite often as a time-wasting one; with partner interrelationships characterised by a lack of trust and commitment and an overriding sense of a bureau-cratic process that achieves significantly less than was hoped for. The private sector in particular had little positive to say about the URP model – with property consultants even having zero scores on two of the four positive attributes of URPs articulated by survey respondents.

A breakdown of the issues

Table 13.1 identifies in greater detail all the main issues that participants raised in interviews. Some quotes are also given in the text below to illus-trate the types of concern raised by respondents.

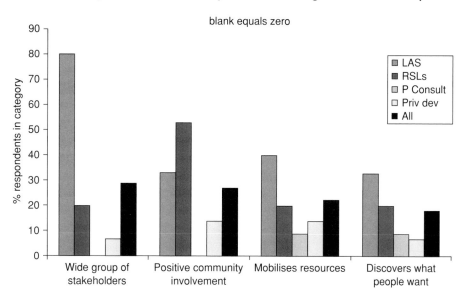

Survey results: The four main pluses of Urban Regeneration Partnerships

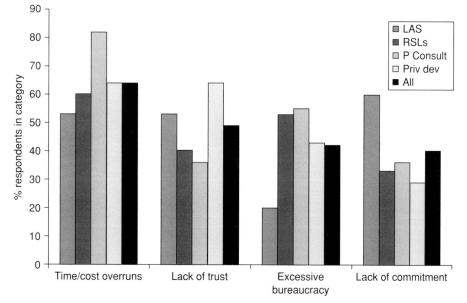

Survey results: The four main nagatives of Urban Regeneration Partnerships

Figure 13.1 Views on the benefits and costs of URPs.

The most frequently cited problem was one of *'efficiency'*, time and cost overruns. Almost two-thirds of respondents felt that they occurred. The overruns could be substantial with, for example, the time delays reported sometimes stretching into years. The reasons for such delays were

Table 13.1 Main issues raised by respondents.

% of respondents by type*	LA%	RSL%	PC%	PD%	Overall%
Negative responses					
Time or cost overruns	53	60	82	64	64
Lack of trust/information sharing	53	40	36	64	49
Excessive bureaucracy	20	53	55	43	42
Lack of commitment of partners	60	33	36	29	40
Too much community consultation/power	20	27	36	50	33
Personalities play key role	40	7	45	29	27
Too many non-representative community leaders	33	27	27	21	27
Lack of clarity of objectives/strategies	7	40	18	36	25
Lack of recognition of social objectives	33	33	9	14	24
Lack of resources to perform effectively	27	27	9	14	20
Poor management/lack of management skills	7	13	45	14	18
Lack of partnership/LA leadership	7	13	27	21	16
Structural/organisational problems	13	33	9	0	15
Cost delays due to planning process	13	0	27	21	15
Lack of recognition of roles	13	20	9	14	15
Positive responses					
Involves wide group of stakeholders	80	20	0	7	29
Positive community involvement	33	53	0	14	27
Mobilises resources	40	20	9	14	22
Effectively finds out what people want	33	20	9	7	18
Positive synergy	20	20	0	21	16
'The best way to do it'	47	13	0	0	16
Democratic method	33	13	0	0	13
Neutral response					
No alternative	7	0	9	7	5

* Local Authority (LA), Registered Social Landlord (RSL), Property Consultants (PC), Property Developers (PD).

varied, relating to the difficulty of waiting for decisions to be made or approved of in the appropriate meetings when they came around; the length of time taken in discussion; the difficulty of reaching clear outcomes; problems with one type of agency reaching a clear view (particularly true of community representatives); or one type of agency refusing to agree to a consensus position for a long period of time.

Property consultants – at 82% – were strongest in believing time delays and cost overruns were significant impediments to URP functioning. This may be because they tend to work in larger schemes where URP governance structures are likely to be the most problematic. Even so, 60% or more of RSL and other property developers also expressed concern about cost and time factors. One private-sector property developer summarised the extent of the potential delays by referring to one case study in the following light:

> We've done two years of consultation, 30 sets of consultation meetings with various bodies – from [firms] to local residents – we present it to council, and we still get planning problems. It gets really frustrating.

More than half of local authority respondents were of the same opinion – the lower percentage response for them might also be affected by the fact that they are less likely to feel the direct consequences of cost over-runs, as their budgets may not be affected. Overall, nevertheless, this issue transcended public–private–voluntary sector divisions.

A significant *lack of trust* between agents that leads to lack of information sharing was the second most-cited response. Almost half of those interviewed had experienced a lack of trust between partners in one form or another. This indicates that the complexity and heterogeneity items identified in the theoretical literature as impediments to co-operative working feature highly in URP practice.

Property developers seem to have had the most experience with a lack of trust, with 64% of those interviewed voicing this complaint. A common explanation was that private property developers are viewed by the public and community sectors in URP circles as solely profit driven and 'in it for the money'. That stigmatises them even though few participants in URPs actually are anti-market economy in general, though some do tend to see urban regeneration as a welfare-state style domain that should be beyond the market. Local authority agents were the next highest, at 53%, in voicing trust concerns. Most of this lack of trust seemed to concern their relationships with community leaders who, according to the respondents, often distrusted everything that local authorities did. The lowest response was from property consultants, which may arise because they rarely sit on partnership boards but rather act as agents for those who do – with whom they directly have a trusting relationship. Nevertheless, property consultants often had jaundiced views of the ability to build up trusting relationships as the following quote indicates:

> Public sector projects are somewhat difficult from the start. There is a general mutual loathing amongst various partners because they've been there before, been burned before, but they have to do it. They usually butt heads from the start.

Excessive bureaucracy, or 'red tape', was the third most important factor. Local authorities were far less bothered about bureaucracy than other agents, perhaps unsurprisingly as URPs frequently mirror their working practices and, so, when they complained about bureaucracy they were generally referring to central government edicts. RSLs and property consultants, in contrast, were the most concerned. As one RSL respondent put it:

> All the regeneration programmes that we've been involved in are just riddled with bureaucracy and administration and politics.

Frequently, other agencies cited local authorities as the cause of the problem, although it was recognised that the rules and regulations of URP practices were often imposed from above by central government or its agencies, or by the need to conform to strict procurement criteria.

A lack of commitment of partners was the next most important concern at 40% of respondents overall. There were sharp variations between agency types to this question, with each agency type tending to blame the others. An RSL respondent, for example, thought regeneration was like a 'honey pot' for many participants:

> With a lot of agencies, they'll remain involved for as long as they have something to gain and when they receive their money, they'll leave.

The greatest overall concern was by local authorities, which may be explicable in that local authorities, as noted earlier, often take the leadership role in formulating URPs and their overall regeneration policies can be highly dependent on their success. Private developers, in contrast, were the most criticised by the other agents for their poor attendance at partnership meetings and for a lack of following through on partnership social objectives and other matters.

Community involvement was also a significant area of concern for a third of respondents with wide variations between types of respondent. This issue was raised by half of all property developers, but only a fifth of local authorities. A pessimistic property consultant stated:

> If the process [community consultation] continues, nothing will get done.

Concern was also expressed that community leaders were not representative of the local community by over a quarter of respondents. Local authorities, again probably because of their initiating role, were the most concerned about this issue:

> You can also have community representatives who aren't representative at all. There's nothing new there.

A related issue was that individual personalities could play an obstructive role in negotiations, because this complaint referred to community representatives in particular. Over 40% of local authorities and RSLs voiced this concern, such as the following local authority person:

> You sometimes get a person from the community that has a purely personal interest. If their personal needs are not met, they can cause an awful lot of problems. It can be a nightmare.

Other issues that were thought to hamper URP effectiveness varied considerably between agency types. All types of property developer were concerned about a *lack of clarity of objectives*, with 40% of RSLs and 36% of private developers voicing concern, in contrast to far lower percentages of property consultants and local authority staff. This may be because these agencies were the ones that had to achieve what are generally the most expensive outcomes, built structures, and, therefore, are focused on the need for timely and cost-effective redevelopment. One private-sector developer complained:

> You never get a strong vision laid down by the executives and politicians; it's not easy to deliver in those environments.

A *lack of recognition of social objectives* similarly concerned those most directly affected by them, local authorities (33%) and RSLs (33%). A local authority respondent said that:

> Developers are looking after their own interests on their own sites. Creating jobs for locals, jobs for different ethnicities, etc. are not the main interests of the developers. We try to get them to realise that these are important issues.

The same two agencies were also most affected by a *lack of resources*. One RSL respondent commented:

> In my experience, working with the politicians is a far more positive experience than working with senior officers . . . Local authority officers are far too stretched and far too under-resourced to actually work properly in partnership.

Property consultants felt most strongly that URPs were *poorly managed* (45% of them, in fact). The views of other agents could be similar as well. According to a local authority respondent:

> Project management skills aren't as efficient as they could be.

While a property consultant commented:

> The delivery of schemes is about good basic management and a lot of the organisations involved simply don't have that.

Property consultants (27%) and private developers (21%) were also bothered by the quality of *leadership*. A third of RSLs were concerned about *structural problems* – particularly central government rules that forced them into partnership arrangements, when they generally preferred to receive direct grants to buy land and build homes themselves. The private sector was most concerned about the costs of *planning delays*.

So far, negative views on URPs have been discussed. This reflects the weight of responses: there were three times as many negative responses as positive ones. The most frequent positive response was that multi-agency partnerships involve a *wide group of stakeholders*, which is necessary for success. The ability to get everyone affected by a project around a table discussing relevant aspects of it was seen as the most important benefit of the URP model, as one local authority officer put it:

> The advantage is that you've got all these people at the table, you've got their brain, their voice, their ideas, and they are a part of the pro-gramme which means they are more likely to support you.

This was closely followed by various community related features such as *positive community involvement*, *effectively finds out what people want*, and *democratic method*. Some also reported *positive synergy*. These elements are illustrated by the comments of two local authority respondents:

> The community has been quite active and vocal over the last few years. It can be challenging, but this is seen as healthy debate.

> It can be slow, people bring different agendas to the table . . . but I don't think any agency has all the answers . . . they can't do it alone.

> It's really useful having all the stakeholders around the table because people learn to understand everyone's view.

> You've got people around the table challenging and questioning in a very healthy way. I think it's developing quite nicely.

Finally, a sense of acceptance of the policy status quo was articulated, which recognised that partnerships may be problematic, but are the accepted way of doing things in urban regeneration. This can be seen in the comments of a local authority and property developer respondent respectively:

Are partnerships efficient? No they're not, but I don't see an alternative.

Working within partnerships is inefficient. It is hard work, but I don't see any other way of doing it at the moment.

There was a much greater division of views between the types of agency with regard to the benefits of URPs than there was on the criticisms of them. Local authorities were by far the most enthusiastic with 80% supporting the stakeholder participation argument; 47% thinking it was the best way to undertake regeneration; and a third, respectively, highlighting community involvement and finding out what people want. Other agents were far less enthusiastic. Over half of RSLs supported community involvement, but were less supportive of other facets of URPs. Property developers often voiced only limited benefits and property consultants generally had little positive to say.

Respondents' overall views of URPs

To obtain an impression of respondents' overall views about URP governance, all the responses of interviewees were scored on a scale from 0 (highly approve of URP governance) to 10 (highly disapprove). Table 13.2 presents some descriptive statistics of the aggregate scores for each type of agency.

In terms of agency types, local authorities were most favourable to the URP model, followed by RSLs. In contrast, the groups dominated by the private sector, namely property consultants and property developers,

Table 13.2 Subjective scores.

0 = highly approve of URP governance; 10 = highly disapprove.

Respondents*	LA	RSL	PC	PD
Mean	4.7	5.3	7.1	6.8
Median	5.0	5.0	7.0	7.0
Mode	3.0	5.0	7.0	7.0
Standard deviation	1.8	1.8	1.0	1.3
Minimum	2.0	2.0	5.0	5.0
Maximum	7.0	8.0	9.0	9.0

* Local Authority (LA), Registered Social Landlord (RSL), Property Consultants (PC), Property Developers (PD).

were, on average, far less favourable. This ranking may be explained by the more social orientation of local authorities and RSLs and the more business-like perspectives of property consultants and developers.

Even the more apparently enthusiastic agency types were, in fact, on average, neutral towards the URP governance structure rather than highly favourable. Moreover, views of local authorities and RSL respondents were the most variable, as can be seen from the greater standard deviations and score ranges for these two groups. This means that individual local authority respondents, therefore, could be as pessimistic as developers.

Conclusions

The views of many of the respondents to the survey of regeneration schemes highlighted the potential weaknesses identified in the theoretical analysis of the governance model. For many, the traditional animosities between the private and community sectors – and also those between local authorities and community representatives – do not seem to have been resolved or smoothed over by the partnership formula. Management and leadership difficulties scored high with many private sector respondents. There was a widespread sense of an inability to move URP objectives forward harmoniously. In terms of benefits, there was a sharp division between the public and voluntary sectors, more widely supporting greater local involvement, and the private sector, which saw little advantage.

The results of only one survey cannot be said to be definitive. Yet, some of the most important private sector developers and consultants in the UK and some of the major RSLs were part of the survey. If urban regeneration involves major property redevelopment, consequently, the views of the respondents suggest that the URP governance model may limit the efficiency and effectiveness of transformations of the UK's rundown urban areas.

The situations where the partnership approach is most likely to work are when partners' initial objectives can be dovetailed together, when trust can be built up, and where efficient management procedures are put in place. This is more likely to occur when there is a common interest in a relatively straightforward, easily comprehensible set of outcomes that do not involve substantial disagreements between partners over who should benefit from the outcomes. Such a combination of features is least likely in large-scale property-led regeneration schemes, where the need to rethink the regeneration model may consequently be greatest.

Note

1 There is a distinction between property developers and private property developers in the results reported below, because there were a small but important number of public and quasi-public developers. On most items, however, the views of both types were quite similar.

Bibliography

Agbola, T. (1987). Institutional constraints on housing development in the urban areas of Nigeria: the land-use degree and building plan approval process. *Habit International* 11(2): 113–120.

Aharoni, Y. (ed.) (1993). *Coalitions and Competition: The Globalization of Professional Business Services*. London, Routledge.

Aharoni, Y. (ed.) (1997). Changing Roles of State Intervention in Services in an Era of Open International Markets. Albany, New York, SUNY Press.

Akerlof, G. A., Kranton, R. E. (2005). Identity and the economics of organizations. *Journal of Economic Perspectives* 19(1): 9–32.

Alexander, E. R. (1992). A transaction cost theory of planning. *Journal of the American Planning Association* 58(2): 190–200.

Alexander, E. R. (2001). A transaction cost theory of land use planning and development control: towards the institutional analysis of public planning. *Town Planning Review* 72(1): 45–75.

Allen, F., Gale, D. (1999). *Comparing Financial Systems*. Cambridge, Mass., MIT Press.

Allmendinger, P., White, M. (2003). Land use planning and the housing market: a comparative review of the UK and the USA. *Urban Studies* 40(5/6): 953–972.

Alston, L. J., Eggertsson, T., North, D. C. (1996). *Empirical Studies in Institutional Change*. Cambridge, Cambridge University Press.

Amis, P. (1984). Squatters or tenants: the commercialization of unauthorized housing in Nairobi. *World Development* 12(1): 87–96.

Anglin, P. M., Rutherford, R., Springer, T. M. (2003). The trade-off between the selling price of residential properties and time-on-the-market: the impact of price setting. *Journal of Real Estate Finance and Economics* 26(1): 95–111.

Arnold, M. A. (1992). The principal–agent relationship in real estate brokerage services. *Journal of the American Real Estate and Urban Economics Association* 20: 89–106.

Arrow, K. (1985). The economics of agency, in Pratt, J. and Zeckhauser R. (eds). *Principals and Agents: The Structure of Business*. Cambridge, Mass., Harvard Business School Press.

Atkinson, R., Cope, S. (1997). Community participation and urban regeneration in Britain. *Contested Communities*. P. Hoggett (ed.). Bristol, Policy Press.

Bain, J. S. (1956). *Barriers to New Competition*. Cambridge, Mass., Harvard University Press.

Balbo, M. (1993). Urban planning and the fragmented city of developing countries. *Third World Planning Review* 15(1): 23–31.

Ball, M. (1983). *Housing Policy and Economic Power: The Political Economy of Owner Occupation*. London, Methuen.

Ball, M. (1988). Rebuilding Construction: Economic Change and the British Construction Industry. London, Routledge.

Ball, M. (1996). *Housing and Construction. A Troubled Relationship*. Bristol, Policy Press.

Ball, M. (1998). Institutions in British property research: a review. *Urban Studies* 35(9): 1501–1518.

Ball, M. (1999). Chasing a snail: innovation and housebuilding firms' strategies. *Housing Studies* 14: 9–22.

Ball, M. (2002). Cultural explanations of regional property markets: a critique. *Urban Studies* 39(8): 1453–1469.

Ball, M. (2003a). Is there an office replacement cycle? *Journal of Property Research* 20(2): 173–189.

Ball, M. (2003b). Markets and the structure of the housebuilding industry: an international comparison. *Urban Studies* 40(5/6): 897–916.

Ball, M. (2004a). *International Survey of Estate Agency Practices*. London, Office of Fair Trading.

Ball, M. (2004b). *RICS Review of European Housing Markets 2004*. Royal Institution of Chartered Surveyors, London.

Ball, M. (2004c). Co-operation with the community in property-led urban regeneration. *Journal of Property Research* 21: 119–142.

Ball, M. (2005a). *The Labour Needs of Extra Housing Output: Can the Housebuilding Industry Cope?* London, Homebuilders Federation/CITB–ConstructionSkills.

Ball, M. (2005b). *RICS European Housing Review 2005*. London, Royal Institution of Chartered Surveyors.

Ball, M., Antonioni, P. (2003). Diversification as a strategy for minimising fluctuations in construction firm turnovers. *Construction Dynamics and Urban Economics*. P. Thalmann (ed.). Basingstoke, Palgrave.

Ball, M., Grilli, M. (1997). *Housing Markets and Economic Convergence in the European Union*. London, Royal Institution of Chartered Surveyors.

Ball, M., Maginn, P. (2005). Urban change and conflict: evaluating the role of partnerships in urban regeneration in the UK. *Housing Studies* 20(1): 9–28.

Ball, M., Morrison, T. (2000). Housing investment fluctuations: an international comparison. *Housing, Theory and Society* 17(1): 3–13.

Ball, M., Sunderland, D. (2001). *An Economic History of London, 1800–1914*. London, Routledge.

Ball, M., Wood, A. (1999). Housing investment: long run international trends and volatility. *Housing Studies* 14: 185–211.

Ball, M., Farschi, M., Grilli, M. (2000). Competition and the persistence of profits in the UK construction industry. *Construction Management and Economics* 18(7): 733–745.

Ball, M., Le Ny, L., Maginn, P. (2003). Synergy in urban regeneration partnerships. *Urban Studies* 40(11): 2239–2254.

Ball, M., Lizieri, C., MacGregor, B. D. (1998). *The Economics of Commercial Property Markets*. London, Routledge.

Ball, M., Morrison, T., Wood, A. (1996). Structures investment and economic growth: a long-run international comparison. *Urban Studies* 33: 1687–1706.

Barker, K. (2003). *Review of Housing Supply. Interim Report – Analysis*. London, HM Treasury: 208.

Barker, K. (2004). *Review of Housing Supply. Final report – Recommendations*. London, HM Treasury.

Barlow, J. G., Duncan, S. (1994). *Success and Failure in Housing Provision: European Systems Compared*. Oxford, Pergamon Press.

Barlow, J., King, A. (1992). The state, the market and competitive strategy: the housebuilding industry in Britain, France and Sweden. *Environment and Planning A* 24: 381–400.

Barlow, J. G., Jackson, R., Meikle, J. (2001). *Homes to DIY for the UK's Self–build Housing Market in the Twenty–first Century*. York, Joseph Roundtree Foundation.

Barney, J. B. (1991). Firm resources and sustained competitive advantage. *Journal of Management* 17: 99–120.

Barney, J. B. (2001). Is the resource-based 'view' a useful perspective for strategic management research? Yes. *Academy of Management Review* 26(1): 41–52.

Barney, J. B. (2002). *Gaining and Sustaining Competitive Advantage*. New Jersey, Prentice Hall.

Barney, J., Wright, M., Ketchen, D. J. (2001). The resource-based view of the firm: ten years after 1991. *Journal of Management* 27(1): 625–641.

Bartlett, R. (1981). Property rights and the pricing of real estate brokerage. *Journal of Industrial Economics* 30: 79–94.

Barzel, Y. (1989). *Economic Analysis of Property Rights*. Cambridge, Cambridge University Press.

Bâtirama (2002). *La plupart des maisons sont construites dans l'illégalité*, http://www.batirama.com/data/12042002/12042002-161715.html

Becker, R. (2005). Companies, does size matter? *Real Estate Confronts the Future*. Swanepoel, S., Dooley, T. (eds). New York, Thomson Learning.

Bertaud, A., Brueckner, J. (2005). Analyzing building-height restrictions: predicted impacts, welfare costs, and a case study of Bangalore, India. *Regional Science and Urban Economics* 35(2): 109–125.

Black, R., Jaszczolt, K., Lee, M. (2000). *Solving the Housing Problem. Lessons from Poland and Hungary in Creating a New Housing Finance System*. Warsaw, USAid Regional Development Office.

Blau, J. R. (1984). *Architects and Firms*. Boston, MIT Press.

Blom-Hansen, J. (1997). A 'new institutionalist' perspective on policy networks. *Public Administration* 75(4): 669–693.

Boelhouwer, P., Boumeester, H., van der Heijden, H. (2005). *Stagnation in Dutch housing production and suggestions for a way forward*. ENHR Conference, Housing in Europe: New Challenges and Innovations in Tomorrow's Cities, Reykjavik.

Bolton, P., Scharfstein, D. S. (1998). Corporate finance, the theory of the firm, and organizations. *Journal of Economic Perspectives* 12(2): 95–115.

Bowley, M. (1966). *The British Building Industry*. London, Macmillan.

Bramley, G., Leishman, C. (2005). Planning and housing supply in two-speed Britain: modelling local market responses. *Urban Studies*.

Bresnen, M., Marshall, N. (2000). Building partnerships: case studies of client–contractor collaboration in the UK construction industry. *Construction Management and Economics* 18: 819–832.

Bridge, A. J., Tisdell, C. (2004). The determinants of the vertical boundaries of the construction firm. *Construction Management and Economics* 22(8): 807–825.

Briscoe, G. (1990). *The Economics of the Construction Industry*. London, Mitchell Publishing.

Brock, D., Powell, M., Hinings, C. R. (eds) (1999). *Restructuring the Professional Organization: Accounting, Health Care and Law*. London, Routledge.

Buckley, R. (1996). *Housing Finance in Developing Countries*. London, Macmillan.

Buckley, R. M., Tsenkova, S. (2001). Housing market systems in reforming socialist economies: comparative indicators of performance and policy. *European Journal of Housing Policy* 1(2): 257–289.

Buitelaar, E. (2003). Neither market nor government. Comparing the performance of user rights regimes. *Town Planning Review* 74(3): 315–330.

Buitelaar, E. (2004). A transaction-cost analysis of the land development process. *Urban Studies* 41(13): 2539–2553.

Buzzelli, M. (2001). Firm size structure in North American housebuilding: persistent deconcentration, 1945–98. *Environment and Planning A* 33(3): 533–550.

Campagnac, E. (1992). Les cadres dans la construction en France: politiques d'entreprise et évolution des professions. *Évolution des professions et politiques d'emploi des cadres dans les entreprises de bâtiment en Europe (France, Grande-Bretagne, Italie).* M. Ball, Campagnac, E., Giallocosta, G. (eds). Paris, Ministère de l'équipement, du logement et des transports, Plan Construction et Architecture.

Campagnac, E., Winch, G. (1995). The organization of building projects: an Anglo/French comparison. *Construction Management and Economics* 13: 3–14.

Campagnac, E., Lin, Y.-J., Winch, G. M. (2000). Economic performance and national business systems: France and the UK in the international construction sector. *National Capitalisms, Global Competition and Economic Performance.* S. Quack, Morgan, G., Whitley, R. (eds). Amsterdam, John Benjamins.

Carley, M., Hastings, A., Kirk, K., Young, R. (2000). *Urban Regeneration Through Partnership: A Study in Nine Urban Regions in England, Scotland and Wales.* Bristol/York, The Policy Press/Joseph Rowntree Foundation.

Chandler, A. D. (1977). *The Visible Hand. The Managerial Revolution in American Business.* Cambridge, Massachusetts, Harvard University Press.

Chandler, A. D. (1990). *Scale and Scope: The Dynamics of Industrial Capitalism.* Cambridge, Mass., Harvard University Press.

Cheshire, P., Sheppard, S. (2002). Welfare economics of land use regulation. *Journal of Urban Economics* 52: 242–269.

Cheshire, P., Sheppard, S. (2004). Land markets and land market regulation: progress towards understanding. *Regional Science and Urban Economics* 34: 619–637.

Cheung, S. N. S. (1975). Roofs or stars: the stated intents and actual effects of a rents ordinance. *Economic Inquiry* 13(2): 56–69.

Chiang, Y.-H., Tang, B.-S. (2002). 'Submarines don't leak, why do buildings?' Building quality, technological impediment and organisation of the building industry in Hong Kong. *Habitat International*: 1–17.

Chiang, Y.-H., Tang, B.-S., Leung, W.-Y. (2001). Market structure of the construction industry in Hong Kong. *Construction Management and Economics* 19(7): 675–687.

Chiquier, L. (1999). *Secondary Mortgage Facilities: A Case Study of Malaysia's Cagamas Berhad.* Washington DC, World Bank.

Cho, Y. (2003). Economic efficiency of multi–product structure: the evidence from Korean housebuilding firms. *Journal of Housing Economics* 12(4): 337–355.

Clark, K., Sefton, M. (2001). The sequential prisoner's dilemma: evidence on reciprocation. *Economic Journal*, 57–66.

Clarke, L., Wall, C. (1996). *Skills and the Construction Process: a Comparative Study of Vocational Training and Quality in Social Housebuilding.* Bristol, Policy Press.

Clawson, M. (1971). *Suburban Land Conversion in the United States: An Economic and Governmental Process.* Baltimore, Published for Resources for the Future by the Johns Hopkins Press.

Costantino, N., Pietroforte, R., Hamill, P. (2001). Subcontracting in commercial and residential construction: an empirical investigation. *Construction Management and Economics* 19(4): 439–447.

CUDS (2000). *Housing Microfinance Initiatives.* Cambridge, Mass., Center for Urban Development Studies, Harvard University Graduate School of Design.

Cullingworth, B., Nadin, V. (2001). *Town and Country Planning in the UK.* London, Routledge.

De Haan, J., Voordijk, H., Joosten, G.-J. (2002). Market strategies and core capabilities in the building industry. *Construction Management and Economics* 20(2): 109–118.

De Meza, D., Lockwood, B. (1998). Does asset ownership always motivate managers? Outside options and the property rights theory of the firm. *Quarterly Journal of Economics.*

De Soto, H. (2001). *The Mystery of Capital. Why Capitalism Triumphs in the West and Fails Everywhere Else.* London, Black Swan Books.

Deaton, A. (2005). Measuring poverty in a growing world (or measuring growth in a poor world). *Review of Economic Statistics* 87(1): 1–18.

Deaton, A., Laroque, G. (2001). Housing, land prices, and the link between growth and saving. *Journal of Economic Growth* 6(2): 87–105.

Degryse, H., Ongena, S. (2002). Bank–firm relationships and international banking markets. *International Journal of the Economics of Business* 9(3): 401–417.

Deng, Y., Gyourko, J. (2002). *Real Estate Returns by Non-real Estate Firms: an Estimate of the Impact on Firm Returns.* Wharton Real Estate Working Paper. Philadelpia.

DETR (2001). *Local Strategic Partnerships: Government Guidance.* London, DETR.

Diamond, J. (2002). Managing change or coping with conflict? Mapping experience of a local regeneration partnership. *Local Economy* 16(4): 272–285.

DiPasquale, D. (1999). Why don't we know more about housing supply? *Journal of Real Estate Finance and Economics* 18(1): 9–23.

Dipasquale, D., Wheaton, W. (1994). Housing market dynamics and the future of house prices. *Journal of Urban Economics* 42: 1–17.

DIST (1999). *Building for Growth: An Analysis of Australia's Building and Construction Industries.* Canberra, Department of Industry, Science and Tourism.

Dixit, A. K., Pindyck, R. S. (1994). *Investment under Uncertainty.* Princeton, Princeton University Press.

Donnison, D. (1967). *The Government of Housing.* Harmondsworth, Middlesex, Penguin Books.

Dowall, D. (1992). From central planning to market systems: implications of economic reforms for the construction and building industries. *Housing Policy Debate* 3(4).

ECB (2005). *EU Banking Structures.* Frankfurt, European Central Bank.

Eccles, R. G. (1981a). Bureaucratic versus craft administration: the relationship of market structure to the construction firm. *Administrative Science Quarterly* 26: 449–469.

Eccles, R. G. (1981b). The quasi-firm in the construction industry. *Journal of Economic Behavior and Organization* 2: 335–357.

Edwards, B., Goodwin, M., Woods, M. (2003). Citizenship, community and participation in small towns: a case study of regeneration partnerships. *Urban Renaissance? New Labour, Community and Urban Policy.* R. Imrie, Raco, M. (eds). Bristol, Policy Press.

Eggerston, T. (1990). *Economic Behaviour and Institutions.* Cambridge, Cambridge University Press.

Etzioni, A. (1995). *New Communitarian Thinking: Persons, Virtues, Institutions, and Communities.* Charlottesville & London, University Press of Virginia.

Evans, A. (2004). *Economics and Land Use Planning.* Oxford, Blackwell Publishing.

Farrell, M. J. (1987). Information and the Coase theorem. *Journal of Economic Perspectives* 1(1): 113–129.

Financial Services Authority (2005). *Mortgage Endowments: Progress Report and the Next Steps*. London, Financial Services Authority.

Findlay, J. F., Gibb, K. (1998). The pricing of estate agency and conveyancing services in Scotland, *Journal of Property Research*, 15(2): 135–151.

Fischel, W. A. (1980). Zoning and the exercise of monopoly power: a reevaluation. *Journal of Urban Economics* 8: 283–293.

Fischel, W. A. (1985). *The Economics of Zoning Laws: A Property Rights Approach to American Land Use Controls*. Baltimore, MD, John Hopkins University Press.

Foley, P., Martin, S. (2000). Perceptions of community led regeneration: community and central government viewpoints. *Regional Studies* 34(8): 783–787.

Frankel, A., Gyntelberg, J., Kjeldsen, K., Persson, M. (2004). The Danish mortgage market. As housing finance evolves, are there reasons to follow the Danish model? *BIS Quarterly Review* 8 (March): 95–109.

Frew, J. R. (1987). Multiple listing service participation in the real estate brokerage industry: cooperation or competition. *Journal of Urban Economics*, 21: 272–286.

Gallet, C. (2004). Housing market segmentation: an application of convergence tests to Los Angeles region housing. *Annals of Regional Science* 38: 551–561.

Gann, D. (1996). Construction as a manufacturing process? Similarities and differences between industrialised housing and car production in Japan. *Construction Management and Economics* 14: 437–450.

Gibb, K. (1992). Bidding, auctions and house purchase. *Environment and Planning A*, 24: 853–869.

Gibson, V., Lizieri, C. (2001). Business change, corporate real estate portfolios and the UK office market. *Journal of Real Estate Research*.

Gilbert, A. (1997). On subsidies and homeownership. *Third World Planning Review* 19(1): 51–70.

Gilbert, A. G., Varley, A. (1991). *Landlord and Tenant: Housing the Poor in Urban Mexico*. London, Routledge.

Glaeser, E., Gyourko, J. (2005). The impact of zoning on housing affordability. *Economic Policy Review. Federal Reserve Bank New York* 9(2): 21–39.

Glaeser, E., Laibson, D., Scheinkman, J., Soutter, C. (2000). Measuring trust. *Quarterly Journal of Economics*, 811–40.

Glendinning, M., Muthesius, S. (1994). *Tower Block. Modern Public Housing in England, Scotland, Wales and Northern Ireland*. New Haven & London, Yale University Press.

Golland, A., Boelhouwer, P. (2002). Speculative housing supply, land and housing markets: a comparison. *Journal of Property Research* 19(3): 231–251.

Grebler, L. (1973). *Large Scale Housing and Real Estate Firms; Analysis of a New Business Enterprise*. New York, Praeger.

Greenwood, R., Hinings, C. R., Brown, J. (1990). Corporate practices in professional partnerships. *Academy of Management Journal* 33: 725–755.

Hall, P. A., Taylor, R. C. R. (1996). Political science and the three new institutionalisms. *Political Studies* 44(5): 936–957.

Hannah, L., Kim, K.-H., Mills, E. S. (1993). Land use controls and housing prices in Korea. *Urban Studies* 30(2): 147–156.

Harding, A. (1997). Urban regimes in a Europe of cities? *European Urban and Regional Studies* 4(4): 291–314.

Harloe, M. (1995). *The People's Home.* Oxford, Blackwell.

Hart, O. (1995). *Firms, Contracts and Financial Structure.* Oxford, Oxford University Press.

Hastings, A. (1996). Unravelling the process of 'partnership' in urban regeneration policy. *Urban Studies* 33(2): 253–268.

HBR (2000). *Negotiation and Conflict Resolution.* Harvard Business Review. Boston MA., Harvard Business School Press.

Healey, P. (1998). Institutionalist theory, social exclusion and governance. *Social Exclusion in European Cities.* Madanipour, A., Cars, G., Allen, J. (eds). London, Jessica Kingsley.

Hickman, B. G. (1973). What became of the building cycle? *Nations and Households in Economic Growth: Essays in Honor of Moses Abramovitz.* New York: Academic Press.

Hilbers, P., Lei, Q., Zacho, L. (2001). *Real Estate Market Developments and Financial Sector Soundness.* Washington, DC, International Monetary Fund.

Hillebrandt, P. (1971). *Small Firms in the Construction Industry.* London, HM Stationery Office.

Hillebrandt, P., Lansley, S. (1995). *The Construction Company in and out of Recession.* Basingstoke, Macmillan.

Holmstrom, B., Roberts, J. (1998). The boundaries of the firm revisited. *Journal of Economic Perspectives* 12(4): 73–94.

Hooper A. N. C. (2000). Design practice and volume production in speculative house-building. *Construction Management and Economics* 18(3): 295–310.

Hsieh, C.-T., Moretti, E. (2002). *Can Free Entry be Inefficient? Fixed Commissions and Social Waste in the Real Estate Industry.* National Bureau of Economic Research NBER Working Paper 9208. Cambridge, MA, NBER.

Hubbard, T. N. (2004). Affiliation, integration, and information: owner incentives and industry structure. *Journal of Industrial Economics* 52(2): 201–228.

Ikejiofor, U. (1998). The private sector and urban housing production process in Nigeria: a study of small-scale landlords in Abuja. *Habitat International* 21(4): 409–425.

Ive, G., Gruneberg, S., Meikle, J., Crosthwaite, D. (2003). *Sector Competitiveness Analysis of the UK Construction Industry.* London, Davis Langdon Consultancy for Department of Trade and Industry.

Jackson, A. J. (1991). *Semi-detached London: Suburban Development Life and Transport 1900–39.* Didcot, Wild Swan.

Jaffe, A. J. (1996). On the role of transaction costs and property rights in housing markets. *Housing Studies* 11(3): 425–434.

Jaffe, A. J. (1998). Housing and real estate economics: an overview. *Housing in Europe: Analysing Patchworks.* Smets, A. J. H., Troerup, T. (eds). Utrecht, Utrecht University: 13–19.

Jaffe, A. J., Louziotis, D. Jr (1996). Property rights and economic efficiency: a survey of institutional factors. *Journal of Real Estate Literature* 4: 137–157.

Johnson, L. (1993). An industry profile of corporate real estate. *Journal of Real Estate Research* 8: 525–540.

Jud, G. D., Winkler, D. T. (1994). What do real estate brokers do? An examination of excess returns in the housing market. *Journal of Housing Economics* 3: 283–295.

Kasura, H. M., Stryk, R. J. (1991). Selling Eastern Europe's social housing stock: proceed with caution. *Housing Policy Debate* 2(4): 1251–1273.

Kay, J. (1996). *The Business of Economics.* Oxford, Oxford University Press.

Kreps, D. M. (1990a). *Game Theory and Economic Modelling*. Oxford, Clarendon Press.

Kreps, D. M. (1990b). Corporate culture and economic theory. *Perspectives on Positive Political Economy*. Alt, J., Shepsle, D. (eds). Cambridge, Cambridge University Press.

Kumar, S. (1996). Landlordism in Third World urban low-income settlements: a case for further research. *Urban Studies* 33(4–5): 753–782.

Kumar, S. (2001). Embedded tenures: private renting and housing policy in India. *Housing Studies* 16(4): 425–442.

Kumar, S. (2002). Round pegs and square holes: mismatches between poverty and housing policy in urban India. *World Poverty: New Policies to Defeat an Old Enemy*. Townsend, P., Gordon, D. (eds). Oxford, The Policy Press.

La Porta, R., Lopez-de-Silanes, F., Shleifer, A., Vishny, R. (2000). Agency problems and dividend policies around the world. *Journal of Finance* 55: 1–33.

Laffont, J.-J. (1999). Political economy, information and incentives. *European Economic Review* 43: 649–670.

Lai Wai Chung, L. (1994). The economics of zoning: a literature review and analysis of the work of Coase. *Town Planning Review* 65(1): 77–98.

Larsen, J., Zorn, T. (2000). An optimal incentive system for real estate agents. *Journal of Real Estate Research* 20(1–2): 49–59.

Le Galès, P. (2001). Urban governance and policy networks: on the urban political boundedness of policy networks. A French case study. *Public Administration* 79(1): 167–184.

Leiblein, M. J. (2003). The choice of organizational governance form and performance: predictions from transaction cost, resource-based, and real options theories. *Journal of Management* 29(6): 937–962.

Levine, N. (1997). Financial development and economic growth: views and agenda. *Journal of Economic Literature* 35(2): 688–726.

Levitt, S., Syerson (2002). Market distortions when agents are better informed: a theoretical and empirical exploration of the value of information in real estate transactions. *Mimeo*. Chicago, University of Chicago.

Levmore, S. (1993). Commissions and conflicts in agency arrangements: lawyers, real estate brokers, underwriters and other agent's rewards. *Journal of Law and Economics* 36: 503–539.

Linder, M. (1994). *Projecting Capitalism: A History of the Internationalization of the Construction Industry*. Westport, Greenwood Press.

Lockett, A., Thompson, S. (2001). The resource-based view and economics. *Journal of Management* 27(6): 723–754.

Lockwood, D. (1989). *The Blackcoated Worker: A Study in Class Consciousness*. Oxford: Clarendon Press.

Lowndes, V., Skelcher, C. (1998). The dynamics of multi-organizational partnerships: an analysis of changing modes of governance. *Public Administration* 76(2): 313–333.

Lui, S. S., Ngo, H-Y. (2004). The role of trust and contractual safeguards on cooperation in non-equity alliances. *Journal of Management* 30(4): 471–485.

Macho-Stadler, I., Pérez-Castrillo, D. (1997). *An Introduction to the Economics of Information. Incentives and Contracts*. Oxford, Oxford University Press.

Mackintosh, M. (1992). Partnership: Issues of Policy and Negotiation. *Local Economy* 7: 210–224.

Maddison, A. (1992). *Dynamic Forces in Capitalist Development: A Long-run Comparative View*. Oxford, Oxford University Press.

Mahoney, J. (2001). A resource-based theory of sustainable rents. *Journal of Management* 27(1): 651–660.

Maister, D. (1982). Balancing the professional service firm. *Sloan Management Review* (Fall): 15–29.

Malpezzi, S. (1990). Urban housing and financial markets: some international comparisons. *Urban Studies* 27(6).

Malpezzi, S., MacLennan, D. (2001). The long-run price elasticity of supply of new residential construction in the United States and the United Kingdom. *Journal of Housing Economics* 10(3): 278–306.

Malpezzi, S., Sa-Aadu, J. (1996). What have African housing policies wrought? *Real Estate Economics* 24(2): 133–160.

Malpezzi, S., Wachter, S. (2005). The role of speculation in real estate cycles. *Journal of Real Estate Literature* 13(2): 143–164.

Martin, S. (2002). *Advanced Industrial Economics*. Malden, MA, Blackwell Publishers.

Mather, C. (1989). Information, intermediaries and sales strategy in an urban housing market: the implications of real estate auctions in Melbourne. *Urban Studies* 26: 495–509.

Mayer, L. B., Sommerville, C. T. (2002). *Irreversible Investment, Real Options and Competition: Evidence from Real Estate Development*. Working Paper 01–02. Centre for Urban Economics and Real Estate, University of British Colombia.

McGreal, S., Parsa, A., Keivani, R. (2002). Evolution of property investment markets in Central Europe: opportunities and constraints. *Journal of Property Research* 19(3): 213–230.

McWilliams, A., Smart, D. (1993). Efficiency v. structure–conduct–performance: implications for strategy research and practice. *Journal of Management* 19(1): 63–79.

Meen, G. (1996). Spatial aggregation, spatial dependence and predictability in the UK housing market. *Housing Studies* 26(2): 240–252.

Meen, G. (2001). *Modelling Spatial Housing Markets. Theory, Analysis and Policy*. London, Kluwer Academic.

Meen, G. (2005). On the economics of the Barker Review of housing supply. *Housing Studies* 20(6): 949–971.

Miceli, T. J. (1988). Information costs and the organization of the real estate brokerage industry in the U.S. and Great Britain. *AREUEA Journal* 16(2): 173–188.

Miles, D. (2004). *The UK Mortgage Market: Taking a Longer-term View. Final Report and Recommendations*. London, HM Treasury.

Milgrom, P., Roberts, J. (1992). *Economics, Organization and Management*. Upper Saddle River, NJ, Prentice Hall.

Miller, C. (2000). Accountability: the challenge for UK voluntary organisations in community development. *Scottish Journal of Community Work and Development* 6: 45–53.

MMC (1997). *Solicitors' Estate Agency in Scotland. A Report on the Supply of Residential Estate Agency Services in Scotland*. London, The Monopolies and Mergers Commission.

Mohr, J., Spekman, R. (1994). Characteristics of partnership success: partnership attributes, communication behaviour, and conflict resolution techniques, *Strategic Management Journal* 15: 135–52.

Molho, I. (1997). *Economics of Information. Lying and Cheating in Markets and Organisations*. Oxford, Blackwell.

Muellbauer, J., Murphy, A. (1997). Booms and busts in the UK housing market. *Economic Journal* 107: 1701–1727.

Mueller, D. C. (2003). *Public Choice III*. Cambridge, Cambridge University Press.

Murdoch, J., Hughes, W. (2000). *Construction Contracts. Law and Management*. London, Spon Press.

Muziol-Weclawowicz, A., Oracz, A. (2004). *Rents in Polish Social Housing*. ENHR International Housing Conference, Cambridge.

NESC (2004). *Housing in Ireland: Performance and Policy*. Dublin, National Economic and Social Council.

Norris, M., Shiels, P. (2004). *Regular National Report on Housing Developments in European Countries, Synthesis Report*. Dublin, The Housing Unit, Department of the Environment, Heritage and Local Government, http://www.environ.ie

North, D. C. (1990). *Institutions, Institutional Change and Economic Performance*. Cambridge, Cambridge University Press.

North, D. (1991). Institutions. *Journal of Economic Perspectives* 5(1): 97–112.

O'Mahony, M., de Boer, W. (2002). Britain's relative productivity performance: has anything changed? *National Institute Economic Review* 179: 38–43.

ODPM (2005). *Planning for Housing. A Consultation Document*. London, Office of the Deputy Prime Minister.

OFT (2004a). *Estate Agency Market in England and Wales. Annexe C: International Research*. Office of Fair Trading, London.

OFT (2004b). *Estate Agency Market in England and Wales*. Office of Fair Trading, London.

Oizumi, E. (2006 forthcoming). *Housing and Social Transition in Japan*. London, Routledge.

Penrose, E. T. (1959). *The Theory of the Growth of the Firm*. New York, Wiley.

Perkin, H. (1989). *The Rise of Professional Society: England since 1880*. London, Routledge.

Pichler-Milanovich, N. (2001). Urban housing markets in central and Eastern Europe: convergence, divergence or policy 'collapse'. *European Journal of Housing Policy* 2(1): 145–187.

Pogodzinski, J. M., Sass, T. R. (1991). Measuring the effects of municipal zoning regulations: a survey. *Urban Studies* 28(4): 596–621.

Pollakowski, H. O., Ray, T. S. (1997). Housing price diffusion patterns at different aggregation levels: an examination of housing market efficiency. *Journal of Housing Research* 8(1): 107–124.

Porter, M. (1985). *Competitive Advantage*. New York, Free Press.

Porter, M. (1990a). *The Competitive Advantage of Nations*. New York, Macmillan.

Porter, M., (ed.) (1990b). *Competitive Advantage: Creating and Sustaining Superior Performance*. New York, Free Press.

Powell, W. W. (1990). Neither market nor hierarchy: network forms of organization. *Research in Organizational Behaviour*. Staw, L. L., Cummings, B. M. (eds). London, JAI: 295–336.

Powell, W. W. (1996). Trust-based forms of governance. *Trust in Organizations: Frontiers of Theory and Research*. Kramer, R. M., Tyler, T. R. (eds). London, Sage.

Prendergast, C. (1999). The provision of incentives in firms. *Journal of Economic Literature* 37(1): 7–63.

Price, R. (1980). *Masters, Unions and Men: Work Control in Building and the Rise of Labour, 1830–1914*. Cambridge, Cambridge University Press.

Priem, R. L., Butler, J. E. (2001a). Is the resource-based 'view' a useful perspective for strategic management research? *Academy of Management Review* 26(1): 22–41.

Priem, R. L., Butler, J. E. (2001b). Tautology in the resource-based view and the implications of externally determined resource value: further comments. *Academy of Management Review* 26(1): 57–67.

Pryce, G. (1999). Construction elasticities and land availability: a two stage least squares model of housing supply using the variable elasticity approach. *Urban Studies* 30(2): 2283–2304.

Pryke, S. D. (2004). Analysing construction project coalitions: exploring the application of social network analysis. *Construction Management and Economics* 22(8): 787–797.

Purdue, N. (2001). Neighbourhood governance: leadership, trust and social capital. *Urban Studies* 38(12): 2211–2225.

Putnam, R. D. (2000). *Bowling Alone. The Collapse and Revival of American Community*. New York, Simon & Schuster.

Quack, S., Morgan, G., Whitley, R., (eds) (2000). *National Capitalisms, Global Competition, and Economic Performance*. Amsterdam, John Benjamins Publishing.

Radner, R. (1992). Hierarchy: the economics of managing. *Journal of Economic Literature* 30(3): 1382–1415.

Raiffa, H. (1982). *The Art and Science of Negotiation*. Cambridge, Mass., Belknap Press of Harvard University Press.

Rajan, R., Zingales, L. (1995). 'What do we know about capital structure'? Some evidence from international data. *Journal of Finance* 50: 1421–1460.

Rajan, R., Zingales, L. (2001). Financial systems, industrial structure, and growth. *Oxford Review of Economic Policy* 17(4): 467–483.

Rajan, R., Zingales, L. (2004). *Saving Capitalism from the Capitalists: Unleashing the Power of Financial Markets to Create Wealth and Spread Opportunity*. Princeton, Princeton University Press.

Rakodi, C. (1991). Housing production and housing policy in Harare, Zimbabwe. *Journal of Urban Affairs* 12(2): 135–156.

Reeves, K. (2002). Construction business systems in Japan: general contractors and subcontractors. *Building Research and Information* 30(6): 413–424.

Reilly, F. K., Brown, K. C. (1999). *Investment Analysis and Portfolio Management*. Englewood Cliffs, Prentice Hall.

Renaud, B. (1995). The real estate economy and the design of Russian housing reforms, Part 1. *Urban Studies* 32(8): 1247–1264.

Renaud, B. (2002). Speculative behavior in immature real estate markets, lessons from the 1997 Asia crisis. Speculation in commercial land and real estate markets. *Experiences from around the World*. Cambridge, Massachusetts, The Lincoln Institute of Land Policy.

Ricketts, M. (1994). *The Economics of Business Enterprise*. London, Harvester Wheatsheaf.

Rindfleisch, A., Heide, J. B. (1997). Transaction cost analysis: past, present, and future applications. *Journal of Marketing* 61(4): 30–54.

Rodney Turner, J. (2004). Farsighted project contract management: incomplete in its entirety. *Construction Management and Economics* 22(1): 75–83.

Rosenthal, S. S. (1999). Housing supply: the other half of the market. A note from the editor. *Journal of Real Estate Finance and Economics* 18(1): 5–7.

Rothenburg, J., Galster, G. C., Butler, R. V., Pitkin, J. R. (1991). *The Maze of Urban Housing Markets. Theory, Evidence and Policy*. Chicago, Chicago University Press.

Rydin, Y. (2003). *Urban and Environmental Planning in the UK*. London, Palgrave Macmillan.

Sah, R. K., Stiglitz, J. E. (1986). The architecture of economic systems: hierarchies and polyarchies. *American Economic Review* 76: 716–727.

Sappington, D. E. M. (1991). Incentives in principal–agent relationships. *The Journal of Economic Perspectives* 5(2): 45–66.

Satterthwaite, D. (2005). *The Scale of Urban Change Worldwide 1950–2000 and its Underpinnings*. London, International Institute for Environment and Development.

Scherer, F. M. (1980). *Industrial Market Structure and Economic Performance*. Boston, Houghton Mifflin.

Schmidt, K. (2003). Ordering systems: coordinative practices in architectural design and planning. *Proceedings of the 2003 International Acm Siggroup Conference on Supporting Group Work*, Sanibel Island, Florida, USA, ACM Press.

Schroeter, J. R. (1987). Competition and value-of-service pricing in the residential real estate brokerage market. *Quarterly Review of Economics and Business* 27: 29–40.

Schumpter, J. A. (1942). *Capitalism, Socialism and Democracy*. New York, Harper & Brothers.

SEU (2001). *A New Commitment to Neighbourhood Renewal: National Strategy Action Plan*. London, HMSO.

Shaw, K., Davidson, G. (2002). Community elections for regeneration partnerships: a new deal for local democracy? *Local Government Studies* 28(2): 1–15.

Shelanski, H., Klein, P. (1995). Empirical research in transaction cost economics: a review and assessment. *Journal of Law, Economics and Organization* 11: 335–361.

Sirmans, G. S., Macpherson, D. A., Zietz, E. M. (2005). The composition of hedonic pricing models. *Journal of Real Estate Literature* 13(1): 3–46.

Skyes, A. O. (1993). Some thoughts on the real estate puzzle. *Journal of Law and Economics* 36(2): 541–551.

Smets, P. (1997). Private housing finance in India: reaching down-market? *Habitat International* 21(1): 1–15.

Smith, A. (1979). *The Wealth of Nations: Books 1–3*. Harmondsworth, Penguin.

Somerville, C. T. (1999). The industrial organization of housing supply: market activity, land supply and the size of homebuilders. *Real Estate Economics* 27(4): 669–695.

Southern, R. (2002). Understanding multi-sectoral regeneration partnerships as a form of local governance. *Local Government Studies* 28(2): 16–32.

Stewart, M., Taylor, M. (1995). *Empowerment and Estate Regeneration: A Critical Review*. Bristol, Policy Press.

Stoker, G., Mossberger, K. (1994). Urban regime theory in comparative perspective. *Environment and Planning C: Governance and Policy* 12: 195–212.

Stone, C. (1993). Urban regimes and the capacity to govern: a political economy approach. *Journal of Urban Affairs* 15(1): 1–28.

Strassman, W. P., Wells, J. (1988). *The Global Construction Industry. Strategies for Entry, Growth and Survival*. London, Unwin Hyman.

Sutton, J. (1997). Gibrat's legacy. *Journal of Economic Literature* 35(1): 40–59.

Swenarton, M. (1981). *Homes Fit for Heroes: The Politics and Architecture of Early State Housing in Britain*. London, Heinemann Educational.

Sydlow, J. (1997). Understanding the constitution of interorganisational trust. *Trust Within and Between Organisations*. Lane, C., Buchmann, R. (eds). Oxford, Oxford University Press.

Taylor, M. (1995). *Unleashing the Potential: Bringing Residents to the Centre of Regeneration*. York, Joseph Rowntree Foundation.

Teece, D. J., Pisano, G., Shuen, A. (1997). Dynamic capabilities and strategic management. *Strategic Management Journal* 18: 509–533.

Tiesdell, S., Allmendinger, P. (2001). Neighbourhood regeneration and New Labour's Third Way. *Environment and Planning C: Government and Policy* 19: 903–926.

Tirole, J. (1993). *The Theory of Industrial Organization*. Cambridge, Mass., The MIT Press.

Tse, R. Y. C., Webb, J. R. (2002). The effectiveness of a web strategy for real estate brokerage. *Journal of Real Estate Literature* 10(1): 121–130.

Turel, A. (2002). *Housing Provision in Istanbul: Dominance of Unauthorised House-building*. Vienna, European Network For Housing Research.

UNECE (1999). *Country Profile on the Housing Sector: Slovakia*. Geneva, United Nations Economic Commission for Europe.

UNECE (2004). *Country Profile on the Housing Sector: Russia*. Geneva, United Nations Economic Commission for Europe.

UN-Habitat (2002). *Rental Housing. An Essential Option for the Urban Poor in Developing Countries*. Nairobi, UN-Habitat.

UN-Habitat (2005). *Responding to the Challenges of an Urbanizing World, UN-Habitat Annual Report 2005*. Nairobi, United Nations Human Settlement Programme UN-Habitat.

Wachter, S. (1987). Residential real estate brokerage: rate uniformity and moral hazard. *The Economics of Urban Property Rights*. In Jaffe, A. (ed.). New York, JAI Press.

Webster, C., Lai, L. W.-C. (2003). *Property Rights, Planning and Markets*. Cheltenham, UK, Edward Elgar.

Węcławowicz, G. (2005). *Large Housing Estates in Warsaw, Poland*. RESTATE, Faculty of Geosciences, Utrecht University.

Wehner, P. (2002). Elephant just a memory. *Estates Gazette* (April): 42–43.

Wells, J., Sinda, H., Haddar, F. (1998). Housing and building materials in low-income settlements in Dar es Salaam. *Habitat International* 22(4): 397–409.

Williamson, O. E. (1975). *Markets and Hierarchies: Analysis and Antitrust Implications: a Study in the Economics of Internal Organization*. New York and London, Free Press.

Williamson, O. E. (1981). The modern corporation, origins, evolution, attributes. *Journal of Economic Literature* 19(4): 1537–1568.

Williamson, O. E. (1985). *The Economic Institutions of Capitalism*. New York, The Free Press.

Williamson, O. E. (1990). A comparison of alternative approaches to economic organisation. *Journal of Institutional and Theoretical Economics* 146: 61–71.

Williamson, O. E. (1996). *The Mechanisms of Governance*. New York, Oxford University Press.

Williamson, O. E. (1999). Strategy research: governance and competence perspectives. *Strategic Management Journal* 20: 1087–1108.

Williamson, O. E. (2000). The new institutional economics: taking stock, looking ahead. *Journal of Economic Literature* 38(3): 595–613.

Winch, G. M. (1989). The construction firm and the transaction cost approach. *Construction Management and Economics* 7(4): 331–345.

Winch, G. M. (2000). Construction business systems in the European Union. *Building Research and Information* 28(2): 88–97.

Winch, G. M. (2001). Governing the project process: a conceptual framework. *Construction Management and Economics* 19: 799–808.

Winch, G. M. (2002). *Managing Construction Projects*. Oxford, Blackwell Publishing.

Winch, G. M. (2005). Internationalisation in business-to-business services: polygamy and promiscuity in architectural practice. *3rd Workshop on International Strategy and Cross Cultural Management*, Vienna.

Winch, G. M., Schneider, E. (1993). Managing knowledge-based organization: the case of architectural practice. *Journal of Management Studies* 30: 923–937.

Wong, P. S. P., On Cheung, S., Ho, P. K. M. (2005). Contractor as trust initiator in construction partnering – prisoner's dilemma perspective. *Journal of Construction Engineering and Management* 131(10): 1045–1053.

World Bank (1993). *Housing: Enabling Markets To Work*. Washington, DC, World Bank.

Xu, T., Tiong, R. L., Chew, D. A. S., Smith, N. J. (2005). Development model for competitive construction industry in the People's Republic of China. *Journal of Construction Engineering and Management* 131(7): 844–853.

Yavas, A. (1994). Economics of brokerage: an overview. *Journal of Real Estate Literature* 2: 169–195.

Yuing, F., Somerville, C. T. (2001). Site density restrictions: measurement and empirical analysis. *Journal of Urban Economics* 49(2): 404–423.

Zhang, X. Q. (1998). *Privatisation: A Study of Housing Policy in Urban China*. New York, Nova Science Publishers.

Zorn, T. S., Larsen, J. E. (1986). The incentive effects of flat-fee and percentage commissions for real estate brokers. *Journal of American Real Estate and Urban Economics Association* 14: 24–47.

Zumpano, L. V. (2002). The possible consequences of bank entry into the real estate brokerage market: what the research tells us. *Journal of Real Estate Literature* 10(2): 243–252.

Zumpano, L. V., Elder, H. V. (1994). Economies of scope and density in the market for real estate brokerage services. *American Real Estate and Urban Economics Association Journal* 22: 497–513.

Zumpano, L. V., Elder, H. V., Crellin, G. E. (1993). The market for residential real estate brokerage services: costs of production and economies of scale. *Journal of Real Estate Finance and Economics* 6: 237–250.

Index

9389